D1491746

FALKLANDS WAR HEROES

FALKLANDS WAR HEROES

EXTRAORDINARY TRUE STORIES OF BRAVERY IN THE SOUTH ATLANTIC

MICHAEL ASHCROFT

Biteback Publishing

First published in Great Britain in 2021 by
Biteback Publishing Ltd, London
Copyright © Michael Ashcroft 2021

ISBN 978-1-78590-714-2

10 9 8 7 6 5 4 3 2 1

A CIP catalogue record for this book is available from the British Library.

Set in Adobe Garamond Pro

Printed and bound in Great Britain by
CPI Group (UK) Ltd, Croydon CR0 4YY

MIX
Paper from
responsible sources
FSC
www.fsc.org   FSC® C020471

'Think where man's glory most begins and ends,
and say my glory was I had such friends.'
WILLIAM BUTLER YEATS

CONTENTS

ACKNOWLEDGEMENTS

It is easy to know where to begin my many thank-yous. They start with my gratitude to the thirty-six men and one woman whose write-ups feature in this book. *Falklands War Heroes* is my tribute to their courage and service, whether they are alive or dead. My thanks in particular go to the many veterans who contributed to this book by granting me interviews so I could fully highlight their actions during the Falklands War. Marica McKay, the widow of Sergeant Ian McKay VC, helped greatly with his write-up, while Jean Messenger, the mother of the late Malcolm Messenger, also assisted me with his. I am grateful for everyone's time and their memories, not all of them fond or easy because, as with all wars, there was a heavy price to pay even in victory.

I must single out one decorated war veteran, Gordon Mather, for special praise. He not only gave me great help with his own write-up – the longest in the book – but he also provided me with many key introductions to other veterans through his former role as chairman of the South Atlantic Medal Association, also known as SAMA 82. As a small gesture to Gordon's generosity of spirit, I have included his favourite quote, from the Irish poet and writer W. B. Yeats, at the start of this book.

Inevitably, especially after the passing of nearly four decades, some of the former service personnel remember the same events slightly differently, so it is important to stress that this book is true to their individual memories. In some cases, where recollections were distinctly hazy, I have relied on individuals' accounts of events from nearly forty years ago, including those given to other authors, rather than trying to make the veterans recall tiny details from so long ago.

A number of people helped me trace former servicemen and my thanks go to Joanne Stevens of SAMA 82, Marie Hurcum of SAMA 82, Louise Dixon of Michael O'Mara Books, Pierce Noonan of Dix Noonan Webb (DNW), Marcus Budgen of Spink, Richard Black of the London Medal Company, Matthew Richardson, Randall Nicol, Stuart Trebble, Brad Porritt and Andy Haslam.

I am grateful to David Erskine-Hill, the curator of my medal collection, for coming up with the idea for this book and for helping to collate the information needed for it. Some time ago, David realised that my Falklands War medal collection had become so formidable that, on the eve of the fortieth anniversary of the war, it should be recorded in a book.

A big thank-you, as always, to Angela Entwistle, my corporate communications director, and her team for their help in promoting this project and for arranging the book launch during the challenges presented by the Covid-19 pandemic.

Once again, I have to thank my publisher, Biteback, for their great assistance in enabling me to bring my passion for gallantry to a wider audience. Remarkably, this is my seventh book in the 'Heroes' series. James Stephens, Olivia Beattie and their team continue to be a delight to deal with.

Two respected medal experts, Pierce Noonan and Richard Black, have generously provided me with help and advice. In particular, as with David Erskine-Hill, they read and corrected the original draft of this book. I should, however, stress that any errors (sadly inevitable in a project of this size) are entirely down to me. Inevitably, too, different sources give contrasting figures for things like the number of casualties in a battle, and I have simply tried to go with the most authoritative source, or sources, when such totals differ.

Several auction houses and their staff have provided write-ups and other documentation relating to many of the medal groups featured in *Falklands War Heroes*. My apologies if I have missed anyone off the list, but the auction houses that have assisted include Bonhams, DNW, Morton & Eden and Spink, while others came through private purchases, including those arranged through the London Medal Company.

A large number of publishers and authors have kindly allowed me to reproduce parts of their work in this volume. All of these are listed in a comprehensive bibliography at the back of this book. My thanks to one and all for this gift.

I have also benefited from a mine of useful information on various websites, particularly www.paradata.org.uk, which champions the brave actions of the Parachute Regiment and Airborne Forces.

Good photographs are vital for a book of this nature. My thanks go to Jane Sherwood, the news editor, EMEA (Europe, Middle East and Africa) at Getty Images, for her thorough picture research. I am also grateful to Christopher Cox, a freelance photographer, who photographed both my medal groups and some of the medal recipients for *Falklands War Heroes*.

Rebecca Maciejewska, the chief executive and secretary of the Victoria Cross and George Cross Association, was typically helpful in assisting me with this book, particularly in relation to the write-up on Sergeant Ian McKay VC.

Last but certainly not least, I am hugely grateful to Simon Weston for writing the foreword to this book. If one man represents the courage of our servicemen and women in the Falklands nearly forty years ago, then surely it is Simon. This is also an appropriate time to thank him, on behalf of so many good causes, for all the incredible charity work he has done over the past four decades – actions that rightly earned him an OBE, and later a CBE. I feel privileged that Simon should put his name to this book.

Simon Weston CBE © Lord Ashcroft

FOREWORD
BY SIMON WESTON CBE

It is incredible to think that nearly forty years have passed since the Falklands War. The conflict between the United Kingdom and Argentina not only ended many young lives; it also changed several more for ever, my own included. I received 46 per cent burns to my body when the troop ship RFA *Sir Galahad* was bombed and destroyed by enemy aircraft while anchored in the inappropriately named (for me, at least) Port Pleasant, off the Falkland Islands, on 8 June 1982. I was the worst injured man on the ship, the worst injured serviceman to make it home alive, and I spent the best part of five years in hospital undergoing more than ninety operations.

People have repeatedly said that I was unlucky, but forty-eight men who died on my ship would have loved to have had my bad luck – they would have loved to have had the problems I faced as I recovered from my injuries. When I went to war, I was a carefree twenty-year-old lad who was proud to have served in the Welsh Guards since I was sixteen and happy to have played prop forward for more rugby teams than I can remember. However, that all ended on the fateful day when our ship was bombed and the resulting explosions turned it into a giant fireball. My physical appearance changed at a stroke, but it took years for me to adapt mentally to the new, reconstructed Simon Weston that I am today:

a former soldier, a wartime survivor, a charity worker and, some say, with great generosity of spirit, an inspiration to others.

I am delighted that Lord Ashcroft, who has championed bravery for the past fifteen years, has chosen to mark the fortieth anniversary of the Falklands War by writing a book that highlights the gallantry of so many British servicemen and women – both those who gave their lives during the 1982 conflict and those who survived.

I have long been an admirer of Lord Ashcroft's work in the areas of valour and the military. He has built up four major collections of gallantry medals, including the largest collection of Victoria Crosses (VCs) in the world. He has supported countless military charities, including making a donation of £1 million to the £7 million Bomber Command Memorial that was unveiled by Her Majesty the Queen in 2012.

Furthermore, *Falklands War Heroes* is the seventh book by Lord Ashcroft in his 'Heroes' series, and it does exactly what it says on the tin: it tells the stories of bravery during the ten-week war through the incredible medal collection he has amassed over the past four decades. This book will bring courageous deeds to a global audience; each write-up has been diligently researched and each story is carefully told. Furthermore, every penny of the author's royalties will be donated to military charities.

I commend Lord Ashcroft for penning an inspirational book about men and women whose valour deserves to be championed for many decades to come. These are heroes of the Falklands War – heroes of my time – and I salute the gallantry and service of each and every one of them.

AUTHOR'S ROYALTIES

Lord Ashcroft is donating all author's royalties from *Falklands War Heroes* to military charities.

LORD ASHCROFT AND BRAVERY

All the write-ups in this book are based on medal groups collected by Lord Ashcroft KCMG PC.

Lord Ashcroft also owns substantial collections of Special Forces gallantry decorations, gallantry medals for bravery in the air and some George Crosses (GCs).

His collection of VCs and GCs is on display in the Lord Ashcroft Gallery at the Imperial War Museum, London, along with VCs and GCs owned by, or in the care of, the museum.

For more information visit:
www.iwm.org.uk/heroes

For more information on Lord Ashcroft's books on bravery visit:
www.VictoriaCrossHeroes.com
www.SpecialForcesHeroes.com
www.GeorgeCrossHeroes.com
www.HeroesOfTheSkies.com
www.SpecialOpsHeroes.com
www.VictoriaCrossHeroes2.com

For more information on Lord Ashcroft's VC collection visit:
www.LordAshcroftMedals.com

For more information on Lord Ashcroft's work on bravery visit:
www.LordAshcroftOnBravery.com

For more information on his general work visit:
www.LordAshcroft.com

Follow him on Twitter and Facebook:
@LordAshcroft

PREFACE

The Falklands War was an extraordinary conflict in many ways. It could easily prove to be the last colonial war that Britain ever fights. Whether or not that is the case, it is remarkable that Britain sent a force of some 20,000 men to fight for a small cluster of islands 8,000 miles away that were home to only 1,820 people – and 400,000 sheep.

This book has been published to mark the fortieth anniversary of the Falklands War. Many books have already been written about the war, all of them offering some insight – large or small – into the events in the South Atlantic during ten weeks from early April to mid-June 1982.

Between 2 April, when Argentina invaded the Falklands, and 14 June, when Argentina unconditionally surrendered and returned the islands to British control, 255 British military personnel, 649 Argentine military personnel and three Falkland Islanders died as a result of the hostilities. In all, 907 lives were lost, while 2,432 men were wounded in battle and many were left scarred, physically and mentally, by their experiences in fighting for islands that covered an area of some 4,700 square miles.

This book is *not* an attempt to shed new light on some of the biggest controversies surrounding the war. For example, should it have been avoided in the first place? Should Britain have strengthened the defences on the Falkland Islands as tensions grew? Did we really need to resort to fighting? Should we have attacked the

Argentine cruiser the *General Belgrano*? Was the battle for Goose Green fought too recklessly? Should we have fought the war differently? And so on. Indeed, most of these controversies have been addressed extensively over the past four decades.

Quite simply, this was a war that Britain fought – and won. Almost forty years on, this book seeks to highlight the courage of many of those who risked, and in some cases gave, their lives for the rights of those men, women and children on the Falkland Islands to continue to live there free of Argentine control. This is a book crammed full of stories of derring-do, in some cases what I call cold or premeditated courage, in other cases spur-of-the-moment gallantry. The common thread that runs through the book is my admiration for the valour of our servicemen fighting a difficult war so far from their homeland. It should not be forgotten, however, that women played an important role in the war too, and one of those heroines, a nurse serving on the hospital ship SS *Uganda*, features as a write-up in this book.

I am often described as a military historian, but I see myself much more as a champion of bravery and a storyteller. This is my seventh book in the 'Heroes' series, and like most of the previous ones it is based on one of my many collections of gallantry and service medals – this one entirely centred on the Falklands War. What makes this collection so exceptional is that the medals cover virtually all the key events that took place in the war: on land, at sea and in the air. The medals also span the full length of the war: from shortly after the conflict started, via all the major battles that were fought and up until it was eventually brought to a close.

INTRODUCTION:
THE BUILD-UP TO WAR

The Falkland Islands is an archipelago in the South Atlantic Ocean made up of East Falkland, West Falkland and some 776 smaller islands. Altogether, they form a land mass of some 4,700 square miles. The islands lie approximately 300 miles off South America's Patagonia coast.

The Falkland Islands is one of fourteen British Overseas Territories, which means it is self-governed but its residents rely on the British government for their defence and their foreign policy. Over the centuries, the islands were 'discovered' and exploited by colonialists. At various times, there have been British, French, Spanish and Argentine settlements on the islands.

Britain reasserted its rule over the Falklands in 1833, but since then Argentina has made numerous claims to the islands. These claims were voiced louder during the 1960s, especially after the United Nations passed Resolution 2065 calling on both countries to conduct bilateral negotiations to reach a peaceful settlement of the dispute. In the 1970s, tensions simmered after the Falkland Islanders made it clear that they wished to remain British.

In 1981, Argentina was ruled by a military junta that included army Commander General Leopoldo Galtieri. During that year, Argentina's previously fragile relationship with America improved, and Galtieri visited Washington before ousting Roberto Viola as President in December 1981.

Galtieri became convinced that seizing 'Las Malvinas', as the Falklands are known in Argentina, would help unite the country and increase his personal popularity. Within a short time of becoming President, he was exploring how to invade the islands using his country's navy and, at the same time, assessing the likely response of Britain and other countries to such an act of aggression.

In early 1982, tensions rose still further, but in the UK Lord Carrington, the Foreign Secretary who was eventually to resign his post three days after the start of war on 5 April, and Richard Luce, the minister responsible for the Falklands, did not believe an invasion was imminent. With government spending under careful scrutiny, they did not see the need to send Royal Navy ships to the South Atlantic to reinforce HMS *Endurance*, an ice-patrol vessel already in the area but which was due for imminent decommissioning.

On 19 March 1982, a group of civilian scrap-metal workers arrived illegally on South Georgia, another British territory in the South Atlantic, and hoisted the Argentine flag. Their arrival at Leith Harbour alerted a British Antarctic Survey (BAS) team, the only British presence on the island, which, in turn, sent messages to London and to Rex Hunt, the Governor of the Falklands. At the time, South Georgia was run as a dependency of the Falklands.

At the request of the British, the Argentine flag was eventually lowered, but when diplomatic niceties were ignored, Hunt, in consultation with the British government, despatched *Endurance* from Port Stanley, the capital of the Falklands, to South Georgia with a detachment of twenty-two Royal Marines. *Endurance* left on 21 March and arrived off the BAS station at Grytviken, South Georgia, three days later.

On 26 March, the Argentine junta apparently decided to bring forward their plan to invade the Falklands, previously intended for much later in the year when they knew *Endurance* would be out of the area. With the situation escalating, the British government decided on 29 March to send two nuclear submarines to the South Atlantic.

By 1 April, appropriately enough April Fool's Day, Hunt summoned two senior Royal Marine officers to Government House and declared, 'It looks as if the buggers mean it.' Later that evening, having made some very basic plans to patrol and defend key targets, the Governor made a radio broadcast to the islanders, saying, 'There is mounting evidence the Argentine Armed Forces are preparing to invade the Falklands.' Having deployed his small force of Marines on the outskirts of Port Stanley with orders to resist an attack, Hunt declared a State of Emergency in the early hours of 2 April.

Minutes later, Argentine commandos landed on the Falklands – at Mullet Creek, 3 miles south of Port Stanley. At 6 a.m., they launched an attack on the barracks at Moody Brook, employing phosphorus grenades and automatic fire against a non-existent force – fortunately, the Marines had left the previous day.

As the Argentine forces advanced on Government House, they were briefly held back by the small force of Marines. During a two-hour gun battle, at least two Argentine soldiers were killed. However, by 8 a.m., despite one of their landing craft being hit by an anti-tank weapon, the Argentine reinforcements streamed into Port Stanley. By 8.30 a.m., and by that point cut off from communications with London, Hunt had surrendered. The British had suffered no casualties, but the Marines had the indignity of being photographed face down on the ground. Hunt, meanwhile, was taken by taxi to the airport and flown by an Argentine Hercules aircraft to Montevideo, the capital of Uruguay. Argentina was firmly in control of the Falkland Islands – but for how long?

CHAPTER 1

OPENING SHOTS

South Georgia and the South Sandwich Islands, like its better-known 'neighbour' the Falkland Islands, is a British Overseas Territory in the South Atlantic Ocean. The islands are remote and inhospitable. The largest island, South Georgia, is just over 100 miles long and 22 miles wide. The chain of smaller islands 430 miles to the south-east of South Georgia is known as the South Sandwich Islands. The area of the whole territory is just over 1,500 square miles, and the Falkland Islands lie some 810 miles west of its nearest point.

At any one time, there is a very small permanent population on South Georgia and no permanent population on the South Sandwich Islands. There are no scheduled flights or ferries to the territory, although cruise ships do sometimes stop to allow their passengers to take a look at the islands, particularly since the dramatic events of 1982.

As with the Falkland Islands, the rights to South Georgia and the South Sandwich Islands have long been disputed. The UK claimed sovereignty over South Georgia in 1775 and over the South Sandwich Islands in 1908. However, Argentina claimed South Georgia in 1927 and claimed the South Sandwich Islands in 1938. In the build-up to the Falklands War, South Georgia was governed as part of the Falkland Islands Dependencies (although this came to an end in 1985, when South Georgia and the South Sandwich Islands became a separate territory).

The troubles in the South Atlantic began on 19 March 1982, when a group of civilian scrap-metal workers arrived at Leith Harbour on board the transport ship ARA Bahía Buen Suceso. *The group did not possess the required landing clearance and then raised the Argentine flag. It later emerged that the scrap workers had been infiltrated by Argentine Marines posing as scientists.*

The only British presence at Leith on 19 March was a British Antarctic Survey (BAS) team, whose leader, Trefor Edwards, handed a message from London to the Commander of the Argentine ship, Captain Briatore, ordering the removal of the Argentine flag and the departure of the party. It was also demanded that the Argentine crew report to the top BAS Commander in Grytviken, Steve Martin.

Initially, Briatore replied that the mission had the approval of the British Embassy in Buenos Aires – a clear lie. The Argentine Captain eventually ordered the lowering of the flag but failed to report to Grytviken. These events prompted the BAS Commander to send a message to Rex Hunt, the Governor of the Falkland Islands. After consulting with London, Hunt was instructed to despatch HMS Endurance *to South Georgia with a detachment of twenty-two Marines. The Marines landed on South Georgia on 31 March.*

Until this point, Endurance *and* Bahía Paraíso, *an Argentine naval ship, played a game of cat and mouse around South Georgia, but then they lost track of each other. And as March gave way to April, matters took a sinister turn…*

KEITH PAUL MILLS

Service: Royal Marines

Final Rank: Captain

FALKANDS WAR DECORATION / DISTINCTION:

DISTINGUISHED SERVICE CROSS (DSC)

DATE OF BRAVERY: 3 APRIL 1982

GAZETTED: 4 JUNE 1982

Cometh the hour, cometh the man. Keith Paul Mills was a 22-year-old Lieutenant in the Royal Marines when he faced the greatest challenge of his life: how to defend a remote British outpost from a much larger invading force. He could not be reckless with the lives of his men, for whom he had a duty of care. For his actions back in early April 1982, he would be decorated with the DSC and feted back home as a war hero.

Mills was born on 5 June 1959 in Abingdon, Berkshire. The middle of three children and the son of an engineer, Mills was just four when his family moved to Harlech, in the north Wales county of Gwynedd, due to his father's work in the nuclear power industry. Later, they moved to nearby Anglesey, where Mills spent the rest of his childhood and was educated at his local primary school and Syr Thomas Jones secondary school, both in Amlwch, the most northerly town in Wales. At his secondary school, he became the first-ever English head boy.

After leaving school at eighteen, he decided not to become an engineer as his father had hoped, giving up the offer of a place at the University of Liverpool to read electronics. Instead, he decided to join the Royal Marines, learning in May 1978 that he had been accepted for officer training at Lympstone, Devon, starting in September of that year. Even before joining the Marines as a Second Lieutenant, Mills was a talented sportsman – a black belt in judo and a keen mountaineer – and he was looking for a job that would challenge him physically and mentally.

On completing his course, Mills was appointed to 41 Commando as a troop Commander, still in the rank of Second Lieutenant. During this period and aged just nineteen, he qualified as a jungle warfare instructor in Brunei. The unit then completed a tour of duty with the United Nations in Cyprus and an operational tour in South Armagh, Northern Ireland, during the height of The Troubles. Next, he was appointed to 45 Commando as a company second-in-command, and he completed Arctic warfare training in Norway. In 1981, he was appointed to the Antarctic patrol ship HMS *Endurance*.

As detailed in the introduction to this chapter, he and his men had been despatched to South Georgia from the Falkland Islands to eject the scrap-metal dealers who had illegally arrived and put up the Argentine flag on 19 March. Again as detailed in the introduction, the situation had become more serious as March turned to April. In fact, when Mills and his men had landed on South Georgia from *Endurance* on 31 March, even then a full-scale invasion of the Falklands seemed an unlikely scenario to the British. Both Captain Nick Barker, in command of *Endurance*, and Mills thought the crisis would probably 'blow over' in a few days. Before dropping off the Royal Marine detachment, Barker told Mills to defend the British scientists but not to alarm them by saying that they were in any danger. Barker also told Mills that there should be no radio communication between them, as that could indicate the position of *Endurance* to the enemy. The rules of engagement for Mills and his men were that they could only open fire in self-defence or in the process of saving a life. The party went ashore with 20,000 rounds of ammunition – just in case.

We now know that the Argentine force planned to invade South Georgia on 2 April but were put off by the terrible weather, including a force 12 gale. However, the Argentine ship *Bahía Paraíso* had entered the main bay at South Georgia that day and had sent a radio communication to the British base saying it would return the next day with a 'very important message'. Mills and his men were, by this point, aware of the invasion of the Falkland Islands, and so they started to 'dig in' and prepare to defend the island. Mills also decided to break radio silence with *Endurance*, radioing, 'The Argentinians have made contact with us and will do so again tomorrow morning. What are our instructions?' Much later in the day, the reply came back from *Endurance*: 'When the Argentinians make contact with you, you are not to co-operate.' However, Mills was understandably left puzzled by just how much of a fight that meant he should put up. He replied, 'Your last message is ambiguous. Please clarify.'

Very early the next day, *Endurance* sent Mills a further message: 'When asked to surrender, you are not to do so.' When Mills relayed this message to his men, there were whoops and hollers of delight; they were up for a firefight, but until this moment they had feared that they would have to surrender without any resistance. Half an hour later, however, yet another message came through from *Endurance*: 'The OCRM [Officer in Charge Royal Marines] is not, repeat not, to take any action that would endanger life.' Mills was thoroughly confused and confided the final message only to Sergeant Major Peter Leach, his second-in-command. Mills told Leach that he had decided not to pass this message on to the rest of the men in case it 'muddied the waters' over what they could and could not do as and when the enemy arrived to take the island. By this point, too, explosives had been placed on the main jetty, ready to be detonated if the enemy invaded.

So, at dawn on 3 April 1982, Mills was in charge of a force of twenty-two Royal Marines, including himself, defending South Georgia and thirteen British scientists. The situation facing him could hardly have been more challenging. The previous day, an Argentine force had invaded the Falkland Islands, forcing Rex Hunt to surrender after a short-lived battle. Meanwhile, *Endurance* was at sea midway between the Falklands and South Georgia, making its way to the latter. Captain Nick Barker was, in turn, in touch with London and getting increasingly frustrated by orders not to try to engage the enemy.

At 10.30 a.m. on 3 April, Captain César Trombetta, on board the *Bahía Paraíso* and leading the Argentine force in the area, radioed over the Channel 16 international frequency to the South Georgia garrison, saying, 'Following our successful operation in the Malvinas Islands, the ex-Governor has surrendered the Islands and dependencies to Argentina. We suggest you adopt a similar course of action to prevent any loss of life. If so, all British troops and government personnel will be repatriated to the UK unharmed.'

Mills asked for 'some time to clarify the situation' – i.e. to consider his response and to radio the *Endurance* for guidance. He had hoped for several hours' grace but was told he had only 'five minutes' to consider his response. In his book, Captain Barker wrote of this moment: '3 April was the day when the feeling of impotence hit hardest. I hated what I had to do only slightly less than I despised those who had brought about this situation.'

Meanwhile Mills, after his five minutes of thought, radioed *Bahía Paraíso* to say, 'I am the British Commander of the military troops stationed on South Georgia. Do not make any attempt to land until we have clarified the situation with our superiors. Any attempt to land will be met with force.'

Later that morning, Barker lost radio contact with South Georgia, writing long afterwards:

We knew that the battle had begun … We were most fearful for Keith and our Marines. The situation they faced was untenable. Their lives depended on an honourable adversary and the common sense to know when to admit defeat. When you join the armed services you accept the risks. But you do not expect to fight, and perhaps die, on some Godforsaken windswept mountainside just about as far from home as you can get. At this point South Georgia seemed unimportant, an irrelevance. What could Argentina do with it anyway?

The Marines were 'dug in' in a position about 100 metres from the shore in a sheltered bay, with a Union flag fluttering nearby. They had placed mines and improvised explosive devices in front of the position where they anticipated the enemy would land. Mills had intended to give them a 'bloody nose' and then withdraw into the mountains, where his men had some basic supplies.

The first the Marines saw of the invading force was the corvette *Guerrico* rounding a point and coming into a cove close to the BAS base. She was supported by an Alouette helicopter hovering above. Initially, Mills marched down to the jetty at King Edward Point with the intention of talking to the Argentine landing party. Instead, the helicopter landed and dropped some eight enemy Marines close by, one of whom raised his rifle in Mills's direction. Mills decided there would be no opportunity to talk, and instead he retreated.

Next, a Puma helicopter from *Bahía Paraíso* attempted to land on the foreshore. Mills ordered his men to commence firing and more than 500 rounds of small-arms fire hit the helicopter from a range of under 100 metres. Trailing smoke, the aircraft pulled away and limped some 1,200 metres to the other side of the bay, where it crash-landed. Next on the scene was another helicopter, again an Alouette, and this aircraft was also hit by British fire and crashed.

Guerrico began blasting away with 40mm guns from the aft-end and a 100mm gun from the bow. The British expected her to stop out of their range and then fire at them from a safe distance, but instead *Guerrico* carried on until she was only 500 metres from the British force. In his official report of the incident, a copy of which I have obtained, Mills later wrote:

> I ordered my men to open fire. The corvette was committed to entering the bay and could not turn around. The first 84mm round fired at the ship landed approximately 10 metres short of its target. The round did not detonate on impact with the water, but did detonate on impact with the ship below the water line. The ship was also hit by a 66mm round behind the front 100mm turret. The ship was also engaged by heavy machine gun and rifle fire.

Mills continued:

The ship then moved right into the bay, about turned, and headed out to sea again at full speed. We engaged the corvette for a second time scoring anti-tank rocket hits on the Exocet and to the main upper deck superstructure. Again she was engaged by heavy machine gun and rifle fire. I was later informed by an Argentine marine officer that we had scored a total of 1,275 hits on the corvette, and had we hit her again below the water line she would surely have sunk.

The corvette then made its way to a position about 3,000 metres away and started to shell our position with her 100mm main armament. What I did not know at the time was that the elevation control on the gun had been destroyed and the ship had to manoeuvre its own position to enable the shells to land accurately on our position. This shelling continued for a period of about twenty minutes. During this time we were continually engaged by heavy and accurate fire from the other Argentine positions.

When the shelling stopped there seemed to be a temporary ceasefire. It was then I realised that a withdrawal for us would be almost impossible as the Argentine troops that had landed earlier on the far side of the bay had moved round to cut off our withdrawal. We had by this stage already sustained one casualty, and I realised that we would sustain many more had we waited until the hours of darkness before attempting a withdrawal. A withdrawal in daylight conditions would have been impossible. Having already achieved our aim of forcing the Argentines to use military force I realised we could achieve no more, and it was at this stage I decided to surrender to the Argentine forces. We were also in the fortunate position at this stage of having pinned a group of Argentine marines down close to our position.

As we had not planned to surrender, we had no white flag, and therefore had to improvise using a green anorak with white lining. On initially waving this article of clothing [at the top of a rifle] the Argentines engaged it with heavy fire. I then waved it again and this time it was not engaged. I realised that I would have to move forward from my position to negotiate with the Argentines as it was unlikely they were going to come to me. I slowly stood up [from the safety of the trench], and remarkably I was not shot. I then moved forward to the Argentine position in the base and was met by an Argentine marine officer. I informed him that his position was desperate as was ours, and unless we ceased firing then he and his men in the position in the base would surely die. We had achieved our aim and if we were to be guaranteed good treatment we would lay down our arms sparing the lives of many of his men who would surely have died had he taken our position by force. The Argentine officer agreed saying that it was a very sensible decision and that he would guarantee good treatment for my men.

After more than two hours of intense fighting, the battle for South Georgia was over. It is believed that the twenty-two Royal Marines faced an overall invasion force of some 300 enemy servicemen. The sole British casualty was a corporal shot twice in one arm. The number of enemy casualties is not known, but it is likely there was a total of around twenty dead and wounded.

Mills and his men assembled on the beach. Along with the rounded-up thirteen scientists, the British party gathered on *Bahía Paraíso*. In an interview at his Devon home, Mills told me that the Argentines had initially been 'twitchy' immediately after the British had surrendered. They could not believe they were facing a force of just twenty-two men and feared they were about to be ambushed.

After a while, they accepted it was just twenty-two of us. Even when we were unarmed, they were still very wary of us, while our guys were a bit worried that we still might all get shot in cold blood. It was all a bit tense. I had to tell the Argentines that we had 'wired up' the jetty and other areas. I didn't want them blowing themselves up now that we were all prisoners of war.

As for Captain Barker on *Endurance*, he arrived on the scene hours later, but by then he could not provide support, later writing, 'It was to our huge regret that all this happened as we were heading east round the southern tip of South Georgia. I had every intention of bringing helicopter support to our Marines by mid-afternoon. We were too late.'

Back home in Britain, the media seized upon Mills's bravery: it was the first bit of 'good news' to come from the South Atlantic. Mills's last stand was likened to the famous defence of Rorke's Drift in 1879 during the Anglo-Zulu War, when a small group of British soldiers held out against a much larger force of marauding Zulus. Newspaper headlines on 5 April 1982 were full of his bravery from two days earlier. The front page of the *Daily Star* carried the huge headline 'Keith Mills, hero', alongside a smaller headline that read: 'Marine who showed Whitehall that the British fighting spirit is still alive'.

After their negotiated surrender, Mills and his men plus the scientists embarked on a voyage to Puerto Belgrano, Argentina, which took a total of eleven days, part of it spent circling the Argentine coast while the enemy decided what to do with its prisoners. Once they landed, the Marines were kept at the port for four more days and were questioned about the conduct of the Argentine forces in South Georgia by some sort of board of inquiry.

Mills became emotional with sheer pride when he told me how a senior Argentine officer, General Carlos Büsser, had insisted on meeting all twenty-two Royal Marines in person. The General told

Mills: 'I have come here today because I have been in Buenos Aires listening to the stories of the defence by British Marines of South Georgia. I am a Marine and I decided that I had to come and meet these men.' Mills continues,

> With that, the General went along the line and saluted each of my men, shook their hands and said, 'If Argentine marines were the same as British marines, we would conquer the world. If there is anything you want, let me know and you will have it.' We made a short list that ended 'Twenty-two one-way tickets to London and twenty-two women.' Büsser said: 'You can have everything on the list except the women and the one-way tickets home you will have to wait for.' Yet the next day we flew out of Argentina.

On 17 April, the British Marines were flown to Montevideo, where they were looked after by the British Consulate. On the morning of 19 April, they were flown back to England in an RAF VC10, landing at RAF Brize Norton, Oxfordshire, on the morning of 20 April. Mills was soon reunited with his then girlfriend, Liz Stananought, later to become his wife.

Mills was awarded the DSC on 4 June 1982, and his citation read:

> Lieutenant Mills was the Commanding Officer of a 22-man Royal Marines contingent despatched to South Georgia on 31st March 1982 to monitor the activities of a group of Argentines illegally landed on the island and to protect a British Antarctic Survey Team based there. On 3rd April 1982 a major Argentine assault began and, following his unsuccessful attempts to forestall the attack by negotiation, Lieutenant Mills conducted a valiant defence in the face of overwhelming odds. In spite of the fact that his unit was impossibly outnumbered, extensive damage was inflicted on the

Argentine corvette *Guerrico*, one helicopter was shot down and another damaged. Only when the detachment was completely surrounded, and it was obvious that further resistance would serve no purpose, did he order a ceasefire, placing himself at great personal risk to convey this fact to the invading forces. Lieutenant Mills' resolute leadership during this action reflected the finest traditions of the Corps.

On the same day, Sergeant Peter Leach was awarded the Distinguished Service Medal (DSM) for his gallantry during the same action.

In a typed letter dated 7 June 1982, Admiral Sir Desmond Cassidi, the Second Sea Lord and Chief of Naval Personnel, wrote to Mills saying, 'Many congratulations on your award of the DSC for the part you played in the defence of South Georgia. As the citation for your award states, your resolute leadership during this action reflected the finest traditions of the Corps. Well done.'

Captain Barker later wrote a hand-written and 'informal' letter to Mills's father, Alan, dated 1 August 1982, in which he congratulated him on his son's bravery:

This was a magnificent action and he richly deserves his D.S.C. There has been a great deal of bravery during this short, sharp war, but Keith set the pace, set the example and gave a very special sense of pride back to the country as a whole. We are all proud of him...

I have also obtained a copy of an internal report that summarises Mills's work between June 1981 to September 1982, which included the period of the Falklands War. It read:

There is usually fun, quick wit and coarse humour when Keith Mills is about. He is irrepressible, enthusiastic to a degree about most things, killing Argentines in particular, and a very good man to have in a 'tight corner'. He is very fit and has boundless energy and a good brain once he has it pointed in the right direction.

Although a carefree, somewhat wild, young officer, he proved to be calm and extremely courageous during the First Battle of Grytviken, his DSC was very well deserved indeed and his maturity when the 'chips were down' was outstanding.

I have thoroughly enjoyed having him on board, he has led his men very well, he has accepted many new habits with grace and should do well in future appointments.

After the war ended, a mountain on South Georgia was named 'Mills Peak' in the young officer's honour. 'A lot of people are fortunate enough to be awarded gallantry medals, but to have a landmark named after you is quite something. I was very touched,' Mills told me.

After the Falklands War, Mills's roles included a second UN tour of Cyprus with 40 Commando, another operational tour of Northern Ireland and training duties. He also represented the Corps, the Royal Navy and the Combined Services at alpine skiing. He was promoted to Captain in 1989, was Adjutant at the Royal Marines Depot in Deal, Kent, at the time when the IRA bombed the barracks, killing eleven Marines from the Royal Marines School of Music and leaving another twenty-one wounded. From 1992 to 1995, he was involved in an officer exchange role with the Royal Netherlands Marine Corps, and in 1995, he was appointed as a liaison officer in Bosnia and Croatia at the height of the Balkan War. Mills left the Marines in the rank of Captain on 4 July 1996. By that point, he and his wife, who were married in 1986, had two children.

A final internal assessment of Mills's work, written in September 1995 just months before he left the Royal Marines, stated, 'Mills is a muscular, fit and dynamic officer brimming over with enthusiasm and energy. Although due to leave the Service shortly on voluntary redundancy, he has not let this intrude on his performance ... His decision to leave the Corps is a sad one, if fully understandable.'

In 2007, Mills and his wife were invited back by the Commissioner of South Georgia to unveil a plaque as part of the commemorations of the war a quarter of a century on. Before leaving for their adventure, he said, 'I haven't been back in twenty-five years. I'm quite excited. I've heard it's changed a bit.' During his visit, Mills flew over the peak named after him in a helicopter, but it was considered too unsafe to land and walk on it.

After leaving the Armed Forces, Mills started a business developing and running care homes for the elderly in east Devon, where he continues to live. He remains as managing director of Doveleigh Care Ltd, which has three award-winning care homes; he has held the position for twenty-five years.

CHAPTER 2

THE WAR AT SEA

On 5 April 1982, just three days after Argentina invaded the Falkland Islands, the British Armed Forces were ordered to sail to the South Atlantic fully 8,000 miles away. On 7 April, the UK announced, rather ambitiously, its intention to impose a 200-mile exclusion zone around the Falkland Islands. It did so knowing that it would be weeks before it could even try to enforce what became known as the 'TEZ' (Total Exclusion Zone), and even then, their task might prove impossible.

In the days just before the invasion, and with the Argentine fleet en route to the Falklands, Margaret Thatcher had discussed the prospect of an Argentine attack with her defence chiefs, including Admiral Sir Henry Leach, the First Sea Lord. The Prime Minister had asked him bluntly: 'First Sea Lord, if the invasion happens, precisely what can we do?' Leach's response was calm and considered: 'I can put together a Task Force of destroyers, frigates, landing craft, support vessels. It will be led by the aircraft carriers HMS Hermes *and HMS* Invincible. *It can be ready to leave in forty-eight hours.'*

This is exactly what happened after the invasion. The Task Force eventually comprised 127 ships: forty-three naval vessels, twenty-two Royal Fleet Auxiliary (RFA) ships and sixty-two merchant ships. Those ships requisitioned for war duties included the giant cruiser SS Canberra, *which set sail from Southampton on 9 April with 3 Commando Brigade on board, and the ocean liner* Queen Elizabeth 2, *which left from Southampton on 12 May carrying the 5th Infantry Brigade. British military actions in the war were given the codename 'Operation*

Corporate' and the Commander of the Task Force was Admiral Sir John Fieldhouse.

When the first ships in the Task Force set sail, there was still a reasonable chance that war could be avoided. However, it soon became clear that the Royal Navy and the men on its ships were sailing to war and that the challenges they faced would be formidable. With no advantage over the enemy on land or in the air, it also became clear that the Royal Navy, the senior service in the Armed Forces, would have to play a key role in the fighting. Indeed, how the navy fared was likely to decide whether the war was won or lost. At the time, the US Navy was said to have assessed the chances of the Task Force recapturing the islands as 'a military impossibility'.

Depending on where it set off from and the size of the ship, the journey to the Falkland Islands was expected to take around three weeks. Most ships stopped off at Ascension Island – a 34-square-mile mound of volcanic rock in the South Atlantic – on the way, to pick up supplies and to prepare for what lay ahead. Meanwhile, a small force had been sent to recapture South Georgia, with the British destroyer HMS Antrim arriving off the island on 21 April. Military actions to recapture South Georgia were codenamed 'Operation Paraquet' (sometimes also spelt 'Operation Paraquat'). This task was achieved on 25 April 1982, with Mrs Thatcher famously telling the nation to 'rejoice' at the news.

On 2 May, the day after two Vulcan bombers had attacked Stanley airfield, the first major loss of the war took place when, in what were to become highly controversial circumstances, the Argentine cruiser General Belgrano was sunk by a torpedo fired from a British submarine. The sinking led to 323 Argentines being killed, while 700 sailors survived. News of the sinking caused shock among the Task Force and the British public, and the incident became a cause célèbre for anti-war campaigners. Opponents of the sinking claimed that the Belgrano was outside the TEZ and sailing away from the conflict. British defence insisted, however, that the Task Force had the right to defend itself against any hostile vessel.

Once the Belgrano *had been sunk, and with British ships near the Falklands particularly vulnerable to attack, it was almost inevitable that Argentina would strike back fast and hard. On 4 May, HMS* Sheffield *was hit by an Exocet missile, which started a fire in the control room. The crew was forced to abandon ship and twenty men died. The* Sheffield *was the first British warship to be sunk in the conflict.*

On 14–15 May, the SAS attacked Pebble Island, which could have given an early warning of the arrival of the British fleet. Three days later, the Argentine junta rejected British peace proposals, and two days after that, on 20 May, United Nations peace talks also failed, thereby ending any real hope of a diplomatic outcome to the crisis.

With a land battle now inevitable, 3,000 troops and a mass of equipment were landed at San Carlos Water, East Falkland, on 21 May, with a view to establishing a beachhead for attacks on Goose Green and Port Stanley. As the Argentine Air Force tried to prevent the landings, HMS Ardent *was sunk with the loss of twenty-two crew. HMS* Argonaut *and HMS* Antrim *were also hit by bombs that failed to explode but nevertheless killed two men. In turn, thirteen Argentine aircraft were reportedly shot down.*

Two days later, on 23 May, HMS Antelope *was hit and later sunk after one of the bombs that had lodged in the ship exploded during bomb-disposal work. In a week of heavy British casualties at sea, HMS* Coventry *was bombed on 25 May, with the loss of twenty men, and on the same day the container ship* Atlantic Conveyor *was hit, with twelve men being killed.*

In June, as the land war escalated, there were further major casualties at sea. On 8 June, as British troops were ferried from San Carlos to Bluff Cove and Fitzroy, ready for the southern offensive on Stanley, the Argentines again mounted a deadly attack. A delay in disembarking troops meant that around fifty men, most of them from the Welsh Guards, were killed by Argentine aircraft which attacked the landing ships Sir Galahad *and* Sir Tristram. *Four days later, as the land war reached its climax, the British destroyer HMS* Glamorgan *was hit by a shore-launched Exocet missile, killing a further thirteen men; another member of her crew later died of his wounds.*

Falklands War Heroes *does not seek to provide a definitive account of the war at sea. That role has already been fulfilled by Admiral Sir Sandy Woodward's* One Hundred Days: The Memoirs of the Falklands Battle Group Commander *and many other excellent books. However, this book does try to provide an insight into the bravery of some of those who served at sea, particularly their gallantry throughout the losses of some of the Royal Navy's finest ships and most courageous men. No less brave were many soldiers from the British Army who died or displayed valour while the ship in which they were being transported came under attack.*

The contribution of the Royal Navy in recapturing the Falklands was immeasurable. Woodward's last signal to the Task Force on 4 July 1982 from HMS Hermes, *then off Port Stanley, said: 'As I haul my South Atlantic flag down, I reflect sadly on the brave lives lost, and the good ships gone, in the short time of our trial. I thank wholeheartedly each and every one of you for your gallant support, tough determination and fierce perseverance under bloody conditions. Let us all be grateful that Argentina does not breed bulldogs and, as we return severally to enjoy the blessings of our land, resolve that those left behind for ever shall not be forgotten.'*

GRAHAM JOHN ROBERT LIBBY

Service: Royal Navy

Final Rank: Petty Officer

FALKLANDS WAR DECORATION / DISTINCTION:

DISTINGUISHED SERVICE MEDAL (DSM)

DATE OF BRAVERY: 25 MAY 1982

GAZETTED: 8 OCTOBER 1982

HM submarine *Conqueror* is best known for sinking the Argentine cruiser *General Belgrano* in an incident that is still controversial nearly forty years on. Yet for crew member Petty Officer Graham Libby, his greatest test came not at the time of the sinking but less than a month later, when he showed outstanding courage as a diver to solve a major problem faced by his submarine.

Graham John Robert Libby was born on 2 December 1958 in Portsmouth, Hampshire. The son of a Royal Navy diver, he was brought up and educated in the city before leaving school at sixteen. As a boy, he had initially wanted to join the fire brigade, but he eventually enlisted in the Royal Navy instead in 1975, aged sixteen. Two years later, he transferred to the Submarine Service, and like his father before him, he became a diver.

By the spring of 1982, when war broke out, Libby had been serving in the *Conqueror*, arguably the most famous British submarine ever launched, for three years. Some 285ft long with a beam of 32ft, the *Conqueror* was ordered on 9 August 1966, just ten days after England defeated West Germany 4–2 in extra time to win the World Cup. The *Conqueror* was built at Cammell Laird's Birkenhead shipyard and was launched on 28 August 1969, then finally commissioned on 9 November 1971. The *Conqueror* was a Churchill-class nuclear-powered submarine with a complement of more than 100 officers and crew.

By late March 1982, after completing a three-month overseas deployment, the *Conqueror* was back at her base of Faslane, situated on the eastern side of Gare Loch, Scotland, home to the 3rd Submarine Squadron. With the submarine in need of some repair work, her crew was given leave. However, just two days before the invasion of the Falkland Islands and with diplomatic alarm bells ringing loud and clear, the men were ordered to return to the boat – and to prepare for war. Libby was one of those on leave at his home in Portsmouth on 1 April 1982. He told Mike Rossiter, the author of the book *Sink the Belgrano*:

I had only been there a few days when there was a knock on the
door and there was this policeman stood there saying, 'You've been
recalled. Make your way to the boat.' It was the morning of April
the first he knocked on the door, and I thought, this is a wind-up,
April fool, so I phoned the boat up in Faslane, and they said, 'Yeah,
it's true – you're recalled.' When I got there it was just a hive of
activity. There were stores on the jetty, there was a complete new
weapons load, everybody was running around, and I thought this is
not a wind-up, this is not an exercise, something is going on here.

The crew received instructions to 'store for war', which meant
taking twice the amount of provisions on board that were needed
for a routine patrol. To start with, all the crew were baffled as
to their destination, but it soon emerged that there was trouble
brewing in the Falkland Islands. Soon, under the command of the
newly appointed Commander Christopher Wreford-Brown, the
Conqueror was sailing for the South Atlantic – but with many of
the crew initially convinced that the dispute would be settled by
diplomacy, not military conflict.

Libby was the submarine's 'scratcher', the crewman responsible for the maintenance of the outer casing. Part of his role was to
ensure that the capstans, winches and cables were all properly secured and that they made no noise when the boat was under way: in
war, such noises could give away the submarine's position, resulting
in it being torpedoed or bombed and all lives on board being lost.
Libby was also the most senior diver on board the *Conqueror*.

He was enthusiastic about the secret presence of fourteen Special
Boat Service (SBS) men on board the submarine. The SBS – men
drawn from the Royal Marines – were not as famous as their SAS
cousins, but they were still respected as an elite and highly trained
force. However, early on in the *Conqueror*'s journey to the South

Atlantic, the Special Forces men also gave him cause for concern. In his interview with Mike Rossiter, Libby takes up the story some time after the submarine left Faslane on 4 April:

> We were heading down, making good speed, when suddenly we heard this massive thumping noise. It sounded like part of the boat was rattling and we thought, 'What the hell is that?' You don't like it because it means you haven't done your job properly, or we have to surface and fix something. And we have guys on the boat that can go round with a little portable device to isolate where the sound is coming from. Because we have to fix it, you can't make those sort of noises when you are operational, you have to be quiet. And we listened and we couldn't pin down what it was. Eventually the noise monitors came back. The banging was the SBS guys doing their exercises in the fore part [of the submarine] where the torpedoes were stored. They were banging against the metal grating and it was being transmitted out to the ocean. It was a hell of a racket. So we had to put rubber mats down whenever they wanted to work out. But to have an SBS unit on board was unusual, and you thought, 'What the hell's going on?' We knew we were going south but we didn't know why these chaps were on board.

Libby also said that once on board, the crew tended to concentrate on the job in hand: 'You didn't forget your family; it's very strange, you have your family but they're over there in England in a box, and you very quickly come down to the only thing that matters is the submarine and the job it's doing and your mates.'

Libby said the crew picked up snippets of information on their journey south – they crossed the equator after just over a week at sea, on 12 April – but they never got the complete picture. 'We'd get told that Mrs Thatcher's doing this and this has happened, and rules of engagement are changing. Although we were never told specifics, you know. You were kept in the picture but you were kept in the little tiny picture in the corner of a big picture.'

After nearly three weeks at sea, *Conqueror* was approaching South Georgia, more than 900 miles south-east of the Falklands. By this point, the British government had decided to retake South Georgia prior to mounting an attack on the Falkland Islands. However, when the assault on South Georgia was planned, no role was given to the SBS men travelling in the submarine. *Conqueror* resurfaced so the men could be picked up by helicopter and transferred to HMS *Antrim*, the navy's county-class destroyer. Just at the worst possible moment, one of the SBS men and Petty Officer Libby were hit by a huge wave that swept them into the bitterly cold sea.

In his book *Secrets of the Conqueror: The Untold Story of Britain's Most Famous Submarine*, Stuart Prebble tells the story:

The ship's helicopter quickly moved into place and lowered its single rescue hoist above their heads. Libby was wearing only his waterproofs and immediately felt the warmth from his body draining away into the frozen sea. The SBS man had on his dry suit, but neither was keen to remain in the water for long. There was a brief exchange of glances between the two men: who would avail himself of the rescue hoist and who would remain in the ice-cold mountainous waves? The question answered itself; both men managed to secure themselves into the harness and were brought back on board at the same time. Libby was put into a bath to try to get his circulation going again, and spent six hours recovering on board HMS *Antrim*. When rescuers removed the trousers of the SBS man they were amazed to see that his legs were pink and the blood was circulating normally. These men had been trained in the Arctic, and a dip in the South Atlantic seemed to be a matter of very little concern. Eventually the men from the SBS were air-lifted successfully by helicopter to the destroyer.

Libby later told author Mike Rossiter about the incident:

> The next thing I know, this wave has come from nowhere, the submarine dipped down, came back up and the next wave swept me, the cargo net and the SBS trooper into the sea. I had the weight of the cargo net on me and as it pulled me down the life-line broke. Which was lucky otherwise I would have drowned. The submarine just kept going – it's such a big beast it can't stop.

As the helicopter hovering above dropped just one line for both men in the water, Libby felt unbelievably cold.

> We sort of look at each other, and he's quite happy sat there in his dry suit, and I'm going blue, and he's sort of looking at me to say, 'I'm going first,' and I'm thinking, 'I'm going first.' In the end we both went in the same harness, I was very close to collapse because of the cold.

Libby was officially classed as a 'survivor' after the incident, which meant he was given new kit – plimsolls and clothes – before being returned to his submarine, which had remained on the surface as engineers tried to repair some communications problems.

Once in the war zone, the *Conqueror* was on the lookout for potential targets, notably the Argentine aircraft carrier *Veinticinco de Mayo*. The dream scenario for the crew of the *Conqueror* was that the aircraft carrier could be sunk before its aircraft successfully attacked British ships in the area. HMS *Splendid*, *Conqueror's* sister boat, did in fact locate the aircraft carrier outside the TEZ, only to lose it again. Next, *Conqueror* was ordered to head south-west of the Falklands to look for the Argentine cruiser *General Belgrano*, which had been bought from the US in 1951 after being active – under a different name, of course – during the Second World War. *Conqueror* was tasked with finding the *Belgrano* and trailing her, as the 'rules of engagement' suggested an attack was not permissible.

On 23 April, the British government made a statement that said Argentine ships might be a target 'if they could amount to a threat to interfere with the mission of British Forces in the South Atlantic'. This went further than the government's earlier statement, which had restricted targets to inside the 200-mile TEZ.

British intelligence passed on information deemed to be of 'excellent' quality to Commander Wreford-Brown that a four-ship Argentine convoy, made up of the *Belgrano*, two destroyers and an oiler, was in his vicinity. Petty Officer Libby was supervising the duty team listening for incoming sonar signals when he detected something at 16.45 GMT – 1.45 p.m. local time – on 30 April. 'The first contact was a heavy – it was a heavy ship. A heavy oiler makes a lot more noise than a warship does,' he told author Mike Rossiter. Despite being over 50 miles away, he could tell from the steady beat of the propellers and the clatter of the diesel engines that this was a slow-moving ship – if it was from the small convoy, it was likely to be the oiler that was on the scene for refuelling purposes. Libby said,

We had to investigate every single contact that we came across. With experience, you can listen to a vessel and know immediately that it was not what we were looking for. We had various fishing vessels as contacts, but as soon as we heard the tanker, we knew this was of interest. I reported it to the control room, the control room told the Captain, and we investigated it further.

The Captain decided to go closer, initially 20 miles nearer, strongly suspecting that his target – the *Belgrano* – would eventually come within firing range. The next morning was 1 May and, although the Captains of both the *Conqueror* and the *Belgrano* were initially unaware of it, the fight for the Falklands had started in earnest.

At 9.49 a.m. on 1 May, the Captain of the *Conqueror* ordered the submarine to be raised to periscope depth, and he was able to see the *Belgrano* minutes later. In fact, he could see her being refuelled by the oil tanker. Throughout the afternoon, the Argentine cruiser was trailed by the British submarine, with Libby and the rest of the sonar team listening to the *Belgrano*'s engine and propeller: both were heard loud and clear beneath the waves. The *Belgrano* was, in turn, moving towards, not away from, the TEZ. The atmosphere on board was tense as the Argentine sailors realised their first taste of military action was probably imminent. Little did they know that the *Conqueror* was only 5 miles away, some 200ft below the surface. That evening Captain Hector Bonzo made an announcement to his crew on the *Belgrano* that he had been instructed to attack the British Task Force, then some 200 miles away.

The final order to 'Sink the *Belgrano*' came on 2 May and was issued by the British War Cabinet. They held a twenty-minute meeting beginning at 1 p.m. with Lord Lewin, the Chief of the Defence Staff, at which he asked permission for Rear Admiral Sandy Woodward to proceed with his (Woodward's) desire to sink the enemy ship even though she was outside the TEZ. Communication problems to the submarine further delayed things, but Wreford-Brown and his crew were soon in a position to carry out their orders.

Once again, Stuart Prebble, who had unique access to crew from the submarine, sets the scene and tells the story:

Later that morning [morning because of the time difference], in the South Atlantic, the Captain announced to the crew that they had orders to sink the *Belgrano* and that after lunch they would be going to action stations. This meant that every man on board would be at his post and ready to do whatever was necessary. This was something they had done countless times in exercise, but this was the first time a British submarine had been on a real combat footing since 1945, and the gravity of the situation was not lost on those in the boat.

Lunch on that day consisted of roast pork with all the trimmings, followed by apple crumble and custard. Grant Louch [Weapons Engineering Rating] had just come off his morning duty and tried to grab two hours' sleep before he would be called to action stations. Needless to say, he did not sleep. 'I remember it being very calm,' he recalls. 'Everyone was doing everything exactly by the book, just as we had been trained to do.'

Libby told Mike Rossiter that the situation had remained calm:

It's a funny feeling because you weren't nervous because this is all you'd ever trained to do. As time went on, you were constantly passing to the Captain the bearings and updating the Captain on its position – it was constant updates and the chatter back and forth was tremendous. And even then we were still going, 'It's never going to happen.' Then I thought, 'Fuck me – we are going to fire.' And people looked at each other and went, 'Fucking hell.' I'll never forget it. And then the boat vibrated, the first one went, moving your cursor around you can hear the fish [torpedo] running away, there's two, there's three, all three are running. And you can hear the Captain asking, 'How long to run?' So the periscope goes up at the last minute and as the 'scope goes up and he puts his eyes to it, *bang*.

Three Mark 8 torpedoes fired at three-second intervals had been aimed at the *Belgrano* and two had hit their target. It was just after 4 p.m. local time on 2 May that the *Belgrano* was hit, when she was situated at 55° 24' south latitude and 61° 32' west longitude. After initially listing to port, the ship began to sink. At 4.24, just twenty minutes after the attack, Captain Bonzo instructed his crew to abandon ship, and once the crew had prepared the inflatable life rafts the evacuation got under way. A total of 323 men lost their lives, many killed in the two initial explosions. At the time of the attack, there were more than 1,000 men on board. It was the first operational sinking attributable to a nuclear-powered submarine.

There was a feeling of euphoria on board the *Conqueror*, but it did not last long. Libby told Mike Rossiter: 'Everybody was on a high because of what we'd done, but it's momentary. We've got to get our heads back on. The threat's now what else is around us, update the skipper on everything so he can plot a way out safely without getting caught.' Having ensured that the attack was successful, Commander Wreford-Brown took the *Conqueror* deep and fast for a sprint away from the immediate area. In fact, the submarine remained at 500ft and changed course to move eastwards. After a short while, she moved south-west, putting 50 miles between the submarine and its stricken target.

In the two days after the attack, the *Conqueror* patrolled the area close by. However, at 12.56 p.m. on 7 May, the company learnt how it felt to be on the wrong end of a surprise attack by the enemy – in this case a low-flying aircraft. With the submarine at periscope depth, the *Conqueror* came under attack from an airborne Mark 46 torpedo which used sonar to home in on its target. The company knew that it could take fully six minutes from the moment of launch to the potential moment of impact. This meant they spent six long minutes wondering if they were about to be hit and sunk. The sudden realisation that the torpedo might have locked on to the nuclear submarine caused Wreford-Brown to undertake a series of dangerous, high-speed manoeuvres. The Captain gave the order for 'full ahead'. This necessitated the engineers to operate the 'battle short switch', which overrides all nuclear-reactor safety measures designed to regulate pressure and temperature within the reactor. Turning these off could lead to a reactor meltdown. 'On this occasion, however, the manoeuvre appeared to be entirely justified, because the instruments soon showed that the torpedo was no longer in pursuit,' Prebble wrote.

Now, though, it seemed that *Conqueror* was being hunted in deadly earnest. The order was given to go to silent routine, which meant that those not on operational duty were encouraged to lie in their bunks rather than walk around, and all non-essential machinery was switched off … Wreford-Brown now threw the boat around from deep to shallow, to very deep, to shallow, at every angle imaginable. [Lieutenant] Sethia had a vivid mental image of the submarine zig-zagging through the water, with some lethal weapon zig-zagging behind in tireless pursuit. Every passing second could bring with it instant annihilation for the submarine and every man on board … After what seemed like hours but was probably only minutes, the submarine appeared to be in the clear; it felt like a very narrow escape.

After surviving that dramatic moment, the *Conqueror* experienced a series of communication problems and as part of an effort to repair the situation, an aerial wire was released into the water. However, this appeared to have become entangled around the propeller and so rather than solving the initial problem, the wayward aerial had created another more serious one.

The position of the aerial wire, or whatever was causing the problem, meant the submarine had to operate at a reduced speed, and there was a noise coming from the propeller as it rotated. By 25 May, and with the submarine patrolling north of the Falkland Islands, there was only one thing for it: the submarine would have to surface – dangerous in itself with enemy aircraft in the area – and a diver, backed up by other crew, would be released into the water. His task was to investigate the problem and try to dislodge the wire.

The sea, however, was both bitterly cold and rough – this was the South Atlantic after all. There was a real danger that the diver might be washed away. Even worse, if an enemy aircraft was sighted, the submarine would have to dive at once, with the diver unable to get back into the submarine in time. The abandoned diver would have no chance of survival – either freezing to death or drowning, as it would be hours before it was safe for the submarine to re-emerge.

The submarine remained on high alert against attacks from the air, even though the Argentines had withdrawn what remained of their surface fleet, including the aircraft carrier, back to home waters. Petty Officer Libby volunteered for the task of trying to solve the submarine's problem, later recalling,

> I was a single man, I was quite happy to go out there because I was all pumped up. We had just sunk a blooming great warship – this could be the icing on the cake, you know? It's just something exciting that I might never ever get a chance to do.

In his book *Secrets of the Conqueror*, Stuart Prebble takes up the story:

> Libby and [First Lieutenant] Tim McClement climbed out onto

the submarine casing, with five other divers for support and back-up. All of the men were attached to the boat by life-lines, but straight away a wave swept Libby and [Lieutenant] John Coulthard into the water. Libby immediately disappeared from sight and, to his horror, McClement caught a glimpse of Coulthard lying apparently face-down in the ocean. For a moment it seemed that his life-line was not attached.

'How are things going up there?' From down in the control room, Wreford-Brown chose that precise moment to ask his first lieutenant for a progress report. For what he says was the only time, McClement chose to mislead his Captain.

'According to plan, sir,' he replied.

The life-line to Coulthard had not broken after all and he was pulled back on board, and Libby also now reappeared at the stern of the boat. Clanking around his body as he was buffeted by the waves was a range of tools and hacksaws which he thought he might need for the task. He edged his way around the submarine to the stern and found that the aerial wire was indeed wrapped tightly around the shaft and blades. Worse still, even though the engines were of course stopped, the propellers were still turning gently, and in danger of severing the diver's life-line back into the boat. Libby worked away with hacksaws, as speedily as he could, cutting off the wire in sections. The need for dexterity meant that he could not wear gloves, and gradually he felt his hands seize up and his entire body being penetrated by the cold. In his position back on the submarine, Tim McClement was constantly scanning the horizon for any sign of an enemy aircraft, knowing that there would be no way of getting Libby back in the boat if he had to give the order to dive. After twenty minutes, and just when his stamina was on the point of giving out, Libby declared the propeller clear and was hauled back inside the submarine.

Wreford-Brown noted in his log that Libby's efforts went 'far beyond the call of normal duty'. Later, the Captain said of the action:

> We surfaced at night and my best diver, Petty Officer Graham Libby, volunteered to dive in marginal weather to clear the wire from the propeller. He was diving in the dark in a reasonably rough sea. He spent twenty minutes struggling to get the wire off. Before he went out, I had to warn him that, if there was an air attack, I would have to dive and this would have given him very little time to get back on board. I think he was outstandingly brave. It is just the sort of thing I would expect from him.

This incident took place three weeks and two days after the controversial sinking of the *Belgrano* on 2 May 1982.

As the *Conqueror* continued her patrols, it was realised that – having left port on 4 April – she could be forced to remain at sea until the fall of Port Stanley. It was not known when this would be, but it could perhaps be as late as 14 July according to some calculations. This meant that food rationing would have to be introduced and the company was told:

> Please help to make things easier at this difficult time by NOT WASTING FOOD, EATING SENSIBLY and NOT GIVING THE CHEFS HASSLE. These restrictions have been introduced so that we can continue to enjoy a balanced diet for the remaining time on board rather than spending the last few weeks on bread and water.

As the *Conqueror* continued to patrol close to the Argentine coast, the Royal Navy sustained further losses due to attacks from enemy aircraft. However, slowly Britain gained the upper hand. With their Armed Forces weakened and demoralised, Major General Mario Menéndez, the Argentine Commanding Officer in the Falklands, surrendered on 14 June. There were celebratory scenes on board the *Conqueror*, and twenty-four hours later she was ordered home to her Faslane base. Her role in 'Operation Corporate', the military action to regain the Falklands, was over.

On 16 June, the submarine's company received a signal from Rear Admiral (later Admiral) Sandy Woodward, saying,

> When the dust has settled on the Falkland Islands campaign it will be seen that the single most significant naval event after the arrival of the Task Force itself was your sinking of the cruiser *Belgrano*. That action brought the Argentine Navy up with a round turn and sent it scurrying to the twelve-mile limit [of its coastline], there to stay for the duration while we got on and fought the air war.
>
> That cool and determined attack was typical of your whole patrol. Well done. Bon voyage. Take a well earned break.

As the *Conqueror* headed home, there was even a mail drop from a Nimrod, which resulted in thirty-four sacks, all full of letters from family, friends and strangers, falling into the sea and being eagerly recovered by the crew, the submarine having recently surfaced. There were newspapers too, including a copy of *The Sun* with its famous 'Gotcha' headline. All the papers not only championed the sinking but specifically named the *Conqueror* rather than simply attributing it to 'a British submarine'.

As Libby told Mike Rossiter: 'As a submariner we've done lots and lots of these patrols, and you're used to coming in very quietly, not allowed to say anything, about who you are, where you've been or what you've done. And now it was all over the papers.'

Conqueror arrived at Faslane to a triumphant reception on 3 July, proudly flying the White Ensign at the stern and the Jolly Roger, embellished with her achievements, at the mast above the fin. After their return to a heroes' welcome, the crew was sent home to recuperate after being at sea for more than fifteen weeks and were told that it would be at least two months before they would be called upon again. But it was not to be. Later that same month, intelligence reports were received that two Polish auxiliary general intelligence vessels were using towed-array sonars in the North Atlantic, and *Conqueror* was tasked with tracking them.

Libby's DSM was announced in *The London Gazette* on 8 October 1982 (although this *Supplement to The London Gazette* was in fact officially dated 'Monday, 11th October 1982'). His citation stated:

Whilst on patrol north of the Falklands [*sic*] Islands on 25th May 1982 a floating wire aerial trapped round HMS *Conqueror*'s propeller causing cavitation and noise to the detriment of her operational effectiveness.

Acting Petty Officer (Sonar) (SM) Libby volunteered to carry out a dive to free the obstruction. With the submarine surfaced he knew full well that if she were detected by Argentine aircraft she would possibly have to dive without recovering him. He was also battered by heavy waves, threatening to part his lifeline and sweeping him away. Nonetheless he succeeded in clearing most of the obstruction, after twenty minutes in dark, freezing, and terrifying conditions, enabling HMS *Conqueror* to continue on her patrol unhindered.

Acting Petty Officer (Sonar) (SM) Libby demonstrated a degree of cold, calculated courage and willingness to risk his life for the benefit of the ship far beyond any call of duty.

Commander Wreford-Brown was decorated with the Distinguished Service Order (DSO), and two other members of the boat's company were Mentioned in Despatches for their efforts to repair the radio mast.

Libby received his decoration in an investiture at Buckingham Palace on 8 February 1983. He told me that he still remembers the occasion fondly:

> It was a brilliant day out. I received my medal from the Queen, and I remember she called me by my first name. She had been incredibly well briefed because she knew I was on a course and she asked me how it was going. She had definitely done her homework and from what I could see she had no notes or prompts from a projector or anything else. She was very impressive – quite remarkable.

As time passed, the sinking of the *Belgrano* came under intense scrutiny. Part of this controversy resulted from the fact that John Nott, the Defence Secretary, made errors when he first reported the position and course of the *Belgrano* when she was torpedoed. In a further statement ten days after his initial report, Nott again made incorrect statements indicating that the enemy ship was just five or six hours from striking at the Task Force and was heading in its direction.

In December 1982, six months after the war had been won, Labour MP Tam Dalyell accused the Prime Minister of deliberately ordering the sinking to prevent an agreement with Argentina and to create the conditions for all-out war. As he put it, 'the *Conqueror*'s torpedoes would torpedo the peace negotiations'. Into the next year, 1983, and beyond, the conspiracy theory grew and grew. This book, which champions bravery in the Falklands, is not the place to go into the details of these conspiracy theories – or to seek to dismantle them one by one. Suffice to say that there were intelligence and military reasons for the government not wanting to go into great detail over the sinking at the time.

After leaving the Royal Navy in 1984, Libby worked for

Hampshire fire brigade at their headquarters in Eastleigh. During his time with the service, his expertise and wide-ranging activities meant that his name appeared in national and local newspapers several times. In July 2008, he was described as an 'inventor' when he assisted an electronics specialist in devising a remote-controlled model helicopter with on-board video and thermal cameras, which was helping fire crews to fight large blazes. Libby was quoted in the *Daily Mirror* saying of the model helicopter: 'The only way to get an aerial shot before was with a hydraulic platform. The helicopter will make tackling fires much quicker.'

As part of his role with the fire service, Libby began to special-ise in rescue techniques used following natural disasters. He was a member of Hampshire Fire Service's urban search and rescue team and the UK international search and rescue team, and he was deployed to Indonesia and New Zealand following large-scale earthquakes and to the Balkans following severe flooding.

He finally retired from the fire service in 2016 after thirty-one years of service. Libby has three grown-up children and five grand-children and lives in the Portsmouth area. Reflecting on the war and the sinking of the *Belgrano* nearly forty years on, he said, 'I have no qualms about what we did. I think we did the right thing. We'd have lost quite a lot more lives on our side without it.'

MALCOLM DAVID MESSENGER

Service: Royal Navy
Final rank: Able Seaman
FALKLANDS WAR DECORATION / DISTINCTION: **N/A**
DATE OF BRAVERY: N/A
GAZETTED: N/A

Malcolm Messenger was serving on HMS *Sheffield* when the Task Force received its first major reverse of the Falklands War. He was injured and buried under debris when the ship was hit by an Exocet missile on 4 May 1982 before managing to dig himself out. Eventually, he was rescued from the burning vessel as he and the rest of the crew were forced to abandon ship.

Malcolm David Messenger was born in Swindon, Wiltshire, on 29 September 1960. The son of a builder, he was an only child. The young Messenger was educated first at Park South Infants and Junior School and later at Churchfields Secondary School, Swindon. Having joined the Sea Cadets while still at school, he joined the Royal Navy on 21 June 1977, aged sixteen.

By early 1982, Messenger was serving in the rank of Able Seaman and was a radar operator on HMS *Sheffield*, a Type-42 guided-missile destroyer and the second ship to be named in honour of the Yorkshire city. She was ordered in 1968 and laid down in January 1970 before being built by Vickers Shipbuilding and Engineering in Barrow-in-Furness. Ironically, at roughly the same time an identical ship, *Hércules*, was being built for the Argentine Navy. During the *Sheffield*'s construction, an accidental explosion killed two dockyard workers and part of her hull was replaced with a section from *Hércules*. *Sheffield*, estimated to have cost more than £23 million to build, was launched by the Queen on 10 June 1971.

On 26 January 1982, she was undergoing maintenance in the Kenyan city of Mombasa when Captain James 'Sam' Salt took over command. In fact, the list of her former Captains included Rear Admiral Sandy Woodward, the Battle Group Commander. In March, the *Sheffield* passed through the Suez Canal in order to take part in Exercise Spring Train, an annual training exercise in the Atlantic. However, after the invasion of the Falkland Islands on 2 April, she was diverted to join the Task Force. She eventually headed for the South Atlantic having already picked up ammunition and other supplies in Gibraltar, and she arrived at Ascension Island on 14 April. Along with other warships, she then sailed towards the Falkland Islands, entering the TEZ on 1 May. After the sinking of the *General Belgrano* on 2 May, Salt ordered the crew of the *Sheffield* to change course every ninety seconds in an attempt to thwart an enemy submarine attack. In fact, just three days later, the danger came from the air, not the sea.

Sheffield's primary role was to screen the two aircraft carriers, *Hermes* and *Invincible*. At dawn on 4 May, the *Sheffield* was about 20 miles ahead of *Hermes* on a cold, clear morning. At 7.50 a.m. local time, she was detected by an Argentine Neptune patrol aircraft, which radioed back her precise position and then verified it again at 8.14 a.m. and at 8.43 a.m. Two Argentine Navy Super Étendard aircraft, both armed with AM39 Exocets, took off from Río Grande at 9.45 a.m. and met with a Hercules to refuel in mid-air just fifteen minutes later. Shortly after 10.35 a.m., the patrol aircraft again gave the two attack aircraft the ship's position and the Super Étendards prepared for a low-level attack to avoid the ship's radar. The ship did not know it was under attack until four or five seconds before the strike, when someone shouted, 'Take cover!' over the intercom to the 281 officers and ratings on board. A missile from one of the two attack aircraft struck the ship on her starboard side amidships at the level of No. 2 deck. The Exocet then entered the forward engine room and travelled aft, passing over the gas turbines before striking the after bulkhead. There was a sheet of flame caused by the missile passing through steel plating, and then the main supply tank caught fire. Captain Salt said later: 'I know it sounds incredible but in ten to fifteen seconds the whole working area of the ship was filled with black, acrid, pungent smoke, mainly from the cable-runs and paint. Then of course it caught on fuel and other combustibles.'

Two frigates, *Yarmouth* and *Arrow*, came alongside to rescue the injured crew, while many of the frigates' crews directed fire hoses on the burning hull. At the same time, helicopters brought sets of breathing apparatus and other fire-fighting gear from other ships. Those on the *Sheffield* helped to fight the blaze in the most grim and dangerous of conditions. They wanted to save not just the ship but her ammunition, including twenty-two Sea Dart missiles and other warheads in the forward magazine. Television crews were on hand to record the scenes as injured men were airlifted to the sick bay on HMS *Hermes*.

After some four hours, those tackling the blaze finally accepted they were fighting a losing battle, and Captain Salt ordered the men to abandon ship. The officers and ratings who tried to get the weapons systems, main generator and other equipment working again formed the bulk of the twenty men who died. Twenty-six men were injured, mainly suffering from burns, smoke inhalation and shock.

News of the tragedy reached Fleet Street by late afternoon London time. By 6 p.m., the Prime Minister knew, and Mrs Thatcher convened an emergency meeting with her senior politicians and advisors. With rumours swirling around that it was the aircraft carrier *Invincible* that had been hit, the decision was taken to come clean about what had happened straight away. Ian McDonald, the Ministry of Defence's acting chief of public relations, was called for a briefing with Defence Secretary John Nott. The main BBC news was interrupted, and the British public learnt the news from the lips of McDonald:

> In the course of its duties within the Total Exclusion Zone around the Falkland Islands, HMS *Sheffield*, a Type-42 destroyer, was attacked and hit late this afternoon by an Argentine missile. The ship caught fire, which spread out of control. When there was no longer any hope of saving the ship, the ship's company abandoned ship.

Some 12 million viewers hung on his every word.

In the House of Commons, Nott came into the chamber shortly before 11 p.m. and spoke of casualties (dead and wounded) –
initially eleven and then, after receiving a note, thirty. There was
a limit to the bad news politicians wanted the public to see and
hear: an interview on 7 May with Captain Salt, along with pictures
of the smouldering hulk plus interviews with survivors, was not
screened until 26 May, by which time the land war was in full flow.

The Sun, which was in the middle of a tabloid circulation war
with the *Daily Mirror*, ran the following headline on 5 May: 'British Warship Sunk by Argies'. The *Daily Mirror*, on the other hand,
ran the headline 'Too High a Price' and urged politicians to find
peace through diplomacy. As the tabloid war escalated, *The Sun*
accused its rival of treason, while the *Daily Mirror* labelled its foe
'the harlot of Fleet Street'.

Unsurprisingly, the attack on the *Sheffield* came as a huge blow
to both the Task Force and the British public. It was clear that the
British fleet was vulnerable to attack and had one or more 'weak
spots', while the enemy air force, with its apparently deadly Exocet
missiles, was clearly no pushover. Many British sailors had died,
and as the Task Force sailed on to the Falklands it was heading for
a war that it could no longer be certain of winning. With the strike
on the *Sheffield* coming so soon after the sinking of the *Belgrano*,
both sides knew they were involved in a full-scale war that was
likely to have heavy casualties on both sides. The rest of the world
watched in disbelief as they observed two unlikely enemies heading for a major conflict over a tiny group of islands few had heard
of prior to April 1982. Only the Exocet salesmen in Paris could
afford to rub their hands with delight.

Admiral Sandy Woodward had reluctantly agreed with the
decision to abandon ship. Navy Commanders had expected the
Sheffield to sink fairly quickly once she was abandoned, but in
the event she refused to disappear beneath the waves. Eventually

a salvage tug, *Irishman*, was ordered to take her in tow with the hope that, if she reached South Georgia or Ascension Island, she could be examined for useful information and her missiles could be saved. Photographs were also taken of the inside of the ship, which showed that the Exocet had not, in fact, exploded and the main damage to the ship had been caused by fire and secondary explosions. However, as the weather worsened, it became harder and harder for the tug to tow *Sheffield*. Finally, by 10 May, she simply had too much water on board to progress any further, and she was sunk between the Falkland Islands and South Georgia fully six days after being hit. Only one dead body was recovered from the *Sheffield*; the remains of nineteen other men sank with her.

To this day, the wreck is a war grave and a protected area under the Protection of Military Remains Act 1986. A board of inquiry in June 1982 criticised the ship's fire-fighting equipment, training and procedure. Furthermore, the fires in the *Sheffield* and other ships damaged by flames prompted a shift by the Royal Navy away from the nylon and synthetic fabrics then worn by British sailors. The synthetics had a tendency to melt onto the skin, causing more severe burns than if the crew had been wearing non-synthetic clothing. Incidentally, it is not known exactly what happened to the second Exocet that was fired from the attack aircraft on 4 May 1982, other than it missed its target, which may have been *Invincible*.

Messenger, then aged twenty-one, had been working in the operations room of the ship when the missile struck. The explosion blew the door in, which knocked him out of his chair, and he was buried under the door and debris. Injured, he scrambled back to his post, but it soon became clear that he and his fellow crewmen would need to be evacuated from the burning ship. Messenger was eventually airlifted by helicopter to *Hermes* and then evacuated home. He received a hero's welcome, first when he landed at RAF

Brize Norton on 25 May and again at his home town of Swindon. Numerous articles were published about him and the loss of *Sheffield*, which his parents kept and collated in a scrapbook. In one article in his local paper, he was quoted as saying, 'It's great to be back – absolutely fantastic. I was in the Operations Room. A door was blown off, it hit me and I was knocked out of my chair. Stuff fell on me. I scrambled up to get to my post.'

Messenger was discharged from the navy in the rank of Able Seaman (Radar) on 30 November 1984 after more than seven years' service. Afterwards, he worked first as an IT consultant and then in the pharmaceutical industry. After the war, he married and was later divorced, but he and his wife had no children, living first in Swindon and later in Nailsea, near Bristol. After his divorce, he moved back in with his mother, but in his final years he was unable to work, suffering from mental health issues and heart disease. Messenger died from heart failure on 7 April 2009, aged just forty-eight.

In an interview at her home in Swindon, Jean Messenger, his mother, told me:

> He was affected very badly by what he had seen and experienced. He didn't like talking about the war, but he did once say to my husband and me, 'Some of my comrades went down below deck to get some fire-fighting equipment. Then I heard them screaming and they never came back. I never saw them again.'

Mrs Messenger added:

> He was a wonderful son. Before my husband died, Malcolm promised him he would look after me and he always did. But when Malcolm was ill himself, I looked after him. I am very, very proud of my son – for the courage that he showed in going to war and now that he has been chosen to appear in this book.

MICHAEL DAVID TOWNSEND

Service: Royal Navy

Final rank: Chief Petty Officer

FALKLANDS WAR DECORATION / DISTINCTION:

DISTINGUISHED SERVICE MEDAL (DSM)

DATES OF BRAVERY: 21 AND 25 MAY 1982

GAZETTED: 8 OCTOBER 1982

Michael Townsend was decorated for outstanding bravery in what became known as 'Bomb Alley', or the Battle of San Carlos. The battle was largely between aircraft of the Argentine Air Force and ships from the Royal Navy. An intense and ferocious fight, it lasted from 21 to 25 May 1982, during the British landings on the shores of San Carlos Bay.

Michael David Townsend was born in Heathfield, Sussex, on 13 August 1943, but he was brought up in Kent. The eldest of three boys, his father had served in the Royal Artillery during the Second World War before becoming a driver and site manager. After attending various primary schools, Townsend attended Morehall Secondary School in Folkestone, Kent. He left school aged fifteen to fulfil his ambition to join the Royal Navy, signing up on 10 February 1959. Initially, Townsend was a junior Marine engineering mechanic, better known simply as a 'stoker'. For the next two decades, he travelled the world with the navy, including several visits to the Falkland Islands.

By 2 April 1982, when the islands were invaded, Townsend, then aged thirty-eight and married with two children, had already served for twenty-three years in the Royal Navy on numerous ships. He was serving in the rank of Chief Petty Officer Marine engineering mechanic (mechanical) when he sailed to the

Falklands on HMS *Argonaut*, a Leander-class frigate that had been part of the Royal Navy since 1967. On the day of the invasion of the Falkland Islands, Townsend and his fellow crew were in Portland, Dorset, following their recent return from a six-month assignment to the Persian Gulf. Within days, they were on their way to the South Atlantic. As Townsend told me in an interview at his home in Yalding, Kent, 'We knew we were going to go and kick them [the Argentines] off.' Townsend's specific role on the ship was fire-fighting and damage-control logistics, so before going to war he had ordered extra fire-fighting equipment.

The *Argonaut* was one of two warships, along with HMS *Ardent*, that escorted troop-carrying merchant ships to the Falklands via Ascension Island over a voyage of more than five weeks. By 21 May, the ship was vulnerable to enemy attack off the Falklands, having just escorted HMS *Fearless* into Falkland Sound. Admiral Sandy Woodward sets the scene in his book, *One Hundred Days*:

> Then it began. An Argentinian light attack two-seater jet aircraft, the Italian built Naval Macchi 339, flying at wave-top height along the northern coast, swung suddenly into the narrow entrance to Falkland Sound, going as fast as he could. The first ship he saw was [Captain] Kit Layman's *Argonaut* and he fired all eight of his five-inch rockets at the frigate, coming on in low and raking the decks with 30mm cannon shells. One rocket hit the Seacat missile deck area and injured three men – one of whom lost an eye; another, the Master-at-Arms, took a piece of shrapnel one inch above his heart.
>
> The attack had been so swift and sudden that the raider was making his escape away to the south-east before any kind of hardware could be aimed at him. As it was, they had a shot at him with a Blowpipe missile from the deck of *Canberra*; *Intrepid* launched a Seacat missile and David Pentreath opened up with the 4.5in. guns

of *Plymouth*. But the Macchi got away doubtless to stagger his High Command with the tale of what he had just seen spread out below him in Carlos Water...

Back in Carlos Water another hour went by before the Argentinians sent in their most lethal and sustained air raid of the day. It would last for just over half an hour and it did great damage. The opening assault was made by six Skyhawks flying extremely low along the north coast, out of sight of all our radars. As swiftly as any of the opening attacks, they came through the narrows at more than 500 knots. There they found Kit Layman's *Argonaut*, from which the crew was desperately trying to evacuate their wounded by helicopter over to *Canberra*. At the last moment the *Argonauts* saw them and opened fire with everything they had, but they had no hope whatsoever of stopping all six. Five made it through, dropping a total of ten thousand-pounders, eight of which exploded in the water close to the embattled Leander Class frigate. The other two hit her, but mercifully failed to explode. The first one hit forward, going through a diesel fuel tank and coming to rest in the Seacat magazine, starting a fire and causing considerable structural damage ... The second bomb wrecked the boiler room turbo generator electrical switch panel and it also wrecked the port boiler turbo force draft fan.

Argonaut was perilously close to the rocks around Fanning Head and still going ahead with effectively no brakes and no steering. With remarkable presence of mind, Sub-Lieutenant Peter Morgan (D.S.C.) raced off the bridge, collecting a couple of ratings as he went, and managed to let go the anchor, which dragged the three-thousand-tonner to a halt, just short of the shoreline. Seconds later they lost all power, there was almost total devastation in certain parts of the ship and, with two men killed in the magazine, *Argonaut*'s war was almost over.

I have obtained a copy of the ship's hand-written engine-room diary for Friday 21 May 1982, which recorded the day's dramatic events succinctly:

> Arrived off Falkland Sound at 0630. 0900 – Action Stations. 1246 – Under attack from aircraft – three casualties. 1312 – Under attack from aircraft. 1432 – Under attack from aircraft. 1540 – Under attack from aircraft. 1726 – Under attack from aircraft – hit by 2x1,000lb bombs, one in the boiler room, port aft corner, the other in forward sea cat magazine. Fortunately neither exploded. Engine and boiler room evacuated. Command damage control … two dead. Ship stopped in the water. Ship was at full ahead when bombs hit and machinery spaces evacuated.

At lunchtime on 21 May, an enemy Pucará aircraft had attacked the *Argonaut*, spraying fire on the deck and injuring three crew. The citation for Townsend's DSM takes up the story of his own involvement in the drama that took place after the major air attack later that day:

> On 21 May 1982, during intensive enemy air attacks, HMS *Argonaut* was struck by two bombs which did not explode, one lodging in the boiler room and the second entering the forward magazine through a fuel tank. Chief Marine Engineering Mechanic Townsend re-entered the boiler room to assess the damage and then organised and carried out the patching of a hole in the ship's hull at the waterline measuring 4ft in diameter. He worked firstly inboard, passing over and working within 5ft of the unexploded bomb, and then hanging over the side of the ship during continuing air attacks and the subsequent tow.
>
> He then, without a break, attacked the flooding and damage

caused by the second bomb. He directed and personally carried out pumping operations above the magazine containing this unexploded bomb and packed with explosives. He continued to search compartments flooded with diesel fuel for almost forty-eight hours.

Chief Marine Engineering Mechanic Townsend worked with no regard for his own safety. His fearlessness and resolute stamina in helping to overcome severe damage was a major factor in saving the ship.

Townsend told me that when the first bomb hit the ship, he was on the second of three decks in the 'switchboard' area, which was used for distributing electricity. 'When the ship was hit, it jumped up and I was thrown across the switchboard and I smashed my face. The force broke my nose and broke three of my front teeth,' he recalled. As a fire broke out, Townsend, wearing standard synthetic overalls, was soon organising the fire-fighting operation as the sea water rose up to their necks, having poured through a gaping hole in the ship. He told me:

Once the bombs hit us, we lost all electrical power. They got the emergency diesel running but the trouble was the young engineers didn't know they were actually sucking in sea water because one of the bombs had gone through the fuel tank. About 350 tons of diesel from the tank was therefore on top of the water on two deck. I had about ten men with hoses to fight the fire for nearly two hours before we put the flames out.

Once the fire was put out, bomb-disposal experts, Staff Sergeant Jim Prescott and Warrant Officer 2 (WO2) John Phillips of the Royal Engineers, from another ship were able to defuse the first bomb and make it safe. Townsend said:

There was so much water from the gaping hole in the fuel tank and magazine that we couldn't pump it out with our equipment, so the rescue tug sent over some large pumps. We managed to get the water level down and that's when we found the [dead] bodies of two of our sailors. At this point I put on a rubber diving suit in order to hang out on ropes to try to patch up the hole in the boiler room. For some of this time, we were still under attack. Initially, I told my stokers and the seamen, 'If we come under attack, drop me in the water.' But the sea was so cold that I soon told them, 'Don't drop me in the water again. I would rather get shot than freeze to death!' At one point, I spent about four and a half hours in near-freezing temperatures, hanging from ropes as I patched up the side of the ship.

Townsend and his team then had to address the second bomb in the magazine. This could not be defused because its nose had been damaged. The men worked day and night for four days to find a way to remove the bomb from the ship and lower it onto the seabed. Townsend said:

The second bomb, which set off two Seacat missiles when it landed in the ship's magazine, could not be defused. Basically, we had to rig up ropes and pulleys to get the bomb up to the second deck level, and then we had to cut a hole in the side of the ship and put the bomb overboard. Most of the ship's company were taken off while we were doing that. I can tell you it was pretty frightening. We were under constant threat of air attack. I was too busy getting on with the job. I didn't sleep for four days. We were given drugs, pills called 'pinkies' and 'blueies', to keep us awake and then, right at the end, to sedate us. After getting rid of the live bombs, engineers came on board to weld up the hole in two deck above the magazine where the forward magazine live bomb had been removed from the ship. A spark from the welding ignited the diesel fumes in the mattresses and clothing in the mess deck and the ship caught fire yet again. We had to fight this blaze for another three hours.

Naval Commanders decided the ship could be saved and should limp back to Britain with a limited crew, including Townsend. The *Argonaut* returned to Plymouth, Devon, in late June, shortly after the enemy had surrendered. 'We were the first ship to return to England. They tried to keep it quiet, but we got in at 9 a.m. on a Saturday morning.' Townsend was met on the quayside on 26 June 1982 by his wife, Mary, and his brother, Barry.

Staff Sergeant Jim Prescott of 49 Squadron Royal Engineers, who had worked with Townsend and his team to defuse the bomb on *Argonaut* on 21 May, was killed two days later while defusing one of two unexploded bombs on board HMS *Antelope*. His colleague WO2 Phillips was badly injured, losing one of his arms.

Townsend's DSM was announced on 8 October in *The London Gazette*. On 22 October 1982, Captain Christopher 'Kit' Layman, who had been in command of the *Argonaut* when the ship was bombed, wrote a hand-written letter of congratulations to Townsend, which even had a joke at the end that was typical of the black humour enjoyed in the Armed Forces. Layman, who had moved on to captain HMS *Cleopatra* and who was decorated with the DSO for his own bravery and leadership in the Falklands, wrote:

Dear Chief Petty Officer Townsend

Very many congratulations on your DSM. I can't think of anyone who deserved a medal more. The citation only tells half the story: if you had not found and extinguished our fire on 21st May we would probably have lost the ship. It is good to see such resolute courage and stamina so well rewarded.

I am not sure where you are at present, but I hope this reaches you. Poor old *Argonaut* is in a fearful mess; what the Argentine Air Force failed to do the dockyard have done very well!

If you come this way before Christmas, or our paths cross in the years ahead, please come and say hello and we'll share a glass.

Yours sincerely,

Christopher Layman

P.S. Why does [General] Galtieri have glass-bottomed boats? Answer: to review the AAF [Argentine Air Force]!

At the time, Townsend later told his local paper:

I don't think of myself as a hero. All I wanted was to get on with my job. The ship was my home as well as that of 250 others. I was paid to do it so I thought I had better get on with it. And 8,000 miles is a long way to swim home.

On 25 November 1982, Townsend attended an investiture at Buckingham Palace, at which he received his DSM from the Queen. He was accompanied by his wife and their two children, Simone and David. (By this point, his son had also joined the Royal Navy and eventually went on to serve for thirty-four years.) 'It was a special day. The Queen basically said, "Well done,"' Townsend recalled.

Townsend decided to leave the Royal Navy after being overlooked for a role he wanted. He was discharged in August 1983, aged forty, and later worked in the pub trade, in agricultural engineering and as a civil servant. He retired from his final role as a civilian Commanding Officer of an army unit aged sixty-five.

When I purchased Townsend's medal group at auction in 2011, it came with some interesting related artefacts and documents. These included two pieces of the unexploded 1,000lb bomb that landed in the forward magazine and set off the Seacat missiles, along with a large aluminium ring that had attached the tailfin to the bomb itself.

Ironically, both the bombs that hit the *Argonaut* were British-made 1,000lb general-purpose high-explosive weapons sold to the Argentine Air Force several years previously. The tailfin is designed to break away from the bomb on impact, at which time the bomb is armed ready to explode. It appears, however, that the enemy made the mistake of not adjusting the timing mechanisms to allow for the extremely low altitudes at which they were dropping the bombs.

Today, Townsend, who now has five grandchildren, carries out voluntary work, including serving on various NHS management boards. He is a keen mountaineer, walker and boating enthusiast. Reflecting on the Falklands War, he told me: 'It was a just war. We had to go down there because the islanders were part of the British Empire. Looking back, I am proud to have played my part.'

JOHN STEVEN LEAKE

Service: Royal Navy
Final rank: Petty Officer
FALKLANDS WAR DECORATION / DISTINCTION:
DISTINGUISHED SERVICE MEDAL (DSM)
DATE OF BRAVERY: 21 MAY 1982
GAZETTED: 8 OCTOBER 1982

John Leake was decorated for incredible courage while serving on board HMS *Ardent*. In theory, he was a civilian Navy, Army and Air Force Institutes (NAAFI) canteen manager, but when the ship came under heavy attack from Argentine aircraft he used his earlier military training to act as a machine gunner, eventually shooting down an enemy plane during a deadly onslaught. Leake was one of only twelve men to receive the DSM for bravery during the Falklands War.

John Steven Leake was born in Erdington, a suburb of Birmingham, on 29 October 1949. One of five brothers, he was educated at Prince Albert Junior and Infant School in Aston. As a teenager, he enlisted in the army and joined the Devon and Dorset Regiment, serving with its 1st Battalion on a tour of Northern Ireland during The Troubles. One of his army roles was as an instructor in the use of general-purpose machine guns (GPMGs).

Aged just twenty-four, Leake left the army and went to work for private security companies, including Securicor at Birmingham Airport. After his spell in the security industry, he planned to join West Midlands Police. However, after arriving early for his interview, he saw an advertisement for a job with the NAAFI. He decided to apply for that role instead and landed it.

When the Falklands War broke out in April 1982, Leake was aged thirty-two and was serving as a canteen manager in the Naval Canteen Service wing of the NAAFI on board *Ardent*, a Royal Navy Type-21 frigate. The ship was ordered to Ascension Island and, after a further three days, on to the Falkland Islands. On the morning of 7 May 1982, Leake was invited to practise on a GPMG, being informed afterwards that he was to take up that role at action stations should active service be declared. While en route to the war zone, active service was duly declared, and Leake voluntarily signed on to the Royal Navy on a temporary basis while also continuing his role as canteen manager.

On 21 May, *Ardent* moved into position in Falkland Sound tasked, as the lead ship, with bombarding enemy positions so as to divert attention from the main landing of British troops at San

Carlos inlet. In an interview with Max Arthur for his book *Above All, Courage*, Leake told his version of the remarkable events leading up to 21 May and of that dramatic day:

We'd just got to Ascension Island when I went up on deck to get some fresh air and saw a Petty Officer sitting on the deck with a manual, trying to work out how to use a General Purpose Machine Gun. I said to him, 'Ah, the good old GPMG.' He said, 'Oh, you know about it?' I said, 'Yes, I used to be an instructor on it in the Army.' He said, 'Well, you can have a go if you want to.' But I said I couldn't because as a civilian I wasn't entitled to carry arms. Later he had a word with the Captain, who said only if active service had been declared and I'd actually signed on in the Navy would I be able to use it. After we'd sailed from Ascension, active service was declared and we were then given the option of signing on with the Navy or getting off the ship and having NAAFI fly us back to England. I had no hesitation – I signed on in the Navy as a Petty Officer. It had to be done under the Articles of the Geneva Convention, stating that I was a combatant; otherwise, had I been captured, I would have been treated as a civilian and not covered by the Convention. But all the time I thought, 'We'll just get near the islands, rattle our sabres and that will be it.'

Then as we approached the Falklands, and the *Belgrano* and the *Sheffield* were sunk, we realised we were close to war and that we were not invincible. The *Sheffield* was a much bigger boat than the *Ardent*. When the news came, everybody went quiet. It was then that we started reflecting on actually going into combat and for a couple of days the ship was subdued. But everyone realised they had a job to do and things soon got back to normal. Every day Captain West would visit each mess in turn and give us a situation report, which was good for morale. I always think the *Ardent* was a one-off ship anyway; such a happy ship.

We were on defence watches when we were told that the *Ardent* was going to lead the ships through the passage between the two islands. The Captain said he didn't know if the channel was mined, but we were going to chance it, and find out. We knew then that we were going to war – the talking was over. But I don't remember having any fears...

Their [the enemy's] first attack came from a Pucará [aircraft], but when we fired the Seacat at it, it veered off. I then went on to the GPMG. For me, taking hold of that gun was the most natural thing in the world. I'd lugged that gun thousands of miles; I'd taken it apart in daylight, darkness, rain and snow. I had such an affinity with it; I'd fired it under so many conditions. But when I left the Army I never expected to use it again, yet here I was, in action again, on a ship.

Then their aircraft really started coming. It was one big mass attack all day. The first few, probably Skyhawks and Mirages, came in from the port side, low and fast. I remember the bows of the ship being straddled by bombs but fortunately she wasn't hit. There were explosions about 50 yards in front of me, where the bombs had missed. But in one of the next few attacks we were hit by a plane that flew over the length of the ship. I could feel further attacks hitting other parts of the ship, but I was so preoccupied that I didn't have time to find out the extent of the damage. It seemed that I was in action all through the day. At one point a couple of lads came up from the aft end, which they told me had been badly hit. They were in a bad state of shock so I got them to sit down by my side and gave them some Nutty bars. Then somebody shouted to us, 'Aircraft bearing green ninety.' I looked over our starboard side and there were two aircraft coming in low. I opened fire on them, but they both dropped their bombs on the ship. Then two more turned up, and this time I hit one. I could see bits coming off his wing and underneath fuselage.

Then more came over and the ship was hit again. At one point I ran out of ammunition. One of the lads had gone to get more but we were under heavy attack and there was nothing else to do but hit the deck. While I was lying there I looked up and there was a Skyhawk coming across. I watched his bombs leave the aircraft and they passed so close to the ship's mast that I thought, 'Christ, this is it.' I felt fear then, because I knew the ship was being badly hit. Then PO Chef Goldfinch, who'd brought me ammunition throughout the attack, shouted, 'Come on, John. We've got the stuff,' and back we went. I could keep going. It's in moments like that when fear seems to spur you on, as long as it is not unreasonable fear, which makes you not know what you're doing. But I did know, so I got back and could keep on firing.

Then, suddenly, the aft end of the ship was covered with one big pall of smoke. I couldn't see anything, couldn't see anything at all, so I moved over to the other side of the ship with my GPMG. It was only then that I realised how much of a tilt the ship was at. She was settling over to starboard. I stood there for a while and watched all the lads coming up from below decks. Then the *Yarmouth* came alongside and we stepped off. I took the gun with me because I was hoping they would give it to me as a souvenir – but I was out of luck. I had to hand it over on the *Yarmouth*. But, even then, there was more to fear, because when we were below decks on the *Yarmouth*, 'Air Raid Warning Red' came over the Tannoy. I realised there was absolutely nothing we could do stuck down below, having spent a day with everything to do. Eventually the *Yarmouth* took us into one of the bays where the *Canberra* was and we were taken in a landing craft to her.

I found out afterwards that the *Ardent* had been hit by seventeen bombs and missiles, plus rockets and cannon fire. I think that with all they threw at us that day it was a miracle we only lost twenty-two men. I thought of the *Coventry*, a big destroyer, which was hit by five bombs and went down in minutes, yet we'd been there all that afternoon being hit, hit and hit, and all at the aft end – I've never worked out how. I often think, 'Why did they sink the *Ardent*?' She wasn't a significant ship, especially when you take into account all the others that were there, like the *Canberra*. Perhaps they were actually out for a kill, and with our main armaments out they knew it was an easy thing. Because there wasn't a lot of fire coming from us, they had a sitting duck.

I suppose if it hadn't been for my affinity with the old GPMG, there wouldn't be a story to tell. I did what I could. I never thought when I left the Army that I'd ever see action again, let alone get involved with it, but I wouldn't have wanted to do anything else in the circumstances.

Those boys on the ship were like a family to me. I remember when I was walking down on the jetty, before the *Ardent* sailed, and saw some of the lads painting the ship. One of them shouted, 'Are you coming with us, John?' I stopped and said, 'Of course I'm bloody coming with you. I'm like a father to all you lads. I wouldn't be able to sleep if I didn't come with you.' Just before we came under attack I brought up stacks of Mars Bars and Nutty and a crate of Gotters, because I thought we might need them. So whenever I could, while the action was on, I'd throw them a Mars Bar or a tin of drink and say, 'I'll be round tomorrow for the money.' I took some movie film of the lads on the way down. I've only played it back twice since. It's wonderful to see all those faces laughing – then suddenly you'll see one of the lads who was killed.

On a happier note, a year after the sinking I got a phone call to say that I had been credited with shooting down a Skyhawk. The pilot had bailed out and they picked him up and took him to Stanley; he said he'd had his fuel tanks hit while attacking the *Ardent*.

On 8 October 1982, Leake's decoration was announced in *The London Gazette*, where his citation stated:

> Petty Officer Leake originally joined H.M.S. *Ardent* as a civilian N.A.A.F.I. Canteen Manager. On the declaration of Active Service he volunteered to enrol as a Petty Officer on 15th May 1982.
>
> On 21st May 1982 HMS *Ardent* came under heavy attack by Argentine aircraft. Using his previous Army training, Petty Officer Leake was stationed as a machine gunner. Throughout the air attacks he remained cool and calm even though the ship was being hit by bombs and cannon fire. He fired large quantities of accurate tracer [ammunition that has a light so it can be seen] at the attackers and inflicted damage on a Skyhawk. His courage, steadfastness and total disregard for his own safety undoubtedly saved the ship from many further attacks and was an inspiration to all those in the vicinity.

Leake was an unlikely war hero, as Admiral Sandy Woodward noted in his memoir:

> I was sure there would be many stories of heroism to come out of it, but of them all, I remain most impressed by the conduct of John Leake who manned the machine gun in *Ardent*. He was not really in the Navy, but, as we say, we are all of one company, the Captain and the NAAFI man. And we all go together.

Leake, who later served on HMS *Sutherland*, was married to Carole and the couple lived in Plymouth, Devon. They had a son together, and she also had two sons from a previous relationship. However, Leake fell ill in his late forties and died from cancer at St Luke's Hospice, Plymouth, on 13 February 2000, aged fifty. He had previously undergone an operation to remove a kidney in an attempt to beat the disease. His funeral took place at Weston Mill Cemetery and Crematorium on 21 February 2000.

PETER HERLICK RENE NAYA
Service: Royal Army Medical Corps
Final rank: Staff Sergeant
FALKLANDS WAR DECORATION / DISTINCTION:
MILITARY MEDAL (MM)
DATE OF BRAVERY: 8 JUNE 1982
GAZETTED: 8 OCTOBER 1982

Peter Naya was decorated for an outstanding act of bravery after the RFA *Sir Galahad* was bombed and set on fire. As a result of the attack on the ship in Bluff Cove, forty-eight men lost their lives, the biggest single loss by the British during the conflict. Had it not been for the courage of Naya and others like him, many more lives would have been lost.

Peter Herlick Rene Naya, who was known by the nickname of 'Pierre', was born in Ocean Road Hospital in Dar es Salaam, the capital of Tanzania, on 4 July 1945, close to the end of the Second World War. He was one of five children, including four sons, born to Jules Rene and Rita Naya, who were strict but loving Catholic parents. The couple had moved from their home in the Seychelles in April 1915 because Jules was in search of better work as a motor mechanic. Just 5ft 8in. tall, slim and handsome, Pierre was good-natured, charming, musical and a strong swimmer. As a boy and in later life, he loved telling stories, jokes and ditties, and was a good mimic. After being educated locally in Dar es Salaam, where he became fluent in Swahili as well as his first language of English, he was a keen fisherman and hunter – often, with his father and brothers, catching fish and wild animals for his family to eat.

In 1964, the family moved from Tanzania to Britain, travelling by ship and with different members going at different times. On 21 June 1964, shortly before his nineteenth birthday, Naya enlisted into the Royal Army Medical Corps (RAMC). It was to be his life for the next twenty-two years, and his younger brother Michael later joined him. The Corps' motto 'In Arduis Fidelis' ('Faithful in Adversity') was an inspiration to all new recruits, and for all of them their careers started with sixteen weeks of intensive training. Naya was trained as an Operating Theatre Technician, and his first posting was to the military hospital in Colchester, Essex, where he would remain for six years. There, he met and married Nina, who was training to become an army nurse. The couple went on to have four daughters: Juliette, twins Ginette and Alison, and Nicola. After a time, Naya's parents moved from south London to Colchester, where his father worked as the foreman for a coal distribution company.

After various home and foreign postings, including working in Hong Kong and Berlin, in early 1982 Naya was working at 22 Field Hospital near Aldershot, Hampshire, training staff to operate in war zones. By this time, his hobbies included painting and making wine. As the crisis grew in the South Atlantic, Naya, then in the rank of Sergeant, was ordered to Southampton on 12 May, where he embarked on the converted luxury liner the *QE2* before heading off to war. On the journey, he wrote letters to his wife, signing them 'Pomme', the affectionate nickname they both used for each other. As they neared the Falklands, Naya and his comrades transferred to the MV *Norland*, as it was deemed too risky to take the *QE2* to the Falklands in case she was attacked. As they headed for Ajax Bay on East Falkland, the weather deteriorated and they were caught in a fierce storm. For the last leg of their journey, Naya and his comrades from 55 Field Surgical Team moved onto *Sir Galahad*.

On the morning of 8 June 1982, *Sir Galahad* and *Sir Tristram* were bombed. The recommendation for Naya's MM takes up the story:

On June 8 1982, whilst at anchor in Fitzroy Sound, East Falkland, RFA *Sir Galahad* was bombed and set on fire by enemy aircraft. Embarked troops included two companies of infantry and the main body of 16 Field Ambulance, men and equipment. At the time of the attack most of the troops were positioned in the tank deck where substantial quantities of ammunition soon began to explode as the fire worked through the ship. Over the course of some two hours 135 casualties, the majority with burns and amputations, were evacuated to the ADS [Advanced Dressing Station] already ashore at Fitzroy settlement.

Sergeant Naya, Royal Army Medical Corps, was standing in the tank deck when he was thrown against a bulkhead by the first explosion and partially stunned. The lights went out and the tank deck began to fill with dense black smoke. A second explosion killed two men behind him, set his large pack alight and scorched the back of his head. Shrugging off the burning material, he managed to lead a third soldier by hand up two flights of stairs to daylight. There he paused to cut burning clothing from other soldiers with his scissors before mounting a third flight to the upper deck. He then helped to carry a man who had lost a leg up to the forecastle, having first dressed the stump and set up intravenous infusion. He treated many more casualties, including another amputee, and set up several more infusions, until all casualties had been evacuated; he left the ship on the last helicopter, later to be evacuated as a casualty himself. After three days only he returned to duty in the Advance Surgical Centre of the field ambulance, where he worked steadfastly through the most intense period of military activity and the passage of many battle casualties.

Sergeant Naya, being a casualty himself, was well aware of the dangers he faced remaining in the stricken vessel and yet, with no thought for his own safety, devoted himself to the care of his injured comrades until such care was no longer required.

Sergeant Naya's conduct throughout showed immense personal courage, courage deserving of formal recognition. He acted in the highest tradition of the Royal Army Medical Corps.

Long after the war, Naya provided a vivid account of the events on 8 June 1982 for Max Arthur's book *Above All, Courage*:

The first inkling I had of us being attacked was this loud roaring, whooshing noise and I looked up just in time to see an aircraft zooming past; it was flying so low you could tell it was going to rocket or shell us. I instantly registered the colour was wrong. It was a dingy, browny, chocolate colour. I shouted 'It's not ours' and simultaneously someone shouted 'Hit the deck', then bang, it struck and all hell broke loose!

The massive orange fireball started the devastation. It burnt blokes, it killed blokes, everywhere there was the screaming of men in agony, pain, shock, fear, panic – it all happened in seconds. I was very bewildered and struggling around totally dazed. It was pitch black and I could feel this intense heat burning the back of my head – then I realized my backpack was on fire, so I pulled it off and beat out the flames. Everywhere around me was in chaos. My first thought was that we'd been wiped out. I couldn't see a thing; all I could smell was the burning metal and flesh and this acrid smoke. It was stifling and the heat was scorching my lungs – all I wanted to do was get out from the tank deck. I knew there was a hatch behind me so I made a beeline for that. Needless to say, there must have been about 100 other people with the same idea, some of whom were in a terrible mess.

I managed to haul myself and pull others and push others up two flights of stairs towards daylight. On the way up to the top deck I grabbed hold of this injured Guardsman – he was in agony but I knew I had to get him up on deck. He kept screaming, 'Mind my leg, mind my leg,' but he'd lost his leg – it was a phantom pain. I tried to pull him up the stairs by his belt but he was too heavy for me and we both fell backwards but I somehow struggled up those stairs with him. How I got him out of there I don't know, it must have been pure adrenalin. I'd got my arm round this poor sod and took him to the bow of the ship to evade the smoke. All the time I was carrying him his bone was hitting the deck and leaving a trail of blood.

It was chaos everywhere on deck. Smoke and flames were billowing up from below, ammunition was going off, and there were blokes running around screaming because their plastic all-weather gear had caught fire and was sticking to them, burning their skin away – it was pitiful to watch them trying to tear it off. That was an awful sight – such pain, such terrible pain. I'd never seen anything like it. They [the injured] were just rolling about on the decks.

This was the fastest my mind had ever worked; I was trying to decipher what was going on and to sort out priorities. I wanted to find the others, my mates, but I couldn't. It felt as if I had been caught up in a big machine that was going round and round. Helicopters were suddenly appearing and men were jumping off the ship onto lifeboats, into the flaming seas; and some were being winched off by helicopter. People were shouting orders, and all the time there were explosions after explosions and flames everywhere.

I didn't have time to think. If they'd attacked us again I wouldn't have known it because there was so much smoke and confusion – it was horrendous. I couldn't see any doctors working (I found out later they'd been taken off before the bomb struck) and I couldn't see any medics working: I thought I was probably the last medic alive. So I thought, 'Come on, Pierre, you're the only medic, get to it.' So I got stuck in with what medical kit I had – a pair of scissors! The rest had been blown to pieces – wiped out.

So I got to my knees and started to cut away at some of the badly burnt clothes to expose the wounds. I became a focus for people – they knew at least someone was there to help. The NCOs were marvellous, keeping everyone calm and bringing the injured men up to me and talking to them while they waited. I began smashing up crates of wood to make splints because there was nothing else. The Welsh Guards who'd survived came by and dropped their field dressings for me; others gave me their intravenous drips or held someone while I got at his injuries. Everyone rallied round – they'd got over the initial shock and were doing all they could to help me.

I didn't have time to look up, I couldn't answer anyone, I'd just say to one of them, 'You grab that, just hold it there and I'll start putting up a drip.' I managed to get a few drips into the very worst, those who'd had legs and ankles blown off. I'd never seen injuries like these – I'd never been in action in all the twenty years I'd been in the Army!

I don't know how I kept a sober head on me at the time. All I remember was fixing guys, trying to put a figure-of-eight bandage round some poor bugger's legs that were smashed, then kicking a pallet to pieces trying to get splints from it – it was all so primitive. I was putting the field dressings over this fellow's stumps, I then grabbed someone's webbing straps to use as a tourniquet on what was left of his leg and used a guy's bayonet to tighten it. Then I looked up at the poor devil and saw his face was swollen to twice its size, like a pumpkin, and was completely black with the flash burn. All the time WO Mike McHale, the other medic and RSM [Regimental Sergeant Major], was organising everything – I was glad he'd survived. He was getting the casualties off the ship; he'd come alongside and say, 'Which one, Pierre, which one?' I'd point them out in order of priority. Then I'd be back on the next. It was decisions, decisions: could I leave him, should I go on to save one who was dying? How much time have I got? Will this bloody ship blow up? Who's next for the chopper? All this was rushing through my mind. I just carried on, totally absorbed, for what seemed an eternity.

A three-ringer Naval officer came up and said, 'Can I help?' So I said, 'Yes, Sir, that one there, shunt him off quick.' The lad had lost a leg and had the other broken, as well as one of his arms. I stuck in a drip but of course we couldn't strap him in a harness as there was this stump. So this Naval officer suggested we use a pallet. We laid the lad out and tried to hook the harness round with rope, but as the chopper pulled it up he rolled off in agony. So we called for the harness again and somehow wrapped it round him and got him up there. He was the last of the severe casualties, so then I started on the burns victims.

All I could do was start cutting the plastic clothing, because it had impregnated their skin and was still smouldering. Where the lads had grabbed hold of red-hot handrailings they had 'de-gloved' the palms of their hands and their skin had bunched up all their fingers, so I had to cut down between the webs to separate the fingers – all this without morphine. Some of the lads were still burning because they couldn't use their hands – there was no water on the ship. If I could have peed on them, I would have; they just needed to be put out, to be cooled down. All that bloody sea and we didn't have any water. It was the exposed areas of the body which really suffered – the face, the neck, the ears, the hair, the hands, whatever was exposed at the time of the flash got scorched. Many of those lads will carry the scars all their life. Some were completely burnt from the neck up, no hair, no eyebrows, all black and swollen. I wouldn't recognise them now.

While I was waiting to get the last of the burns cases off, I could see one particular lad who was in pain. There wasn't a thing I could do for him except loosen his collar where the plastic had burnt into his neck. He was holding his fingers apart where I'd just cut them and he was standing there bewildered and exhausted. I had a packet of cigarettes so I lit one and put it in his mouth and the pleasure of his grin was wonderful – he just stood there holding his blackened and bleeding hand in the air, puffing merrily away.

Later I met blokes who, the moment they hit the beach, started smoking for the first time in their lives – it was the heat of the moment! The adrenalin was flowing something shocking. It was like being very high, but it wasn't a good high, it was a fearful thing – I'd never seen such horror in all my life.

Slowly we got them all off. Those chopper pilots performed miracles. They were unbelievably brave – time and again they came back.

I'd realized I'd been on my knees for probably over an hour, tending to the wounded, with the heat of the deck burning into my own skin. But we'd done it, we'd got everyone off [who was still alive]. Then I thought, 'OK, you can get off now,' but all the lifeboats had gone. Then for the first time I looked over the side of the ship to see where we were – I'd never done this, we'd been down in the tank deck when it happened, so I never did see the land. Now I could see it and it looked like a long swim. I stood on the side of that ship on this beautifully clear day and realized that I'd survived and now, after all that, I was probably going to drown in the icy water. I knew the survival time in the water was about five minutes. I knew I'd had it. Then there were more explosions, bullets started whizzing about – and I'd lost my helmet in the initial blast. I thought, 'I can't just stand here. I've got to get off or I'll get it in the head,' so I started to take my boots off. Suddenly a Naval officer came out of the smoke and shouted, 'A chopper's coming.' I was almost the last man off that ship but I have never been more grateful to a pilot in my life – I was so grateful I put the sign of the cross on his visor. He just smiled – he was so young – but they saved our lives that day, they saved over 300 lives. As we veered away from the ship I began to tremble and shake like a leaf. I'd survived, I'd got my hands, my legs, and I was in one piece.

Naya went on to explain how he later stood on a cliff and looked at the stricken *Sir Galahad* as tears rolled down his cheeks. The ship's crew had expected her to explode at some point but instead she burnt for days. He said his overall impressions of the war were of pain and death, the sheer desolation of the Falklands and the humility of people involved in the war. He remained working in the war zone until the Argentine surrender and then stayed for a further two weeks before going to Port Stanley Hospital and eventually returning home.

'I feel humble, and lucky, that I survived,' he told Max Arthur, author of *Above All, Courage*. Naya ended his interview for the book praising the frontline soldiers:

When people talk of heroism I think of the Paras and the Marines and the other people who had to fight the enemy, tooth and nail and eye to eye. It takes real guts to do that, it really does. As far as I'm concerned, heroism is a bit like madness. You have to be mad to face an enemy like they did. You have to be completely detached from the situation as it presents itself at the time. You have to jump in with both feet but be completely switched off. You know, it's a deliberate act, and you know you might get killed. But you do it. You're either very brave or mad – there is no logic. I certainly don't consider myself a hero. I just did my job.

Naya was undoubtedly traumatised by the shocking events that he witnessed on *Sir Galahad*, and he was unable to discuss his feelings with family and friends.

He attended his investiture at Buckingham Palace on 8 February 1983, accompanied by his wife and his mother. It was a day of great pride: he enjoyed meeting the Queen and looking at the wonderful paintings on the palace walls. He was discharged from the army in the rank of Staff Sergeant on 20 June 1986, after completing twenty-two years' service.

Next, he worked in a management role for the NHS before enjoying his retirement with his wife on Portugal's Algarve. The couple bought a town house in Lagos, which Naya renovated, and at night classes he got his small boat skipper's licence. Eventually, however, Naya's health deteriorated, and he suffered from diabetes and heart attacks. After a triple heart bypass operation in Lisbon, he initially seemed to recover well – only to die suddenly in his wife's arms on 6 October 2012, aged sixty-seven. At his funeral on the outskirts of Lagos, his coffin was draped with an RAMC flag.

CHIU YIU NAM
Service: Royal Fleet Auxiliary
Final rank: Seaman
FALKLANDS WAR DECORATION / DISTINCTION:
GEORGE MEDAL (GM)
DATE OF BRAVERY: 8 JUNE 1982
GAZETTED: N/A

Chiu Yiu Nam was one of the most modest unsung heroes of the Falklands War – yet also one of the bravest. He was decorated for an act of outstanding gallantry in fighting a fierce fire on *Sir Galahad*, and his courage is estimated to have saved at least ten lives. He was one of only three recipients of this decoration from the Falklands.

Chiu Yiu Nam was born in 1949 in Guangdong Province, mainland China, and little is known of his background or exactly when he joined the RFA. The RFA was founded in 1905 with the role of delivering worldwide logistic and operational support to Royal Navy military operations. Its members are the uniformed, civilian branch of the Naval Service, staffed by merchant sailors. Chiu represented one of the last generations of locally recruited sailors – others were from places such as Goa and Malta – who had helped man the Royal Navy's ships for hundreds of years.

On the afternoon of 8 June 1982, Chiu was serving as a seaman on the RFA *Sir Galahad*, one of five landing ships logistics that ferried troops and stores around the islands and were manned by British Merchant Navy officers and Hong Kong Chinese crewmen. Chiu, as one of the helicopter flight deck party, was also trained in firefighting.

In an attempt to outflank Argentine positions, *Sir Galahad* and her sister ship *Sir Tristram* had been sent to Port Pleasant, on the south coast of East Falkland, and elements of the Welsh Guards were waiting to disembark when the ships were attacked by five Skyhawk jets of the Argentine Air Force. Three aircraft dropped bombs on *Sir Galahad*, one of which penetrated an open hatch, its explosion generating a fireball that swept through the tank deck, where there were many troops and where ammunition and petrol were stowed. A second bomb exploded near the galley area, killing Chiu's friend, the ship's butcher, Sung Yuk Fai, and injuring many others.

As the stores on the tank deck began to ignite and explode, causing intense local fires, the master of *Sir Galahad*, Captain Philip Roberts, was reluctantly considering when to give the order to abandon ship. Chiu, meanwhile, realised that there were men trapped inside. Wearing a protective asbestos suit, he fought his way through the smoke and flames into the bowels of the ship, where he was confronted by scenes of confusion and devastation. After leading out one man, he went back for another. He continued to return, bringing men to safety until he realised that there was no one left alive. Only then did he obey the order to abandon ship. In all, forty-eight seamen and soldiers were killed and many more badly burnt. Of those who survived, at least ten owed their survival to Chiu.

Chiu was remarkably modest about what he had done; he is not believed to have told any comrades about his actions. Even on the journey home in the tanker *British Test*, Captain Roberts asked his crew about their role during the bombing of *Sir Galahad* and no one, not even the modest hero himself, came forward with information about Chiu's gallantry.

However, much later Lieutenant Colonel Johnny Rickett, Commanding Officer of the 1st Battalion, the Welsh Guards – who had disembarked the night before the air attack – interviewed his guardsmen and some of them provided information about an unknown rescuer whose identity had been hidden behind a protective hood. The man had fought his way time and again through the smoke and flames in order to lead men to safety. The rescuer had only obeyed the order to abandon ship when he was sure there was no one left alive. Further inquiries revealed that this had been Chiu. Even then, he remained reluctant to discuss his role – or to be recognised officially for his bravery.

Still, Chiu's outstanding courage was formally acknowledged even though, as he was a foreign national, there was no official announcement in *The London Gazette*. Vice Admiral Sir James Kennon, who was chief of fleet support, in a letter dated 13 June 1983, told Chiu:

> I was delighted to learn that Her Majesty the Queen has awarded you the George Medal in recognition of your extremely brave actions in saving the lives of several soldiers in the aftermath of the bombing of RFA *Sir Galahad*. Your courage and total disregard

for your own safety was an inspiration to all those who witnessed or have since learnt of your deeds on that awesome day. You have brought great honour to yourself and to the Royal Fleet Auxiliary.

In July 1983, Chiu agreed to fly from Hong Kong to London, where the Queen invested him with the decoration. His mother accompanied him on the visit and the couple were photographed outside Buckingham Palace, with a smiling Chiu holding his decoration aloft with his left hand. This photograph appeared on the front page of the *Daily Telegraph* on 27 July 1983.

Chiu, who never married, retired from the RFA in 1989 for health reasons and lived with his mother and younger brother in Hong Kong. He declined an invitation to fly to London for the twenty-fifth anniversary of the Falklands War but was flattered to receive a letter from Margaret Thatcher at a reception organised by the local branch of the Royal British Legion.

Mrs Thatcher, by then Baroness Thatcher, wrote the following letter on House of Lords headed notepaper, dated 8 June 2007:

Over these coming days, we here in Britain will be remembering and honouring those who fought so bravely to liberate the Falkland Islands and their people. For those who served in the South Atlantic this will be a special time; a time to reflect on the suffering and the sadness, and on memories of friends and colleagues who did not return. But it is also a time to celebrate remarkable achievements and outstanding courage.

Twenty-five years ago, on 8th June, you found yourself amidst the blazing wreckage of RFA *Sir Galahad*. Heedless of the imminent danger you were in, you worked to save the lives of others as the flames took hold. Your courage that day ensured that many more families were spared the grief of mourning. And your actions are a reminder to us all of the best and of the noblest aspects of the human spirit. Britain will never forget your service or your heroism. Thank you again for all you have done and please accept my warmest good wishes on this special day.

Chiu also met the Duke of York when the Queen's son visited Hong Kong in 2010, and in 2011 he met the Earl of Wessex, the Duke's younger brother. Chiu, who spoke very little English, communicated with both princes through an interpreter.

Chiu died in Hong Kong on 14 February 2012, aged sixty-two. Locally entered seamen like Chiu did not receive pensions, and when he died he was dependent on monthly financial assistance from the Hong Kong government. His cremation on 24 February 2012 was paid for by the Hong Kong and China branch of the Royal British Legion. I think it is disgraceful that men like Chiu, who risked their lives for Britain and for wider freedoms, did not – and do not – receive a pension in recognition of their long service.

An online tribute to the war hero from the RFA's Historical Society ends with the words: 'Mr Chiu, for his bravery, can quite correctly be described as a Hero of the RFA.'

JEUNE MARIE HALL (NÉE HENDY)
Service: Queen Alexandra's Royal Naval Nursing Service (QARNNS)
Final rank: Senior Naval Nurse
FALKLANDS WAR DECORATION / DISTINCTION: **N/A**
DATE OF BRAVERY: N/A
GAZETTED: N/A

Selfless and dedicated to her job, Jeune Hendy was one of some forty female nursing staff who courageously served on the SS *Uganda*, a floating hospital that was anchored in and around the Falkland Islands during the height of the war. After some of the fiercest battles, up to 160 casualties a day – from both sides – were treated on the hospital ship, some suffering from horrendous injuries.

Jeune Marie Hendy was born on 20 February 1956 in Fareham, Hampshire, the younger of two children. She attended St Anne's Secondary Modern School in Fareham, and from the age of eight she had wanted to be nurse. 'Every teddy and doll I owned had a bandage on them,' she recalled of her childhood. After leaving school at sixteen, she worked in a hospital as a cadet nurse for two years. She joined the Queen Alexandra's Royal Naval Nursing Service (QARNNS) working in the Royal Naval Hospital Haslar in Gosport, Hampshire, in 1974, aged eighteen. By the spring of 1982, she had already served a foreign posting in Malta, and at the time of the Falklands invasion, she was working at the Royal Naval Hospital Stonehouse in Plymouth, Devon. On 2 April she was on holiday in Wales and got a call to return to Plymouth because war appeared to be looming.

For a time, Hendy was on standby to go to war, and she spent several days training for the possibility. Soon she was informed she was off to war and would serve on the SS *Uganda*. The ship had been built in 1952 as a passenger liner and later specialised in educational cruises. After the invasion of the Falkland Islands on 2 April 1982, the *Uganda* was requisitioned for military duty and therefore discharged her 315 cabin passengers and 940 school children in Naples, Italy. School children could be heard singing 'Rule Britannia!' as she arrived in the dock. The *Uganda* was given a three-day refit in Gibraltar in preparation for her new role as a hospital ship. In accordance with the Geneva Convention and to prevent her coming under enemy attack, the ship was painted white with eight red crosses. *Uganda* left Gibraltar on 19 April 1982, with a team of 136 medical staff including twelve doctors, operating theatre staff and some forty nurses from the QARNNS.

In an interview at her Devon home, Hendy recalled that she was excited by the prospect of going to war.

At that stage, I felt 'this is what I joined the service for'. Also, there is no greater feeling as a nurse than you are doing your job to the best of your ability in challenging situations. But, for all of us, as soon as we flew out on a Hercules to Gibraltar we realised this was going to be a very different experience. We were well-trained and well-qualified, but when we arrived in Gibraltar we had to transform a passenger ship into a hospital ship. This was make do and mend in the extreme. Also, most of us had never been to sea before so we were a little apprehensive. All the equipment that came on board was not labelled for some reason, so we unpacked all these boxes thinking, 'What's this? What's that?' It was all a bit daunting. I think we were in Gibraltar for about five days making various preparations, and we quickly realised that this was nothing like the nursing that we had been used to. On the voyage down to the Falklands, we were all incredibly busy, ripping everything out and changing it. I was allocated to the operating theatre but I wasn't an operating theatre nurse. Our living accommodation was cramped with three of us in a cabin. We were each allowed fifteen seconds maximum in the shower each day because water was so scarce. We had the Royal Marine Band on board. Their role was to be stretcher-bearers, but they did so much more than that. They helped us with everything; they were fantastic. There were about forty bandsmen on board and they were our complete and utter backbone, our rock.

In theory, Argentina was committed to not attacking a hospital ship, but it was a war zone and the ship was always in danger of being attacked by accident, or even deliberately. Hendy and other nurses forsook their crisp uniforms for their war duties and instead wore shirts, trousers and 'woolly pulleys' to combat the chilly, often sub-zero, temperatures.

The *Uganda* stopped at Ascension Island to pick up additional supplies and then sailed on towards the war zone.

> It really hit us when HMS *Sheffield* was attacked, and after that it was full speed ahead to the Falklands. As nurses our first thought was, 'Those poor lads [on board *Sheffield*]. What on earth has happened to them? What condition are they [the injured] in?' We were impatient to get there.
>
> As we got nearer to the Falklands, some of the inadequacies of our conditions became apparent. For example, we didn't have suitable footwear. So they sent out plimsolls, but the smallest shoe size was a seven and I am a five and a half, so my shoes were like flippers. I was never nervous about the dangers – that's not in my mentality – but I was apprehensive as to how we would cope as nurses with all the inadequacies of the ship.

After arriving in the 200-mile TEZ, the *Uganda* received her first casualties on 12 May. By 31 May, she had 132 casualties on board. Hendy said:

> The first day was orderly chaos as we were all finding our feet. For example, an oxygen cylinder fell over because it hadn't been secured properly. We had a sterilising unit that was quickly nicknamed 'Vesuvius' because the damn thing was always blowing and not doing what it was supposed to do. One of the early casualties told me that when they saw our ship arrive with its Red Cross flag, the wounded were lifted psychologically. The men thought, 'If we can get onto that ship, we will be safe.' And that was such a nice thing for him to say.
>
> The wounded came onto the ship by helicopter, and the Royal

Marine bandsmen would bring them down on stretchers. They were then put in a triage area, where their wounds were assessed. The less badly wounded would go to a ward for treatment; those with severe burns went down to the old dormitories which formed the burns unit; and others with serious wounds went straight into the operating theatres. In the operating theatre, where I was based, we had three operating tables and we were all working as a team close together. From the operating theatre, a lot of men went on to intensive care.

We saw so many men in terrible pain and in shock who arrived looking war-torn and not in good condition. The hardest thing for me was seeing so many young, fit men with missing limbs or limbs that were so badly injured that they had to be removed. In some cases, we had to take their boot off still with their foot in it and throw it over the side because there was nowhere to store body parts. It was very distressing: you knew life for them would never be the same and that their careers in the military were over. Some of the burns were terrible too. One man with terrible facial burns was crying and grabbed my arm and said, 'I used to be handsome but now I am never going to look normal again.' The work was relentless. We worked every day, four hours on, four hours off, day and night.

On their busiest day, staff on the hospital ship treated 160 casualties, but more typically, when the fighting was at its height, they would welcome between forty and seventy wounded men. In total during the war, doctors, nurses and medical assistants in the ship treated 730 casualties, including 150 wounded Argentine servicemen. Staff conducted 504 surgical operations on board. In homage to the television series *M*A*S*H*, *Uganda* was nicknamed 'NOSH' – Naval Ocean-going Surgical Hospital.

Hendy told me:

It was mentally and physically exhausting – the hardest nursing any of us had ever done. I remember one day when I was on what was called 'red watch'. I had just done my four hours on, and I had got into bed and over the Tannoy it announced, 'Red Watch, at the rush go to the operating theatre.' The operating theatre had flooded in bad weather conditions, and it took us for ever to sort it all out. Then afterwards we were back on duty and everyone was so, so tired.

Typically, an operating team consisted of a surgeon, an anaesthetist, a nursing sister and junior nurses. Hendy said that equipment shortages meant lots of things had to be used over and over again after being sterilised. 'Sometimes the surgeons put their rubber gloves on and they would disintegrate because they had been recycled so many times,' she recalled. Hendy said that there were only three occasions when she broke down in floods of tears.

One chappie, who was Special Forces, had to have his leg amputated. But because of his medical history, he couldn't have a general anaesthetic; he had to have a local, spinal anaesthetic. While the surgeons were removing his leg, he was still conscious but there was a screen in place so he couldn't see exactly what was happening to his leg. My job was to sit and hold his hand, and this brave man said to me, 'You poor nurses. I bet you don't know what to talk to us about while men like me are having their legs chopped off.' His bravery got to me and made me tearful and he said, 'Oh, don't be upset.' And I thought, 'This is the wrong way around. Why are you reassuring me?' He was such a wonderful man.

On another occasion, we had been under a lot of pressure and then sometimes funny little things can tip you over the edge. We had finished in the operating theatre, and we had to go on to Seaview Ward at the front of the ship. There were very badly injured chaps there and the beds were close together and it was very quiet. Then this one chap who had lost his arm started to cry as we walked in. I was just about to go across and comfort him when a Marine in the bed opposite said in a really loud voice, 'I don't know what you're whingeing about. On my birthday, I got shot up the arse.' It was the way he said it and suddenly the whole ward started laughing, including the man who had lost his arm. And I was very emotional because I thought, 'You unbelievably brave men – what you have been through and yet you still have a sense of humour.'

Another time, I was with another nurse and we were very, very tired. We walked into Seaview Ward and someone had set up a television with a video and they were watching the Monty Python film *Life of Brian*. As we walked in, the person in the film was singing the line, 'Always look on the bright side of life'. Then all of the men started singing the same line at the top of their voices. I was speechless. I looked at all these poor men who had been through so much, and yet here they were all singing, 'Always look on the bright side of life'.

On board, Hendy was often known by her nickname of 'Buttons', given to her because she was always 'as bright as a button'. She said, 'I never cried because I was frightened, but the three times I cried on board was because I couldn't believe the amazing bravery of all these badly wounded chaps.'

Hendy and other medical staff treated injured enemy prisoners as well as British servicemen.

I don't know what they had been told about us, but some of the young Argentinian soldiers seemed incredibly frightened. One chappie looked terribly worried and so I was trying to reassure him. He then had to have some surgery done on his leg and I came into the operating theatre with him. He had his leg pinned and plated and then it was set in what is called 'Portsmouth cement' and it sets hard in the fresh air. But a piece of cement dropped to the floor and so I made him a little penguin out of it, which I gave him when he came round after his operation.

When, days later, he was being transferred over to an Argentinian ship, he was shouting for me and so someone came to find me. He showed me that he still had the little penguin I had made him, and he gave me his rosary beads, which was quite a momentous thing. I waved him off and then I kept the beads for many, many years.

Hendy was on board the ship when the ceasefire was announced over the Tannoy following the Argentine surrender.

I can remember everyone was incredibly happy. The nurses were all photographed toasting the victory, and even though I don't drink alcohol I joined in the celebrations. During the whole war, we only lost three men [once they had arrived on board] under very difficult conditions on the ship. It was sad to lose these men, but we were glad not to have lost more.

After the surrender was announced, Hendy became the first naval nurse to set foot on the Falklands when she jumped on board a landing craft that was taking supplies to a beach from *Uganda*. She did so because she did not want to go home having not stepped on one of the islands. 'I thought, "I have not come all this way not to set foot on the Falkland Islands,"' Hendy said. In fact, a few days later, there was an official tour to the islands for the nurses. However, even after the ceasefire, Hendy and the medical team still had new wounded coming in as a result of soldiers standing on mines.

On the voyage home, Hendy and other nurses reflected on their work after saying goodbye to their final patients.

I am not religious, but we all went to the side of the ship and said a really deep prayer for the badly injured men. As nurses, we were all going back a little bit older, a little bit wiser, a little bit more experienced, but there were so many chaps going back massively disfigured, some with missing limbs and who would not be able to do the job they were trained for again. All the nurses just sent some messages up to the sky.

Hendy also left a message in a glass bottle, which she threw off the ship and which had her contact details inside. Months later Engelbert, the man who found the bottle washed up in the African country of Sierra Leone, replied to her.

The *Uganda*, which was given the call sign of 'Mother Hen' in the Falklands, was given a warm welcome by crowds when she returned to Southampton on 9 August 1982, 113 days after she had sailed to join the Task Force. During that time, she had sailed 26,150 miles. Hendy was met at Southampton by her parents, Ken and Rita, her older brother Brian and other family members. When they returned to her parents' home, neighbours had organised a street party in her honour. 'It was absolutely wonderful, but I thought I hadn't deserved it. However, the Falklands War had brought the country together,' Hendy recalled.

On 25 September 1982, *Uganda* returned to her role of educational cruising. However, that November she was chartered for two years to serve as a store ship between Ascension Island and the Falklands. After a refit, including a new helicopter deck, she left Southampton on 14 January 1983 to sail to the South Atlantic. She was laid up in 1985 and scrapped in 1992.

Hendy did a further twelve years with the QARNNS after arriving back from the Falklands. For her work, she was awarded a long-service medal. Hendy married aged thirty-three, and the couple had a daughter together before their marriage ended after two years. Later, she nursed her ill parents for several years, as well as doing some civilian nursing. She then spent some time as an estate agent before working in a mental health hospital.

Today, Jeune Hall (her married surname) lives in Exmouth, Devon, with her grown-up daughter, Amy. Hall works as a steward at the Royal Marines base at Lympstone, Devon. Reflecting on her war service nearly forty years on, she told me:

> If someone said, 'Would you do it all again?', my answer would be, '100 per cent, yes, without question.' What makes you want to be a nurse is to help people who are ill, or who are in pain, or who have terrible injuries, or who are frightened. It was the experience of a lifetime and I feel privileged to have been a very tiny part in the war effort. I have always been passionate about the military, but my admiration for what they go through escalated even more as a result of what I experienced and what I saw.

CHRISTOPHER JAMES POLLARD

Service: Royal Navy

Final rank: Lieutenant Commander (in the Royal Naval Reserve)

FALKLANDS WAR DECORATION / DISTINCTION:

MENTIONED IN DESPATCHES (MID)

DATE OF BRAVERY: 25 MAY 1982

GAZETTED: 8 OCTOBER 1982

Chris Pollard experienced the highs and lows of war within the space of just a few hours on 25 May 1982. While serving as the Royal Navy master gunner on HMS *Coventry*, he underwent 'the most exhilarating experience I have had' when shooting down two enemy aircraft that were attacking his ship. However, later that day he suffered 'the worst moment of my life' when he watched the *Coventry* sink, with the loss of nineteen men, having been hit by enemy bombs. For his bravery that day, he was Mentioned in Despatches.

Christopher James Pollard was born in Leeds, West Yorkshire, on 17 June 1955. He was the eldest of five children, with four younger sisters. His father, who worked as a machinist for a railway engine manufacturer, had completed his national service in the Royal Navy on the battleship HMS *Duke of York*. Young Pollard attended Coldcotes Primary School, Coldcotes County Secondary School and finally Foxwood Comprehensive School, all in Leeds. Because his father had served in the Royal Navy, Pollard had long wanted to follow in his dad's footsteps. However, he told me:

> As a working-class kid from a council estate, I had never expected to go to the Royal Navy College at Dartmouth. But then, after Cubs and Scouts, I went into the Sea Cadets, where I had a very good training base, and one thing led to another. I applied for a scholarship to Dartmouth when I was thirteen but didn't get it. However, then I applied for a short-service commission in 1972 and this time I passed the interview board and did get in.

Pollard entered the Royal Naval College, Dartmouth, in January 1973, aged seventeen. From 1973 to 1974, he was a Midshipman undergoing training for his navy role. During this period, Pollard served two tours in Northern Ireland on gun-running patrols. After completing the gunnery course at HMS *Excellent*, he was appointed as master gunner in HMS *Eskimo* in 1975 and served on the West Indies Station, which operated out of Belize, during internal turmoil in Guatemala in 1976. In an echo of events six years later, the *Eskimo* was sent to South America, in Pollard's words to 'put the frighteners' on Argentina because one of their destroyers had fired across the bows of the research ship *Shackleton* in an unprovoked incident as tensions in the Falklands mounted.

In the summer of that same year, Pollard served on *Eskimo* as the escort for the Queen's visit to America to mark the bicentennial of American Independence. However, he left the Royal Navy in order to work as a contract officer in the Sultan of Oman's Navy from 1978 to 1979, during which time he served on gunboats for two patrols in Dhofar Province. During this episode, he spent much of his time in the Strait of Hormuz chasing Iranian smugglers.

In 1981, he rejoined the Royal Navy and served during the Falklands War in the rank of Lieutenant and as the master gunner on HMS *Coventry*. The *Coventry* was a Type-42 destroyer laid down by Cammell Laird at Birkenhead, Merseyside, on 29 January 1973, and launched on 21 June 1974. The ship cost just under £38 million to build. *Coventry* was ordered to sail to the Falkland Islands on 2 April 1982, the day of the Argentine invasion of the islands. The ship left the Gibraltar area on that date and on 25 April was joined by the Battle Group. In an interview for this book, Pollard revealed to me a little-known fact: while acting as an advance group well after passing Ascension Island, the *Coventry*'s steering motors had burnt out, meaning the ship lost the use of her rudders. Instead, she had to be steered by her main engines and by hand pumps. Pollard said:

> This was not easy when travelling at 25 knots, and when we hit severe gales we knew that because of the loss of power the ship was in danger of rolling over if she had turned sideways onto the heavy seas. If that had happened, no one would have got out.

On 1 May, the *Coventry* became the first British ship to enter the TEZ, and in fact remained in it – always at the front of the fleet under the threat of attack from the air, from the surface or from submarines – until 25 May. A week after entering the TEZ, *Coventry* was tasked with bombarding enemy-held Port Stanley with her 4.5in. gun and also with engaging enemy resupply aircraft with her Sea Dart surface-to-air missile system. On the 11th, she made her first confirmed 'kill', shooting down a Puma helicopter of 601 Assault Helicopter Battalion.

The attack on HMS *Sheffield* on 4 May and the subsequent heavy casualties understandably had a knock-on effect for the companies of other British ships in the TEZ. In writing home on 7 May 1982, Pollard began his letter:

Hello!! Well I am still in one piece and intend to remain so. The shock of the *Sheffield* has now worn off and morale is slowly improving, people cheered up when we finally got the final casualty figures and knew who'd copped it – my mate is safe and so I feel much better. We have had an analysis of what happened amidst all the confusion and I am now confident I can cope with the flight profiles of the missile carriers and shoot them down. Even so we are all very jumpy and receiving alarms on [seeing] patches of cloud, [and] this is not doing a lot for our sleep. I am averaging seven hours a day but this is in snatches of 1–2 hours and is frequently broken by alarms.

Pollard also kept an occasional diary, and his entry for 11 May noted that at 11.02 a.m., the ship's company got their first glimpse of the Falkland Islands, but they were not impressed by what they saw. 'What a dump. It looks like Wales on a wet Sunday after England have beaten them at Cardiff Arms Park and all the pubs have run out of beer. It also smells of sheep droppings,' he wrote.

25 May is traditionally a national holiday in Argentina: it commemorates the 1810 revolution that ended with the country's independence from Spain. On 25 May 1982, the Argentine Air Force was determined to leave its mark – while *Coventry* was deployed, along with HMS *Broadsword*, a Type-22 frigate, to protect

troopships landing men and equipment on the Falkland beaches. They were positioned on the north-west of Falkland Sound, off Pebble Island, and it was hoped they would pick off enemy aircraft attacking British ships in San Carlos Bay. However, at 12.30 p.m. the two ships were attacked by a wave of Argentine Skyhawks. It later emerged that the *Coventry's* radar system was 'blind' to the low trajectory of the attack aircrafts' approach.

Pollard, who was on watch in the ship's operations room, used a computer link with the *Broadsword*, which had a better radar system. He put this to good use, shooting down two of the enemy planes in the first two waves of attack that day. In an interview with the Coventry-based *Evening Telegraph*, he said years later, 'it was like looking for a needle in a haystack' trying to shoot the aircraft down. However, he quickly appeared to master the computer system during two successive attacks. He said:

> On both occasions, I managed to pick off the leading planes, which I later realised must have been the attack leaders, and the rest of them cleared off. Looking back, that's why they came back [later in the day] – this time for us. They knew they had to knock us out.

Pollard went off duty at 4 p.m., only for action stations to be sounded again at 6 p.m.: all crew were ordered to their battle posts as word came through that a third wave of Skyhawks was on its way. Pollard takes up the story: 'We knew we could pick them off, but they also knew what we were capable of. It was a strange sensation. Very faintly on the horizon we could see their shimmering exhaust trails fizzing over the wave tops as they came for us. After that everything happened very quickly.'

Pollard and his comrades, who were on the starboard side, started firing at the attacking Skyhawks, and they put up a barrage of flak before the planes diverted towards *Broadsword*, leaving the crew of *Coventry* struggling to get their guns low enough. One bomb hit *Broadsword* before the enemy aircraft flew off into the distance.

As soon as they'd gone, I told the men to get ammunition and reload the guns. I ran across to the port side to find out why the machine gun had jammed. Up on the bridge wing, a young sailor began shouting and I turned around to see two more planes. It was as if everything was in slow motion. I remember seeing the British insignia on the bombs as they were released, because they were British-made. As the planes went overhead, I shouted to sailors to get down. Then, through my clenched eyes, everything went white as the first of the bombs exploded. The deck heaved as the ship was lifted out of the water, it felt like my knee sockets were getting ripped out. There was smoke coming out of the port side when I looked over. Then, between the main mast and the funnel, the ship just exploded. One of the bombs must have been delayed, and it blew the guts out of the ship. There was a hole in the deck with flames billowing out. The ship was starting to lean over by about 10 degrees, and I could see the men everywhere climbing out of the hatches. We eventually managed to clear [unjam] the machine gun and then test-fired it, which sent everyone scurrying for cover again.

Pollard, somewhat modestly, failed to detail quite how brave he and his gun crew had been during this deadly enemy attack. However, the *Coventry*'s Commanding Officer, Captain David Hart Dyke, later wrote in his book, *Four Weeks in May: A Captain's Story of War at Sea*:

Lieutenant Chris Pollard, who was directing the close-range guns from the exposed position of the bridge wings, declined to duck for cover as the enemy aircraft closed at eye level and one of them strafed the ship with cannon fire. He then ordered the gun crews to stay at their posts and keep firing, which they did without question.

Within minutes of the *Coventry* being hit, the order was given to abandon ship, but the crew could not launch the lifeboat because the ship was listing so much. Amidst a thick, acrid smoke, some of the crew started slipping down the bridge and onto the upper deck. Pollard recalled how the Chinese men who worked in the ship's laundry were clustered on the upper deck in a daze and disorientated. 'God knows how they made it out,' he said. 'We managed to calm some of them down and get them into life jackets and survival suits.'

The lifeboat was launched from *Broadsword*, which had only received minor damage from the bomb that hit her. Pollard said he swam to a life raft, dragging with him what he thought to be a wounded shipmate. However, upon reaching the raft he discovered that the man, a laundry man, was already dead. Hanging on to the side of the already crammed life raft, he awaited the arrival of a lifeboat from the *Broadsword*. As the two safety boats collided, he received a blow to the head and was taken into the lifeboat and then onto *Broadsword*, where a sailor on the ship grabbed Pollard to prevent him falling back into the lifeboat.

Pollard later reflected on his wartime experience:

I didn't feel the euphoria at the time when we won the war … I still have nightmares about [Captain Jorge Osvaldo] García, one of the pilots I shot down. I later found out that his body was washed up on a beach still in his life raft nearly two years after the war. At four o'clock that day when I shot those planes down, it was the most exhilarating experience I have had. But only hours later, as I watched the *Coventry* go down, that was the worst moment of my life.

Coventry had been struck by three bombs just above the water line on her port side. One of the bombs exploded beneath the computer room, destroying it and the nearby operations room. A second bomb entered the forward engine room, exploding beneath the Junior Ratings' dining room. The third bomb did not explode. Of *Coventry*'s company of 280 men, nineteen were killed and twenty-five injured that day, with the wounded taken to either the field hospital ashore or the hospital ship SS *Uganda*. Furthermore, one of the most seriously wounded men, who received a fractured skull, died less than a year later.

Those wanting to know more about the involvement of the *Coventry* and her crew in the war should read the book written by Hart Dyke, who received burns in the attack. In fact, *Four Weeks in May* was later turned into a BBC documentary, called *Sea of Fire*. Hart Dyke, father of the award-winning comedy actress Miranda Hart, described the moment the bombs struck: 'There was a vicious shockwave, a blinding flash and searing heat ... the force and the shock of the impact shook my whole body to the core. All power and communication were lost, the ship was stopped, burning furiously and beginning to roll.' The Captain made it to a life raft and was taken to *Broadsword*, from where he witnessed his ship's final death throes.

In an article for the *Independent* newspaper just ahead of the twentieth anniversary of the Falklands War, Captain Hart Dyke gave a fascinating insight into his feelings and the effect the conflict had on his life. He wrote:

HMS *Coventry* was a guided missile destroyer. We were a thorn in the side of the Argentinian Air Force, and they ganged up against us to take us out. Nineteen of my sailors were killed, and the rest of us by some miracle swam to the life rafts to be picked out of the water by helicopters. At the time you can keep going, but it took me about two years to recover.

It's very sad that we had to go to war. This conflict should have been solved by the politicians through negotiation: the military had been warning them for years that it shouldn't have to become a military operation. Because they failed to keep the military presence in the Falklands, politicians sent the wrong signal to the Argentinians, so we had to do it the hard way.

In the end it was worth it because we were preserving freedom for British people. You have to take risks to do this. A British sailor doesn't fight well unless he believes in the cause. We had extremely high morale because we did believe, and even though we were 8,000 miles away we could feel the support from home. The nation was behind us and so, against the odds, we won. In a way, I couldn't believe we were asked to do it, but you have to go for it. It's what you are trained for, and I wouldn't have missed it.

The *Coventry* sank off Pebble Island the day after the attack. A Ministry of Defence press release on the sinking of the ship, dated 9 June 1982, said that in

> only four weeks of war [the *Coventry*] had shot down seven fighter bombers, a troop-carrying helicopter, sunk a patrol craft, and controlled numerous Sea Harriers which accounted for several more aircraft.
>
> The country can be proud of the Ship's Company of HMS *Coventry* who performed magnificently and with great bravery throughout a very arduous campaign. They remain an intensely happy, efficient team and united to a man. It will be a sad and emotional day when we have to leave each other and depart for other ships.
>
> We will all have proud and happy memories of a great ship. At

the same time we will never forget our lost friends who also contributed so much to the battle.

Today, the wreck site is protected under the Protection of Military Remains Act. Five months after the ship sank, a team of navy divers conducted an underwater survey of the ship, which lies more than 300ft below the surface. This eventually led to Operation Blackleg, in which a team of divers recovered classified and other vital documents and equipment from the wreck. After the war, a cross to commemorate crew members who lost their lives was erected on Pebble Island. There is also a commemorative plaque at Coventry Cathedral, and another at nearby Holy Trinity Church.

No crew member of the *Coventry* received a gallantry medal for their role on 25 May, but Chief Petty Officer Aircrewman M. J. Tupper was awarded the DSM for his part in the helicopter rescue of the *Coventry* crew. Pollard was Mentioned in Despatches (MID) for his bravery in *The London Gazette* of 8 October 1982. Pollard emphasised to me that he considered his MID a distinction awarded not just to him personally but to the entire gunnery division of HMS *Coventry*. 'It was very much a team effort,' he stressed.

After the end of the Falklands War, and with the *Coventry* no more, Pollard was posted as a Lieutenant to HMS *Nottingham* before retiring from the navy in 1986. Immediately after leaving the military, he worked for two different breweries as an area manager. During this period and beyond, he served in the rank of Lieutenant Commander in the Royal Naval Reserve before retiring from this role in 1998.

In 1992, Pollard joined the Sultan of Oman's Royal Yacht Squadron, where he served on the royal yacht and the royal support ship and also acted as Operations Officer from 1992 to 1993. In recent years, he has been semi-retired, doing other part-time roles – currently he has turned his hobby into his job and works part-time as a cook.

Today, Pollard lives in Hull in the East Riding of Yorkshire. He is divorced with three grown-up children and three grandchildren. Reflecting on the Falklands War nearly forty years on, he told me:

I am very proud of what the navy achieved. It was remarkable to go from a standing start to a full-blown war in just one week and achieve what we did. Very few organisations in the world could have done it. I feel sadness too for the people who didn't come back – friends and comrades – but, unfortunately, that's war.

MALCOLM GEOFFREY COOPER

Service: Royal Navy
Final rank: Chief Petty Officer
FALKLANDS WAR DECORATION / DISTINCTION: **N/A**
DATE OF BRAVERY: N/A
GAZETTED: N/A

Malcolm Cooper survived a deadly enemy attack on his ship, HMS *Antelope*, that eventually killed two men and injured many more. He had to suffer the trauma of seeing the bodies of his shipmates flying through the air and, later, his ship exploding and eventually sinking. During an episode that left him feeling 'lucky to be alive', he tended to a bomb-disposal expert after the man's arm was virtually blown off, before leaping to safety. In the long term, he has suffered from post-traumatic stress disorder (PTSD), receiving flashbacks to that dreadful day decades later.

Malcolm Geoffrey Cooper was born in Plymouth, Devon, on 14 December 1960. The son of a Royal Navy sailor, he had five sisters. He left Barne Barton Secondary School in 1977, aged sixteen. Cooper had a job lined up as a hotel chef, but before taking on the job he walked into a Royal Navy recruiting office and was, as he later joked, 'press ganged' into joining as a junior seaman. He trained to be a gunner, specifically a missile aimer.

His first ship was HMS *Eskimo*, based in Chatham, Kent, and his first deployment was to the Caribbean, where he spent six months 'island-hopping'. After three years on the *Eskimo*, Cooper took a shore-based job in Portsmouth before volunteering to join HMS *Antelope*, a Royal Navy frigate. He was aged twenty-one and in the rank of acting Leading Seaman when the Falkland Islands were invaded on 2 April 1982. At the time, he and his shipmates were in Portland, Dorset, on a training exercise. The Captain came over the Tannoy and announced, 'Stop everything. Full ahead to Plymouth.' On the way to Plymouth, there were rumours among the crew that the ship might be heading to the Falkland Islands but most of the sailors had no idea where they were located. 'Initially, most of us thought they were on the top of Scotland and there must be some Russian involvement,' Cooper recalled. When the ship arrived in Plymouth, there were already preparations for the *Antelope* to embark on the 8,000-mile voyage to the Falkland Islands, via a stop-off on Ascension Island. She sailed from Devonport, Plymouth, on 5 April, a grey, misty morning, followed by HMS *Alacrity*. Both ships were bound for the South Atlantic to take part in 'Operation Corporate'.

Antelope was a Type-21 frigate whose keel was laid down by Vosper Thornycroft in Southampton in March 1971. She was commissioned in July 1975 and was the only ship of her class not to be fitted with Exocet missiles. Typically, she had a ship's company of 170. *Antelope*'s arrival in the war zone was delayed because on the voyage from Ascension to the Falklands, she and another ship, RFA *Tidespring*, were tasked with transporting Argentine prisoners of war (POWs), including Special Forces men, back to Ascension Island after their capture in South Georgia. There were some

180 POWs on *Tidespring* and just one on *Antelope*: the legendary Captain Alfredo Astiz, who had earlier been linked to several atrocities in Argentina. Having played a key role in Argentina's 'Dirty War', he was later branded the 'Blond Angel of Death'. Cooper spent time on board with Astiz, having been tasked with minding him. 'He came across as a real gentleman – a really nice guy. He was clever and charming,' Cooper told me.

Antelope finally arrived in the area of operations on 21 May 1982, and by then the war was already well under way and men and ships had been lost. 'Everybody was scared,' said Cooper. 'We realised this was not a game. We had heard about the loss of the *Sheffield* and we knew people were dying.' On 23 May, *Antelope* was tasked with carrying out air defence duties at San Carlos Water, protecting the beachhead that had been established two days earlier. In the early hours of 23 May, the ship took up her assigned patrol line south of Fanning Island at the head of what had become known as 'Bomb Alley'. The ship went to 'action stations' at 10 a.m., and that afternoon its Lynx helicopter took part in a successful raid on an enemy cargo ship. Shortly after the helicopter returned to the *Antelope*, four enemy aircraft were spotted flying over nearby Fanning Head. Soon afterwards, they returned and the *Antelope* came under attack, first from one pair of enemy Skyhawk fighter-bombers, then from the other.

Cooper's specific role was as an aimer of the Seacat missiles on board *Antelope*. However, when the ship was attacked by the fighter-bombers, Cooper was on the starboard side. He told me:

I went into the ship's magazine after the first pair of planes attacked us. They dropped about twelve bombs in all and two hit us but neither exploded. It was like being in a washing machine. One bomb, from the second pair of aircraft, landed about 15ft below me and the plane that dropped it hit the ship's mast and blew up above me. It was out of control with its wings shot off. There were flames everywhere but nothing hit me.

That enemy pilot was killed in the incident, but the others managed to fly off. Cooper continued:

We now had a situation where we had two unexploded 1,000lb bombs in the deck, one had entered through the port side, the other through the starboard. The one from the port side went through the Petty Officers' mess and ended up in the sailors' mess close to my bed. When the bomb came in, it bounced around inside of the ship and started fires. When the firefighters were tackling the blaze, one of the Chinese laundrymen came up asking to get hot water for his tea – he had been below deck and he was blissfully unaware the ship had been hit!

The other bomb into the starboard side went into the ship's fridges and that set off the gas alarms. For a moment, crew members thought they had been subjected to a gas attack. One member of the ship's company was killed in the attack: Steward Mark Stephens. A second crewman received serious injuries; a third, minor injuries. At 6.30 p.m., the ship moved up San Carlos Water towards the anchorages. The seriously injured Rating was transferred to the Ajax Bay dressing station, and two bomb-disposal experts were embarked on *Antelope* from HMS *Argonaut*. The two men seemed fairly confident that they could deal with the two bombs, but most of the crew were evacuated away from where they were working, some onto the flight deck and others down into the helicopter hangar.

Suddenly, however, there was a huge explosion on the ship that lasted some five seconds. The bomb the men had been working on had detonated, killing Staff Sergeant Jim Prescott and badly injuring WO John Phillips, both of whom served in the Royal Engineers. Once again, Cooper takes up the story:

> The bomb-disposal men were talking over the Tannoy and they tried three times to put clamps on the bombs and defuse them. On the third occasion, the bomb just went off. There were flames everywhere and lots of people flying through the air. I was sat under a helicopter fuel pump and my reaction was, 'I haven't been hit, so I will stay where I am.' Others ran onto the flight deck, but the shrapnel was coming down and hitting some of those on the flight deck. The hangar started filling with smoke and we started making our way out. Then I bumped into the bomb-disposal man [Phillips], whose arm was hanging off, and I tried to help him. The people on the front half of the ship were cut off from the rest of us because the ship was on fire. They couldn't get down to us and we couldn't get up to them. People on the flight deck launched life rafts but the life rafts exploded because of the heat. However, a landing craft managed to get alongside the ship and many of the crew leapt into it from 15 or 20ft high, some breaking legs and arms. Others climbed down a rope to get away from the flames and were picked up by a boat waiting underneath them. For many it was a choice of jump and break a leg, or stay and get blown up. I jumped from about 15ft but was not injured. Because I was covered in blood from trying to help the bomb-disposal man, people thought I was a casualty but I was not, in fact, hurt.

Minutes later, there was another huge explosion on the *Antelope* but nobody was killed because everyone had managed to abandon ship. The blast had been caused when the main magazine exploded. Cooper was standing in a landing craft about 300 metres away at the time and recalled, 'It was a shocking moment and a sound

I will never forget. That explosion resulted in the iconic photographs that people still remember nearly forty years on.'

Casualties were treated at Ajax Bay and those not injured, including Cooper, were later taken to HMS *Fearless* and two other ships. *Antelope* burnt all night and then broke in half and sank the next day, still with the body of Stephens on board. That same day, however, the crew of the *Antelope* were still in danger. Cooper said: 'The Captain of the *Fearless* was giving a running commentary of the air raids coming in. We kept worrying we would come under attack again and the side of the ship would be blown in. We had about seven air raids that day.'

That evening, the survivors from the *Antelope* were cross-decked to MV *Norland*, the North Sea ferry that had been requisitioned as a troop carrier. Later, they were transported to South Georgia and cross-decked again, this time onto the *QE2*. Along with other survivors from the *Coventry* and the *Sheffield*, they then sailed for home and a heroes' welcome at Southampton. Cooper said the return journey was eased because before the *Antelope* sunk, someone had managed to retrieve the beer money from the Sailors' Mess, and it had to be spent before the *QE2* reached Britain. 'We filled a cabin with beer and had to drink it all in just twelve days!' he said.

Reflecting on his part in the conflict, Cooper said:

My war was very fast and very violent. It was a fast learning curve. Many left the navy after their experiences, but I stayed on. My favourite saying after the war was: 'It's too late to ask me how to do something when the shit has already hit the fan.' By that I meant, when it's quiet, you should ask how something needs to be done and I, or someone else, will show you. Don't wait to ask only when there is a crisis.

The two bomb-disposal experts who had tackled the bombs on the *Antelope* were later decorated for their bravery. Staff Sergeant Prescott, who was killed aged thirty-seven, was awarded a posthumous Conspicuous Gallantry Medal – the only such gallantry medal for the war. WO (later Captain) Phillips was awarded the DSC, an award traditionally reserved for the Royal Navy and rarely given to the army in the modern era. Despite losing his left arm, Phillips returned to his bomb-disposal work the following year. A memorial was later erected on the Falkland Islands for those who died on HMS *Antelope* and HMS *Ardent*. The memorial is 25ft high and has a brass plaque that reads: 'To the memory of the brave men of HMS *Ardent* and HMS *Antelope*.'

Cooper remained in the Royal Navy until December 2000, completing twenty-three years' service and retiring in the rank of Chief Petty Officer. During that time, he served as an unarmed observer in Cambodia from 1992 to 1993 during the brutality of the Khmer Rouge, the ruthless Communist Party regime that killed well over a million of its own people. At one point, Cooper and a Canadian observer were held hostage for several hours – only to be released in exchange for a volleyball and a net, the sport loved by many Cambodians. 'A volleyball and a net was all my life was worth!' Cooper joked, adding more sombrely, 'We were shot at almost on a daily basis.'

Shortly after completing his work in Cambodia, Cooper had returned to the Falkland Islands in 1997, while serving on HMS *Somerset* along with two other members of the *Antelope*'s former company. The men went ashore and laid a wreath in memory of those who had died on the ship in 1982.

After leaving the Royal Navy, he worked as a security guard for the Ministry of Defence's Guard Service, retiring early in 2021 after a major cancer operation. Today, Cooper lives in Suffolk with his second wife. He has two daughters and a son from his first marriage.

It was only some six years ago that Cooper realised he was suffering from PTSD:

I started having some problems. Then, and still now, I can be sat in a room with my eyes shut, and when I open them the room is full of smoke – or, at least, that is what I see. I am reliving what I saw back in May 1982. I have seen a psychiatrist and received therapy – but when I was talking about things, it opened up a can of worms. However, my therapy has helped me to deal with the past.

CHAPTER 3

SPECIAL FORCES RECCES

The SAS was formed in 1941 during the Second World War. Its role was to launch hit-and-run raids against enemy targets, initially in North Africa and later in mainland Europe. The key role played by the 'SAS Originals', as the early members were later named, ensured that 'The Regiment', as the SAS is often known, eventually became an important and permanent part of the British Army. By 1982, the potential uses of the SAS in war had expanded from its role of four decades earlier: it was no longer seen only as a hit-and-run raiding force but also had potentially vital reconnaissance, or 'recce', roles. With its offensive capabilities, a small, highly trained, well-equipped force was seen as the best way forward.

Since the 1940s, the SAS has performed a number of covert roles, including several on foreign soil, but the Falklands War was the first time since the Second World War that the SAS was to play a part in a large-scale conflict. In 1982, the Director of the SAS was General Peter de la Billière, who had only two years earlier played a key role in the siege at the Iranian Embassy in central London. As he wrote in his autobiography, Looking for Trouble: SAS to Gulf Command: *'The seizure of the Falkland Islands by Argentina in April 1982 burst on us suddenly. I think everyone in Britain was taken by surprise, not least the Foreign Office. Nevertheless, the moment we heard that South Georgia had been occupied, we – the SAS – took urgent steps to make sure that we had a role in any conflict that might develop.'*

As the situation escalated, de la Billière noted, 'Our most pressing need was for intelligence about conditions in the Falklands. In particular, we needed to know the texture of the landscape at that time of year.' The SAS Director called on Sir Cosmo Haskard, a former Governor of the islands who was in London, and others to provide such local insight. Lieutenant Colonel Michael Rose, the Commander of 22 SAS, was equally as keen as de la Billière to ensure the SAS played its part.

Continuing the story in his autobiography, de la Billière wrote, 'In the general chaos of mobilization Mike Rose managed to jump the gun, very much as he had done at the start of the Iranian Embassy siege. Without any official permission, he took "D" Squadron to Brize Norton [RAF station, Oxfordshire] and got them on board an aircraft; before anyone in authority realized where they were, they had arrived at Ascension Island, 4,000 miles down into the South Atlantic and half-way to their target. Soon I too was on my way there…'

'D' Squadron played an important role in the recapture of South Georgia. In the early part of the war, it soon became apparent that the key role for 'G' Squadron, which had not been far behind in joining their fellow SAS men in the war zone, also lay in reconnaissance. The plan was to get Special Forces units onto the Falkland Islands before the main Task Force arrived. However, without back-up units in place this was highly dangerous for the men involved. De la Billière wrote, 'Back in the United Kingdom, my role was to liaise and advise at the highest level, for some of our proposed operations were highly sensitive, and needed not merely military approval but political backing from the top. Our plan to infiltrate reconnaissance teams, for instance, carried a high risk: if anything went wrong and people were captured, the whole British game would be given away, for it would be clear that an invasion was being mounted.'

Members of the SBS also played a role in reconnaissance, having as already stated been heavily involved in the recapture of South Georgia.

The Special Boat Section (which became the Special Boat Squadron in 1977 and the Special Boat Service in 1987) had been formed in 1940. Its reconnaissance roles on the Falkland Islands, as a result of the men's training, centred on the beaches and coastal areas, while the SAS men focused on the inland areas. The reconnaissance teams were to hide and report on Argentine troop positions, movements and morale. Typically, four-man patrols were inserted by helicopter at night, at least 20 miles from their objectives. The countryside offered virtually no natural cover – no trees nor bushes nor folds to hide in – and the usually brutal weather conditions were no more helpful to the men.

In his autobiography, de la Billière was particularly generous in his praise for 'G' Squadron: 'From the beginning of May, three weeks before the main assault, helicopters flew them blind into remote spots in the Falkland hills, and there they lay up in thoroughly unpleasant conditions, watching tracks, depots, troop deployments and aircraft movements, and determining which sites would be most suitable for the landing. It was a measure of their skill and discipline that none of the patrols was found or captured.'

The aim of this chapter and Chapter 5 is not to tell the story of the SAS's and SBS's full involvement in the war. That task has already been accomplished in books by the likes of Lieutenant General Sir Cedric Delves, Lieutenant Colonel Ewen Southby-Tailyour and General Sir Peter de la Billière – see the bibliography for details. Instead, I am seeking to provide a snapshot of the bravery of SAS and SBS men with my individual write-ups in these two chapters. Some would argue that the write-up on John Pettinger in this chapter should go elsewhere in the book because he was a member of neither the SAS nor SBS. However, the reconnaissance role that he played as a member of the Parachute Regiment was virtually identical to that played by the SAS and SBS patrols, and so I believe his write-up sits most comfortably here. The offensive operations of the SAS / SBS will primarily be dealt with in Chapter 5.

JOSEPH GORDON MATHER

Service: Army (SAS)

Final rank: Captain

FALKLANDS WAR DECORATION / DISTINCTION:

MILITARY MEDAL (MM)

DATES OF BRAVERY: 1–28 MAY 1982

GAZETTED: 8 OCTOBER 1982

Gordon Mather was decorated with the Military Medal (MM) for prolonged gallantry during a daring mission lasting an extraordinary twenty-eight days behind enemy lines, while serving with 'G' Squadron, 22 SAS Regiment. He led a four-man patrol in the most brutal conditions on East Falkland in order to gain valuable intelligence on Argentine positions. After completing a formidable thirty years of military service with 'exemplary' conduct, he played a key role with the South Atlantic Medal Association – SAMA 82 – eventually chairing the group for seven years.

A coal-miner's son, Joseph Gordon Mather, always known as Gordon, was born on 27 February 1947 in Aylesham, a Kent coal-mining village that lies between Canterbury and Dover. He was educated locally, first at St Joseph's Catholic Primary School in Aylesham and later at St Thomas' Catholic Primary School in Canterbury. He recalled:

> The expectation for the majority of the village boys of my generation on finishing school was to follow our fathers and brothers down the mines. Many of the girls from the village naturally married local boys. It was and remains a wonderfully close-knit community. Aged sixteen, I saw an army advert for what was then called the 'Boys' Service', and I saw kids of my age canoeing, climbing rocks and skiing. I thought that would be an adventurous life, and so it proved!

I left school in 1963 aged sixteen and joined the army. I was never given a choice of cap badge and found myself a member of the Royal Corps of Signals as a 'boy soldier'. It was a curious twist of fate which started me on a career path which did indeed prove to be adventurous. On reaching the age of eighteen, I set off for my first posting as an adult soldier to the then divided city of Berlin – then the most decadent place in Europe – and I was a kid from a coal-mining village, so it was good fun!

After two tours in Germany serving with the British Army of the Rhine (BAOR), he was posted to 264 (SAS) Signals. Mather takes up the story:

I said to my Troop Sergeant, 'What exactly do 264 do?' He replied, 'They are in direct support of the SAS.' And I said, 'Who and what are the SAS?' because in those days very little was known about our Special Forces; indeed, few people had ever heard of them. He said knowingly, 'You'll soon find out.' I turned up in Hereford in 1969 not knowing what I was walking into.

Mather then completed foreign tours as a signaller with one of the four SAS squadrons, and later became a fully badged SAS member after qualifying for selection in 1974. Serving in 'G' Squadron, he completed operational tours in Oman and Northern Ireland.

When the Falkland Islands were invaded on 2 April 1982, Mather was aged thirty-five and was a Troop Sergeant in 'G' Squadron. At the time, he and his 'G' Squadron comrades were attending internal courses at Hereford, and Mather was on an Arabic course. He recalled:

Our Egyptian instructor turned on the television and we learnt that the Falkland Islands had been invaded. Word soon came through that the course was cancelled and we should prepare to deploy. We were chuffed to bits – there was a fight on and naturally we would be involved. But a couple of days later we were told we were not even on the order of battle – we were not going to war. It seemed it was going to be a Royal Navy operation and they would take their infantry – the Royal Marines – but that soon changed when our Commanding Officer rang the Commander of 3 Commando Brigade in Plymouth.

The SAS stand-by squadron in April 1982 was 'D' Squadron. And so, they departed RAF Brize Norton for the nine-hour flight down to Ascension Island. The Officer Commanding (OC) 'G' Squadron only had two of his four troops available for 'Operation Corporate', as the other two were deployed on other sensitive commitments. 'G' continued their training, and when it was decided that they too were needed, they were also flown to Ascension Island, where they joined the Amphibious Task Force. As Mather put it:

'D' Squadron pulled the best straw, if you like, because they got the direct action roles, the business of 'breaking things'. 'G' Squadron were tasked with the vital role of gathering Intelligence that would inform the direction of the campaign throughout, including where to land at the start. We embarked on a Royal Fleet Auxiliary ship, RFA *Resource*, and settled in for the journey south. The Squadron Commander and his small HQ team were based on HMS *Hermes*; this was very opportune as he was quickly able to establish regular access to the Naval Task Force Commander. Some days later, the Squadron Commander cross-decked to us and explained, 'We will initially deploy seven four-man patrols on the Falklands, both East and West Islands.' Each patrol was taken aside and given its target area. Although I knew X patrol was to my right and Y patrol was to my left, I didn't know what their targets were. This is a normal procedure for operational security reasons, in case we were captured and interrogated. It was a typical SAS operation conducted on a need-to-know basis. I remember waking up one morning and speaking to one of the crew. He said, 'We are now in the Total Exclusion Zone.' He continued that for the first time in I don't know how long, the Royal Navy had hoisted its battle ensign.

'G' Squadron patrol insertions were to be by Sea King helicopters provided by 846 Royal Naval Air Squadron. Coincidentally, the OC of 846 was co-located with OC 'G' Squadron on board HMS *Hermes*. This resulted in an excellent liaison between the two groups. Shortly after arriving off the Falkland Islands, Mather had to liaise with his pilot to plan the insertion. Mather was full of praise for the work of the helicopter pilots, who had to insert his and other patrols at night, flying at dangerously low levels to avoid detection. They had only recently been issued with night-vision goggles, which today are standard military equipment, and practised with them, landing and taking off from the ships on the journey south.

From memory, the insertion flight was about 120 miles and the final approach was very low indeed, but they did a superb job. Someone had produced a technical report which allowed the pilot to plot his insertion route, hopefully avoiding the enemy radar systems. I decided on an eight-figure grid reference point from which I could then walk into my area of operation, thus avoiding possible compromise by the helicopter's presence. Part of the difficulty of course was that we had no idea where the enemy may be. That was the mission of the 'G' Squadron patrols: where are they [the enemy]?; how many are they?; what weapons systems do they possess? and so on. As a patrol Commander, I had a number of considerations – for example, the weather. We spoke to friends in the Royal Marines who had previously served on the Islands during the winter months and asked how long they thought we might sustain a patrol for. They advised that given the expected weather conditions, seven days, if necessary perhaps stretched to ten days. The Squadron Commander decided for a number of reasons, not least of all to mitigate the risk to the very valuable air assets available, that we should limit the number of insertions and extractions. He briefed us that 'G' Squadron patrols would initially insert for a minimum of fourteen days, if required. In the event, I received my resupply on about day eighteen.

So the weather was going to be brutal: how does this affect my preparations? Of course, everything that we would need to survive, communicate and perhaps fight with had to be carried, for example food. We had the standard British Army Arctic ration pack; one pack feeds one man for one day but it weighs three and a half pounds, so fourteen days' rations equals 49lb per man, just food, and of course that much food doesn't fit into an army bergen! So we had to cut down on rations. No problem with a good diet, but the combination of the weather conditions and the ground we would have to cover would have a debilitating effect on the body.

How much spare clothing to take? Every man would carry his own sleeping bag rather than share. In the event of compromise, perhaps the patrol is split and in escape and evasion mode for an extended period – a sleeping bag could be a life-saver. We wore standard issue army boots and uniform, no Gore-Tex available, though we did get a Gucci waterproof jacket with our resupply, thanks to the Quartermaster emptying all the outward-bound shops in Hereford! We each carried AR-15 semi-automatic assault rifles, 200 rounds of ammunition, along with hand and smoke grenades. As standard procedure, the patrol commander or signaller always carries a white phosphorus grenade to destroy code books

Investiture day, 1 March 2016:
Simon Weston with his CBE
at Buckingham Palace.

Keith Mills DSC outside
Buckingham Palace on
4 November 1982 after
being invested with his DSC:
he was accompanied by
his father Alan and his
mother Sheena Humphreys.

A photograph of Keith Mills and
his small detachment of Royal
Marines, taken shortly before
the Argentine invasion of South
Georgia; Mills is standing,
second left.

Keith Mills photographed at his home in Devon in 2021. In early April 1982, at the age of twenty-two and with twenty-one Marines under his command, he faced off the initial Argentine landings on South Georgia, his detachment shooting down two enemy helicopters and seriously damaging the corvette *Guerrico*. It was a remarkable achievement and quickly hit the headlines back home.

Keith Mills's honours and awards, including his DSC on the left. They reflect active service in Northern Ireland, the Falklands War, Cyprus, Bosnia and the former Yugoslavia.

ABOVE LEFT The stricken Argentine cruiser *General Belgrano* is captured on camera on 2 May 1982 after being torpedoed by the British submarine HMS *Conqueror*. It proved to be a highly controversial action, with opponents claiming the enemy cruiser was operating outside the Total Exclusion Zone, but defence ministers insisted the Task Force had the right to defend itself under any circumstances.

ABOVE RIGHT Submarine HMS *Conqueror*'s Jolly Roger provides the backdrop to a trio of shipmates, with Petty Officer Graham Libby DSM on the left. He displayed remarkable courage in exiting the submarine in diving gear to clear an aerial wire that had entangled itself around the propeller. He recalled; 'I was quite happy to go out there because I was all pumped up. We had just sunk a blooming great warship – this could be the icing on the cake, you know?'

Smoke billows from the stricken destroyer HMS *Sheffield* after she was hit by an Exocet missile on 4 May 1982; she foundered a few days later after the loss of twenty lives. Able Seaman Malcolm Messenger later recalled how a party of his shipmates went below deck to recover firefighting equipment, 'then I heard them screaming and they never came back'.

ABOVE LEFT Chief Petty Officer Michael Townsend and his family outside Buckingham Palace on the day he received his DSM. He displayed marked gallantry over a protracted period aboard the badly damaged HMS *Argonaut*: 'I didn't sleep for four days. We were given drugs, pills called "pinkies" and "blueies", to keep us awake.'

ABOVE RIGHT Michael Townsend today: 'At one point I spent about four and a half hours in near-freezing temperatures, hanging from ropes as I patched up the side of the ship.'

RIGHT Petty Officer John Leake DSM deep in thought on returning to Southampton on the *QE2* in June 1982. He was serving as a civilian Navy, Army and Air Force Institutes canteen manager on HMS *Ardent* in April 1982, but he was given a temporary appointment as a Petty Officer owing to his ex-army skills with the general-purpose machine gun. Amidst bombs and cannon fire, he went on to damage and down an Argentine Skyhawk.

The stricken RFA *Sir Galahad*. The ship was later towed out to sea and sunk as a war grave.

Sergeant Peter Naya of the Royal Army Medical Corps, who was awarded the MM for his gallantry aboard the RFA *Sir Galahad*. A secondary explosion partly stunned him and scorched the back of his head, but he nonetheless set about the task of treating the wounded, among them two soldiers who had lost limbs: 'I became a focus for people – they knew at least someone was there to help.'

Chiu Yiu Nam of the Royal Fleet Auxiliary with seven men from the Welsh Guards whom he saved from the blazing inferno aboard the RFA *Sir Galahad* in June 1982. He is holding his GM, as presented to him at an investiture in July 1993. 'Your actions', Margaret Thatcher later told him, 'are a reminder to us all of the noblest aspects of the human spirit.'

Jeune Hall (née Hendy). A naval nurse, she served with the operating theatre staff on the hospital ship SS *Uganda*. She broke down in tears on three occasions, never out of self-pity but rather on account of the stoicism displayed by her seriously injured patients: in one of the ship's wards, she found them watching a video of the Monty Python film *Life of Brian* and merrily singing 'Always look on the bright side of life'.

Christopher Pollard DSC, a naval Lieutenant who was Mentioned in Despatches for his gallantry in command of the exposed close-range guns flanking the bridge of HMS *Coventry*: 'He declined to duck for cover as the enemy aircraft closed at eye level and one of them strafed the ship with cannon fire.' Each year, he lays a wreath in front of the commemorative plaque at Holy Trinity Church, Coventry, which is dedicated to the ship's fallen.

An Argentine bomb explodes aboard HMS *Antelope* on 23 May 1982, killing the bomb disposal man who was trying to defuse it. His fellow Royal Engineer was seriously injured and Chief Petty Officer Malcolm Cooper went to his assistance: 'Because I was covered in blood from trying to help the bomb disposal man, people thought I was a casualty but I was not, in fact, hurt.'

Investiture day: Gordon Mather and his daughter Katherine admiring his MM.

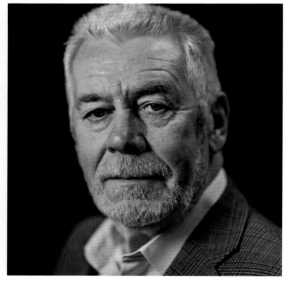

Gordon Mather MM, who was decorated for his gallant leadership of a four-man SAS patrol in enemy-occupied territory. Over a period of twenty-eight days in the harshest of conditions, he and his men amassed vital intelligence, mindful that they 'could not have been extracted from any predicament caused by enemy action'. He recently retired as chairman of the South Atlantic Medal Association, or SAMA 82.

The honours and awards of Warrant Officer Kevin James of the Royal Marines, including his QGM on the left. The riband of his South Atlantic Medal bears an oak leaf to denote the Mention in Despatches he won for his gallant service as a member of an SBS reconnaissance team in the conflict. He had earlier been awarded the QGM for rescuing a wounded comrade in Northern Ireland.

ABOVE LEFT Sergeant (later Captain) John Pettinger of 3 Para, who was awarded the DCM for his gallantry as a patrol commander tasked with gaining information on the Argentine forces holding Mount Longdon in June 1982. He completed six close-target reconnaissance missions, in one of which he had to make a rapid departure by walking through several occupied enemy trenches: 'Nobody stopped us.'

ABOVE RIGHT Lieutenant (later Lieutenant Commander) Rodney 'Fred' Frederiksen, a Fleet Air Arm Sea Harrier pilot who operated from HMS *Hermes*, photographed alongside the Argentine aircraft he shot down over West Falkland in May 1982. Earlier, he had led the way over Goose Green, destroying or damaging three enemy aircraft on the ground. He was Mentioned in Despatches.

Jeffrey Glover, a Flight Lieutenant in the RAF who was the only British pilot captured by Argentine forces during the conflict. His Harrier was hit by a missile, forcing him to eject from the aircraft, badly injuring himself in the process. Thirty years later, he met the Argentine who had shot him down, describing him as 'a smashing chap'.

Glover went on to fly with the Red Arrows and was awarded the Queen's Commendation for Valuable Services in the Air.

Captain Jeffrey Niblett of 3 Commando Brigade Air Squadron, Royal Marines. He was awarded the DFC for his bravery piloting a Scout helicopter in the battle for Goose Green and Darwin in May 1982. He supplied ammunition and collected casualties under fire, and on one occasion – displaying 'exceptional flying skill' – he evaded four cannon and rocket attacks from an Argentine Pucará.

if required. In the event, each man had to carry about 130lb worth of equipment.

Long before their mission, Mather and other patrol Commanders had been warned that they were on their own if compromised and attacked. Under normal circumstances, they could expect a Quick Reaction Force to come to their support if they got into a 'contact' (a firefight) or other difficulty. However, these patrols were the first troops on to the Falklands and the Task Force was still on its way, so there would be no back-up. 'That helped concentrate the mind a bit,' said Mather.

On 1 May, we deployed into my chosen eight-figure grid reference drop-off point. We took two nights to move cautiously into our area. The whole point of us going ashore was to observe and report what we could see. To start with, I was somewhat surprised, and to be honest disappointed, that the area appeared to be clear of enemy. Of course, for me to report, 'This area is clear' is good intelligence for the planners. It's almost as useful as me saying, 'There are hundreds of enemy soldiers here.'

Communicating their information back was far from easy. They were issued with the standard PRC-320 HF (high-frequency) radios using 'hand-speed Morse [code]'. The messages were encrypted with the now old-fashioned one-time pads; it was a slow but secure system. The radio set weighs in at approximately 25lb and each battery 6lb, so they had to decide how many batteries to carry. The antennae systems consisted of 4x4ft poles screwed together with a long copper wire called a 'sloping wire' – hardly the most covert equipment. The receiving station was some 4,000 miles away on Ascension Island because they feared squadron headquarters – on HMS *Hermes* – might be sunk. Ascension then relayed messages to and from *Hermes*. The patrols had also been told that the enemy direction-finding equipment was 'sophisticated', which increased their chances of being caught. Mather said:

> I would radio information perhaps daily or every two days – we had to stay in touch to pass on the information we had obtained and to indicate that we were OK. But because of the difficult communications conditions, we could be on the radio for twenty or thirty minutes at a time and we were worried by the direction-finding capability of the enemy. So, two guys, one signaller and one other man, would move away from our base for about an hour, set up the antenna, send and receive, take down the antenna and then come back to the patrol base. The next time the other two would go out in a different direction, set up, send and receive, dismantle and then come back. We hoped that it would mean the enemy could never identify exactly where our base was situated. But it also meant we were moving a lot, which is not great, but it was safer that way.
>
> Unfortunately, this complicated system, combined with the lack of immediate air support, did not allow us to exploit [engage] any immediate opportunity targets. Later on in the war, however, 'G' Squadron patrols were able to call in air support, which led to the destruction of a substantial enemy AVGAS [aviation fuel] dump, an Argentine Chinook and three Huey helicopters, which, when added to the twelve destroyed by 'D' Squadron, led to a very satisfying Regimental contribution of sixteen [enemy aircraft] to the overall effort.
>
> The key to our success was based on the thorough, extremely demanding, SAS selection process, much of which is based on carrying heavy weights and navigating over difficult ground both by day and night. This was combined with very high standards of

field craft, best use of ground and camouflage and concealment. All movement was carried out at night. When static during daylight hours in our observation positions, we would make best use of the limited cover available from the rocky outcrops.

The conditions, as expected, were severe – it was very, very cold, particularly at night. Rain most days and always strong, bitterly cold winds. But this isn't meant to be a sob story about lack of kit or the weather. It simply reflects both the equipment of and the conditions faced by all of the ground troops following the landings on 21 May. The ground proved, at times, tough-going, particularly over the infamous Falkland Island 'Stone Runs', formed by fields of large boulders at times stretching for several kilometres. We were in darkness, carrying huge weights in driving rain and poor visibility, so it was a dangerous business, and I was concerned that if one of us was to fall and suffer a severe injury, it would be extremely difficult to get the casualty evacuated, particularly during those initial weeks before the main landings.

Had we been faced with a problem like this, the priority would be to get the casualty into a warm, dry shelter. The obvious solution would be to seek shelter in a farm. But this raises a number of concerns. Firstly, I would need to find and then observe the farm for perhaps twenty-four hours to confirm that it wasn't occupied by the enemy. Secondly, given what we knew of the appalling atrocities carried out by the Argentine military against their own population during the 'Dirty War', how might they treat Islanders who they suspected of aiding and abetting enemy Special Forces? Do I have a duty of care? Of course I do. Fortunately, the situation never arose.

Mather added:

We observed our targets through binoculars. The closest we got to the enemy was about 400 metres when we were around Mount

Kent – but I never felt we were in immediate danger of being spotted and engaged by the enemy. The Squadron Commander, who had oversight of all of his patrols and importantly was co-located with the Task Force planners, was able to move his patrols as and when required. In my case, for example, following my initial deployment to the area of Bluff Cove, which I later learnt was one of the potential landing sites, he ordered me to move to the area of Mount Challenger and Mount Kent.

Mather said that, despite the conditions, he never had to motivate his men because they were all tremendously fit, professional and resilient:

Yes, of course, when you are on day twenty-one or whatever it is, cold and soaking wet, you might look at each other and say, 'I would rather be in our favourite pub in Hereford.' But basically you just get on with it; heads never went down.

Occasionally, I would tune the radio to BBC World Service and find out what was happening. On 21 May, they reported that 'British forces have landed on the Falkland Islands'. We looked at each other and that raised a bit of smile. We thought; 'We are not alone – the cavalry have come!' Then we heard another report saying there had been a terrible accident – a helicopter had crashed into the sea off the Falklands killing some twenty people. I remember saying to my guys, 'Those poor sods have come all this way to be killed in a traffic accident.' What we didn't know at the time was that we knew every man on board [in fact, the SAS had suffered their biggest single loss of life in their history].

On arrival in the area of Mount Kent, I was ordered to RV [rendezvous] with a patrol from 'D' Squadron, commanded in fact by the Squadron Commander. I briefed him on what I knew about that patch of ground. 'G' Squadron patrols had patrolled that general area for weeks now and it was apparent that [Mount] Kent, which dominates the approach to the prize of Stanley, was in fact only relatively lightly held by the enemy. The Squadron Commander moved his squadron forward, and they were almost immediately involved in heavy fighting with elements of the Argentine Special Forces who had been moved up as reinforcements. This bold move forward by 'D' Squadron, it has been said, helped prevent a Monte Cassino [the famous Second World War battle fought in Italy] on the way to Stanley.

In fact, the unusual and rather amusing circumstances in which two SAS patrols, one from 'G' Squadron and the other from 'D' Squadron, came across each other are described by Lieutenant General Sir Cedric Delves in his book *Across an Angry Sea: The SAS in the Falklands War*, first published in 2018. Mather was at the centre of the incident as described colourfully by Delves, then a Major in 'D' Squadron, who witnessed it all. Delves wrote:

Billy Cormack saw him first; I had sensed Billy stiffen, his weapon coming up slowly. He drew my attention to the man four hundred metres or more to our front. The soldier had emerged as if from nowhere, walking briskly, out in the open, armed with what looked like an M16 or Armalite, wearing a belt kit, low slung. He had a high-stepping gait, leant-back, and covered the ground fast and positively.

'One of ours?' queried Billy.

Could be, we all agreed, the others having moved to get a better look, all of us taking care not to reveal ourselves. We continued to observe him, intrigued. He appeared to be making his way systematically, progress generally in our direction, moving back and forth, mainly to rock outcrops and any other likely places of concealment. Searching? For us?

'It's Gordon. Gordon Mather,' Gerry said with conviction. I didn't know Gordon, a member of G Squadron, but accepted Gerry's word for it, although still inclined to caution. What was he doing moving about like that in the open, apparently on his own?

He came closer. Definitely Gordon. We let him come up to us, so as not to break his pattern of movement, before quietly announcing our presence. He didn't break step and continued across, stopping a yard or two short. We remained in cover. He too played his part, gazing nonchalantly into the distance, not facing us as he spoke.

'Good morning,' said Clive Lowther quietly, with the faintest hint of irony. Always polite and calm, was Clive. Gerry joined in, gently teasing Gordon about Standard Operating Procedures (SOPs).

Gordon took the banter well, in the good-natured spirit it was intended, explaining that first he had been told to meet us miles away near Mount Harriet. That had been for the previous night. Then, early that morning he had received instructions to make an RV this coming early evening east of Mount Kent, roughly where we were. He hadn't expected to meet us until after nightfall, when he thought our helicopter due. I was surprised, too, having arranged for G to vacate our operating area, not come into it.

'Gang fuck,' somebody muttered out aloud. An expressive if inelegant phrase with wide utility meaning on this occasion that someone, somewhere, somehow had got their wires crossed, obliging Gordon to make a risky move during daylight hours. Could it have been me? I didn't think so; more likely a change of plan that had yet to come down to us. Actually, it was just as well he had made contact in daylight; at night, it could easily have resulted in a 'blue on blue' shoot out, should we have been unaware of the patrol's presence.

At the end of their 28-day mission, the longest of the war, Mather and his three men were picked up at an agreed rendezvous point and flown by helicopter to a ship anchored off the Falkland Islands. Mather said:

> The helicopter deposited us on the darkened, deserted deck and took off. I told my guys in a whisper to unload their weapons. I was whispering because, of course, we had got so used to it over the past four weeks. A ship is a complicated place for a soldier to be at the best of times. At night and in blackout conditions, it becomes challenging! I told my guys to stay on deck and I would go and find help. I walked down a gangway and, eventually, heard a fairly loud noise coming from behind a steel door. I opened it to discover it was the POs' [Petty Officers'] Mess. A number of them were there enjoying a pint of beer.
>
> I remember one of them, pint in hand, looking at me and seeing what must have been an extraordinary sight: a dirty, bearded, slightly gaunt and bombed-up character blinking in the light. I seem to remember someone saying, 'What the fuck is that?' Fortunately, there was a member of 'D' Squadron HQ there who rushed over and pushed me back out of the door. We gathered up the other guys and went below deck to meet up with the rest of 'G' Squadron. They took all our kit off us, stripped us naked and put us in a shower with disinfectant and a toothbrush, and then got us clean clothes and a mug of rum. We then went to see the Boss, who gave us the tragic news that the helicopter crash had involved friends from both 'D' and 'G' Squadrons. As he told us the names of the dead, it was bit of a downer to say the least. We knew them all, friends and colleagues, men we had served alongside on other operations. The death of a friend is a terrible thing, but it seemed more tragic to lose good friends in an incident like that. We had all had friends killed on operations – killed fighting. That's tragic but it happens doing your job, doing what you are paid to do. Doing something you love. To die in a helicopter crash seemed so much worse.

I woke up the next morning and one of the sailors said to me, 'Are you one of the SAS guys that arrived last night?' I nodded and then he added, 'We are "goalkeeping" tomorrow.' I said, 'Sorry, but I don't know what you mean?' He said, 'I thought as much. We are in this Sound, which we have nicknamed 'Bomb Alley'. Every day the Argie fighters [aircraft] come round that headland to attack us. So each day we put a guard ship out there, broadside on to attract the attention of the fighters. It's our turn tomorrow.' So we all decided there and then to go back to shore as soon as possible!

But, in all seriousness, we were so impressed with the crews, many of them just eighteen or nineteen years old. Their ships were being attacked daily by waves of determined, skilled enemy fighters, but, in the finest traditions of the Royal Navy, they simply got on with it, doing their duty without complaining. It was very, very impressive.

As the Task Force prepared for what would prove to be the final battles of the war, Mather and his men were given further roles.

We were tasked to carry out a reconnaissance patrol along the high ground to the area of Mount Low, north of and very close to Stanley. One of our aircraft thought he had been 'painted' [located] by a radar in the area. I took a six-man patrol to try to locate the radar, and if identified then perhaps we could mount a squadron attack on it and its defenders.

Moving at night, along the high ground towards the target area, we came across a number of abandoned enemy trenches and at the far end of the ridge line what appeared to be a platoon-strength enemy position in trenches but no radar. We plotted the position and moved back to the squadron position. Events then unfolding prevented any action taken against this position.

On the night of 13 June, 'G' and 'D' Squadrons and some Royal

Marine rigid raiders combined to take part in a joint operation to support our friends in 2 PARA [2nd Battalion, the Parachute Regiment] – the only unit to fight two battles in the war. As part of the final battles of the war, 2 PARA would assault the enemy positions on Wireless Ridge, on the outskirts of Stanley. We would help by engaging the enemy in depth, much further down the ridge. Given the time available, the 'cunning plan' had to be pretty basic: essentially, make some noise, draw attention to ourselves. We did attract their attention, and with it a shed full of fire, including 120mm mortar and fire from a number of 30mm twin-barrelled anti-aircraft guns. One hell of a lot of enemy fire! It became quite challenging for a time. Afterwards, we withdrew to the heights of Murrell Ridge with good views down to Stanley. Our efforts helped 2 PARA, we only wished we could have done more, something beyond simply taking fire from them to us. A lot of us had served in the Airborne Forces, some actually with 2 and 3 PARA – so there was a particular closeness. I am glad we were there for them, and in there right to the end.

The next morning, one of the guys observing Argentine troops withdrawing to Stanley suddenly said, 'There's a white flag flying in Stanley.' The enemy had surrendered. 'G' Squadron withdrew back to RFA *Sir Lancelot* for about five days before flying out to Ascension Island and, eventually, back to the UK.

Mather was out of the country when he learnt that he had been decorated for his bravery in the Falklands. The citation for Mather's MM, announced in *The London Gazette* on 8 October 1982, stated:

Sergeant Mather commanded a four-man patrol tasked to provide vital information on enemy dispositions and installations on East Falkland as a prelude to the repossession of the islands.

Inserted by helicopter from the Naval Task Force at a distance of 120 miles from the islands, he maintained observations of the enemy movement and dispositions in the Bluff Cove, West Stanley, areas for a period of twenty-eight days. In a totally hostile environment, with the only protection from ground and air search provided by the skill and stealth of his patrol, the reporting by Sergeant Mather was both accurate and timely.

In order to obtain the detail of the enemy disposition, he was required to move his observation position to close and often obvious positions to gain the intelligence required. This he did with great courage and skill knowing that if compromised his patrol could not have been extracted from any predicament caused by enemy action. In addition he communicated his information in an environment where the enemy were known to possess a Direction Finding capability.

The leadership and example shown by Sergeant Mather were in the highest traditions of his Regiment and the Army.

Mather said of the MM announcement:

It was an enormous privilege to be selected to represent the important contribution made by 'G' Squadron during this extraordinary conflict. It resulted in higher public profile for me than I had expected or would have wished. My name was released by a MoD press officer as serving with the SAS rather than with my parent unit [Royal Corps of Signals] as was the practice at the time. This had never been done before. It was, apparently, a deliberate decision by the MoD to inform the public that The Regiment [the SAS] had taken part in the war.

The Prince of Wales sent Mather a telegram that read: 'On receiving the news of your award I send you my warmest congratulations.

I have the greatest possible admiration for the gallantry you displayed and for the way in which you maintained the very highest
tradition of the Regiment.' He also received a letter of congratulations from the Princess Royal, the Colonel-in-Chief of the Royal
Signals.

Mather later attended his investiture at Buckingham Palace with
his wife, Pat, and their eldest daughter, Katherine, then three years
old, who slept through the ceremony. In 1983, Her Majesty the
Queen and the Duke of Edinburgh came to Hereford to meet the
men who had taken part in the campaign. Mather recalled:

> Her Majesty came to our group and spoke not to us soldiers but
> rather to our wives. She said, 'It must be very difficult to be mar-
> ried to these [SAS] men. I sometimes think the wives should get
> the medals.' Not for the first time, I suspect, the Queen absolutely
> nailed it. As a mother, she recognised how difficult it was to be left
> at home when family members – in her case her son Prince Andrew
> – went off to war. I thought it was a wonderful thing for her
> to say.

Mather was also chosen by his parent unit to be the subject of
a painting by the war artist Peter Archer, in a striking image of
the then Sergeant as an armed, uniformed, bearded man peering
over a mountain ridge as he observes enemy positions. As well as
the original, 1,000 prints were made of the painting, called 'Contact, Wait Out', and were widely circulated by the Royal Corps of
Signals, which had commissioned the work. 'It could have been
any SAS soldier, but it just happened to be me,' said Mather, with
great modesty.

Mather remained in the SAS for another eight years. He had
been due to be discharged from the army in August 1987 after more
than twenty-four years' service, but he was in fact offered – and

he accepted – a commission in the Royal Corps of Signals. He was eventually discharged from the army in the rank of Captain in 1993 after what Mather said was 'thirty years' service, man and boy'. During his final six years back in the Corps, he completed a three-year tour of Northern Ireland.

After leaving the army, Mather worked in the security business – known as 'The Circuit' – for more than two decades until fully retiring from work in 2015. During this time, Mather also took on a role with the SAMA 82, whose patron is the Prince of Wales. SAMA 82 is a registered charity with the motto 'From the Sea – Freedom'. Formed on 2 April 1997, the fifteenth anniversary of the arrival of Argentine forces in the Falkland Islands, its aim was, and is, to promote a sense of pride and comradeship among the veterans of the South Atlantic campaign. Mather became a member, then a trustee and finally served as the chairman of SAMA 82 for seven years until 2020.

Another honour came for Mather when he learnt that a troop had been named in his honour – Mather Troop – as part of an army modernisation programme. The Mather Troop passing-out parade took place in October 2002, and Mather was asked to attend the event hosted by 2 Army Training Regiment in Lichfield, Staffordshire.

Mather has returned to the Falklands twice since 1982, including in 2012 for the thirtieth anniversary of the war, when he was accompanied by fifty veterans and next of kin. The group were on the island for a week, and Mather recalled:

It was a memorable and very moving experience. We stayed with the Falkland Islanders in their homes and visited many of the battle sites. On Remembrance Sunday, a very moving service was held in Stanley Cathedral. I spoke with one Falkland Islander and I asked her what she thought about us veterans returning year after year. She replied, 'While you are here this week, Gordon, we will take care of you. And when your children come to the islands, our children will take care of them. When your grandchildren come, our grandchildren will take care of them too because this is a debt that we can *never* repay.'

It was a wonderful thing to hear and reflects the continuing close friendship between us veterans and those special, proud, fiercely independent folk living in the Falkland Islands.

Today, Mather and his wife have two grown-up daughters, Katherine and Helen, who are both teachers, and also two grandsons, Johnny, ten, and James, six, who, in Katherine's words, will 'follow Granddad into the SAS over my dead body!'

Four decades on, Mather still looks back with immense pride on the professionalism of the Task Force:

The reason we were successful was that at the end of the day we were better than the enemy. We were the best trained Army in the world, supported by the finest Navy, Air Force and Merchant Fleet in the world, without whom 'Operation Corporate' could not have succeeded. We were better than them because we got the basics right. Great leadership from the most senior to the most junior rank – we had leaders, mostly very junior leaders, who led from the front. Add to this, outstanding acts of courage and self-sacrifice from men who have been rightly decorated for their actions. But there were hundreds of members of the Task Force on land, sea and in the air, including Falkland Islanders, who performed extraordinary deeds under fire, whose brave actions will never be formally recognised. It was a privilege to serve alongside such men and women.

THOMAS COLLINS
Service: Royal Marines (SBS)
Final rank: Colour Sergeant
FALKLANDS WAR DECORATION / DISTINCTION:
MILITARY MEDAL (MM)
DATE OF BRAVERY: MAY 1982
GAZETTED: 8 OCTOBER 1982

Sergeant Tom Collins was awarded the MM for what he described as 'a classic SBS operation', one that took place well in advance of the large-scale operations to retake the Falkland Islands. His four-man team had been dropped into the heart of enemy territory after a 250-mile journey from their troop ship in a Sea King helicopter. They flew at no more than 50ft to prevent detection from enemy radar. At one point, they realised they were being chased by a 'hostile' – Argentine – helicopter, but it peeled off, apparently in the mistaken belief that the Sea King was a 'friendly' aircraft.

Born in Preston, Lancashire, in 1943, Collins was the eldest of three children and his father was a truck driver. He enjoyed an unorthodox military career, not joining the Royal Marines until he was twenty-eight, in 1971; after leaving school aged fifteen, he had previously worked as a carpenter for thirteen years. Within two years of signing up with 45 Commando, he was seeking selection for the SBS, eventually joining in 1973, aged thirty. 'From the moment I joined the Royal Marines, I wanted to go into the Special Forces – for me, it was the only way to go,' he told me. For the next nine years, Collins said he and his SBS comrades 'made a nuisance of ourselves here and there', essentially travelling to various parts of the world on secretive and security-sensitive roles. 'I loved my job from the start. It was an interesting career,' he said.

Then, in May 1982, Collins's training, skills and nerve would be put to the ultimate test. Collins and three others had been dropped in the dead of night with enough food for three weeks, an armoury of weapons and a clear mission: to recce the area around San Carlos Bay to see if it was the right location for British forces to land with the aim of recapturing the Falkland Islands. The drop-off point, where the men had first to unload their kit and then to drop 10ft to the ground from the hovering Sea King, was at Campito, high above San Carlos Bay in the north-western area of East Falkland.

Collins was in charge of the team that would spend an estimated three weeks gathering information on enemy positions and possible landing sites in and around San Carlos Bay. Their only contact with the main British force was to be through Morse code. Lengthy daily messages were not an option in case they were intercepted by Argentine listening posts. Instead, they sent just the signal 'Tango Charlie' (Collins's initials) twice a day to the British base on Ascension Island, to indicate they were alive and well. 'It was a daunting task. Our role was to gather intelligence and assess whether this was a good place to start the invasion,' Collins told me. 'When we landed we expected trouble, but in the end we didn't have any firefights.'

The four-man team was equipped with rocket launchers, rifles, handguns and hand grenades. They suffered a major setback early on in their mission when the BBC – in an act of astonishing stupidity and recklessness – reported that Special Forces were on East Falkland, apparently disguised as local farmers. This led to a huge increase in Argentine patrols all over the island, but still the men remained undetected. The SBS team also heard, but could not see, HMS *Sheffield* being hit by an enemy Exocet missile on 4 May. At the time, the SBS team thought, and hoped, an Argentine target had been hit, but they heard on the BBC's World Service that the ship was British and that the loss was a major setback for the Task Force.

Their own mission had, in fact, almost ended before it had begun. On the first night, they found a small, cramped cave and camouflaged the entrance by putting plants on top of chicken wire. But at first light the next day, an Argentine helicopter hovered just feet above their hideout, so low that one of the SBS men could read the serial numbers on the chopper's rockets. 'The down-draught from the enemy helicopter was causing the camouflage material on the front of the OP [observation post] to come adrift,' Collins said. 'Fortunately, it left before causing any serious risk of seeing us.' From their hideout in the cave, the four-man team went out with cameras, and also used sketches and written descriptions to build up a picture of the area.

According to Collins:

The first day was very dry and fine, but things changed for the worse from then on. For the first week, we didn't have any more dry days. Although the OP was in the perfect position for viewing the whole of San Carlos Water, the high winds drove the constant rain directly into our position. I suppose the best way to describe the area was the South Atlantic's version of Dartmoor.

After more than two weeks – and following another increase in enemy patrols – they radioed asking to be picked up from a pre-arranged spot at nearby Rookery Point. 'Things were getting a bit hot. We decided to get out so that we didn't lose [by being killed or captured] the information we had gathered. Also, to have got into a firefight might have compromised any invasion plans,' Collins said. They waited to be picked up in a new hideout beneath a grassy bank in the middle of a penguin colony. By then down to their final food supplies, even the birds began to look appetising.

The SBS team went to the pick-up spot every night at an agreed time, but it was not until their third visit that the Sea King came in and lifted them to safety. In the end, San Carlos Bay was chosen as the invasion point on East Falkland for 3 Commando Brigade on 21 May 1982.

Collins and his SBS comrades remained in the war zone until the end of the conflict, carrying out other secretive recce missions behind enemy lines. 'We did quite a few little jobs here and there,' he said. 'During one recce, the RAF bombed an area that they thought might be used by the Argentinians as a landing strip, but they accidentally hit a civilian house, injuring a child. We saw that happen,' Collins said.

After returning from the Falklands and when back in the UK, Collins learnt that he had been awarded the MM – a decoration that came as a complete surprise.

> I'd just got back from a fitness run. I'd had a shower and was half-dressed when the Sergeant Major shouted, 'Oi, get in here,' and I was told that I had been awarded the MM. To start with it didn't really sink in what was happening, but then they went into the details and of course I felt very proud.

Collins's MM was officially announced on 8 October 1982. However, his surname was spelt wrongly as 'Collings' in his citation. Collins received a telegram from the Duke of Edinburgh, the Captain General of the Royal Marines, which read, 'Many congratulations on your well deserved honour.' Collins, his wife and two of their sons attended an investiture at Buckingham Palace, where he received his honour from the Queen. 'She was very knowledgeable about what I had been doing, which surprised me. Someone had clearly briefed her very well. Our conversation seemed to go on for a long time, though it probably wasn't as long as it felt,' he said.

After the war, Collins and his team were nicknamed the 'Interflora Squad', first by their comrades and later by the media. This was because they spent so much time picking fresh foliage – each night they went out to search for new plants to place on their hideout so they would blend in with the landscape.

Collins left the SBS in 1993 after more than twenty-two years' service. After taking a year off, he worked as a budget manager for the Ministry of Defence, retiring from that job in 2008, aged sixty-five. In 2021, when he moved house and cleared out his garage, he was delighted to find his patrol reports from his role in 1982, including a report on HMS *Sheffield* being hit by enemy bombs. Today, Collins lives in the West Country. He and his wife have five grown-up children, thirteen grandchildren and eight great-grandchildren.

KEVIN MICHAEL JAMES

Service: Royal Marines (SBS)

Final rank: Warrant Officer

FALKLANDS WAR DECORATION / DISTINCTION:

MENTIONED IN DESPATCHES (MID)

DATE OF BRAVERY: MAY 1982

GAZETTED: 8 OCTOBER 1982

OTHER DECORATIONS / DISTINCTIONS:

QUEEN'S GALLANTRY MEDAL (QGM)

Kevin James was Mentioned in Despatches (MID) for his courageous service behind enemy lines with the SBS in the Falklands War – having three years earlier been decorated for his courage, including when coming under fire, in Northern Ireland.

James was born in Westbury-on-Trym, near Bristol, in 1949 and joined the Royal Marines in April 1967, aged seventeen. During a long and distinguished career, he served variously in 3 Commando

Brigade based in Singapore, and 41 and 45 Commandos, both based in the UK, in addition to serving in the SBS.

Few servicemen are awarded a gallantry medal after being shot at by law-abiding members of the Royal Ulster Constabulary (RUC) and the Scots Guards before holding up hospital staff at gunpoint. But then, WO Kevin James was no ordinary serviceman, and when he was faced with what to do with a wounded comrade he took the law into his own hands.

It was while serving as Corporal in Northern Ireland that an undercover operation was compromised and a comrade was shot and seriously wounded by republican terrorists. When James's Queen's Gallantry Medal was announced in *The London Gazette* on 27 March 1979, the entry said only: 'In recognition of service in Northern Ireland during the period 1 August 1978 to 31 October 1978.'

It was only many years later that the extraordinary events of an evening in October 1978 became public knowledge through a book, *First Into Action*, written by ex-SBS man Duncan Falconer. The incident happened when James was serving with 14 Intelligence Company, the secretive surveillance organisation, in operations in Northern Ireland.

After his comrade had been shot seven times, leaving him fighting for his life, James drove him at great speed to the nearest hospital. However, his driving was so wild that he ended up being fired on by both the RUC and the Scots Guards, the local army unit, which suspected him of being a terrorist. They were shooting at the wheels of his car in order to try to apprehend him.

James eventually screeched into the hospital car park and came to a halt outside the main entrance. He dived out of the car, gun in hand, and ran inside. Covered in blood, he grabbed a wheelchair and pushed it outside to the car. He dragged his badly injured comrade out of the car and into the chair. The man was still alive but slipping in and out of consciousness. James charged up the ramp with the wheelchair and burst in through the entrance doors once again, ordering – at gunpoint – doctors and nurses who he suspected were Catholic and who he feared might be opposed to the British military, to care for his friend.

I recounted this incident in detail in my book *Special Forces Heroes*, first published in 2012. At the time, James admitted to me that it was an unconventional way for anyone to be awarded a gallantry medal, but he said that if he had stopped to explain what was happening, his comrade would have died:

> They [the RUC and the army] thought I was one of the bad guys so they were entitled to take pot shots at me. It was seven minutes of pure bliss. I loved it. The adrenaline was flowing and it was what I had trained all my life to do. I never again met the man whose life I saved and I don't even know his real name. He not only survived but he served his full twenty-three years in the Army.

This, however, was not the end of James's bravery displayed while serving Queen and country. It was for his service in the SBS during the Falklands War that he received an MID, announced in *The London Gazette* of 8 October 1982.

Unlike many in the Armed Forces, James knew exactly where the Falkland Islands were prior to April 1982, and this was because of his working role. In an interview for this book, he explained to me:

> As a communicator in the SBS, we often did exercises trying to communicate with the Falklands using Morse [code] and HF radio. So I knew where the islands were situated, deep in the South Atlantic.
>
> After the Falkland Islands were invaded, I was actually at my own leaving do in a pub in Spetisbury, Dorset, because I had been posted to Arbroath [Scotland] to the Maritime Counter Terrorism

Unit. But the CO [Commanding Officer] came into my bash and said, 'Right, stop everything, gentlemen. Be at the Royal Marines [base], Poole, at 6 a.m. tomorrow. We are off to the Falklands.' After some preparations, we actually sailed from Portsmouth on 8 April. We were initially on RFA *Stromness*, but we then cross-decked later that night to another ship, RFA *Resource*, because we were SBS and they didn't want the press and everyone else to know our location. We sailed to Ascension Island and we didn't stop there; we carried straight on down towards the Falklands. When we approached the TEZ we cross-decked to HMS *Hermes* in order to launch our operations.

The original recommendation for James's MID, which was not made public but which I have obtained, stated:

Special Boat Service patrols, each comprising of four men, were deployed to the Argentinian held East Falkland Island three weeks before the main landing in order to find suitable beaches and landing areas. The enemy knew the patrols were somewhere on the island and deployed troops, helicopters and EW [Electronic Warfare] means to attempt to detect them, but failed. With the Battle Group 200 miles away and the Task Force still on Ascension Island, the patrols could expect little immediate help if found and probably unsympathetic handling. However, they were not found. Each patrol remained hidden on a mainly bare island, carried out its task and brought back valuable information which allowed the Commander to decide on the landing area. In every patrol, each man was under considerable strain, not knowing whether he would be found at any moment whilst having to live under physically very demanding conditions. The men engaged in these operations showed a high degree of courage and resourcefulness beyond that normally expected.

Sergeant James was landed in East Falkland Island on 3 May 1982. During his patrol, he came into close contact with the enemy and his patrol became split. He was withdrawn with only half his team on 8 May 1982 but, on 12 May 1982, returned to the same area to find his missing men. His route took him again through the enemy locations he had previously reached and, on 15 May 1982, he went forward to search for the missing men and by chance saw them. During a tense half-hour, he approached and made himself known to them and was nearly shot in the process. He then conducted a skillful [sic] withdrawal. Sergeant James therefore successfully conducted two difficult patrols within a short time. He is recommended for the award of a Mention-in-Despatches.

James recalled the night that he had been flown into the war zone from HMS *Hermes* in a Sea King helicopter:

I was in charge of a four-man team: we were a Sergeant [James himself], a Corporal and two marines. At the time, the Air Commander told me it was the longest helicopter flight in history – well over 200 miles – to drop off combatants into a war zone. It was also one of the first times that [British] pilots were using night-vision goggles in a war situation. We were tasked with observing the enemy and the entrance to Berkeley Sound. We landed at Volunteer Lagoon and we had to watch the big inlet where, under one of the plans, the advancing fleet might have landed before striking for Stanley.

Once the helicopter landed at Volunteer Lagoon, we jumped out with all our kit. I cut a piece of turf out of the ground and gave it to the crewman and told him to take it back to the ship as a souvenir. We then, as was normal practice, watched our landing site from a safe distance and, sure enough, within twenty minutes or so an enemy patrol came along and we then followed them – tagging along behind them – to their HQ. Where I had intended to site my OP [observation post] was actually an Argentine battalion HQ. Within twenty-four hours, we had established that there was a battalion HQ and one company on Diamond Rock and two companies forward on Mount Brisbane overlooking Volunteer Lagoon – where there was a big sandy beach which was under consideration to be used as a [British] landing point.

I then split my team into two – inadvertently – because myself and a Marine had gone forward to observe Diamond Rock, near Mount Brisbane. Although we had been warned about it in advance, the light was very strange, apparently because of the lack of air pollution and other factors. So a hill that I thought was very large and a couple of miles away was, in fact, a small hill very close, only a couple of hundred metres away. What happened was that me and the other guy got caught in the open as the sun came up, and so we dug a quick scrape and camouflaged ourselves. We were only about 150 to 200 metres from their battalion HQ and stayed there all day, back to back. When we pulled back that night, the other two guys, thinking we had been compromised or captured, bugged down. That's how we got split up.

The next day we set off in pursuit of the other two but never found them. So that night, under Mount Brisbane, we dug a hide into the ground above a stream and we stayed there until the 8th [of May], when I was withdrawn. At one stage, an enemy helicopter hovered just above us and I thought we had been discovered. The crewman was hanging out of the door and he was so close that I was going to shoot him with my pistol. But, in fact, he was just helping the pilot to fix a position – he was talking into his throat mic [microphone] and he hadn't seen us even though he was only about 50ft above us. It was a very close call.

James said that his eventual rendezvous with the other two men from his original patrol was not coincidental. 'In the original briefing, we were given a fallback RV position to meet up on a particular night. So I knew exactly where they would be that night provided they had not been compromised.'

That landing on 12 May was also eventful, as James described to me:

This time I was with another team [four-man patrol] but it was so foggy that the pilot couldn't see the shore. So he had to helocast – a difficult technique to insert troops by helicopter without fully landing. When we jumped out, we landed in the sea, so we were soaking wet and very cold. We then found an LUP [lying up position) and then, at daybreak, I could hear this scraping sound. I looked around this peat mound that we had dug into, and I could see enemy troops digging in about 150 metres away. That was another close call.

A couple of days later I went to our agreed RV position at the agreed time. The Corporal [from his original four-man patrol] came out with his rifle and poked it into my chest before he was confident that it was me and that I hadn't been compromised and was leading an Argentine patrol to capture him. Of course, we were relieved to see each other and to know everyone in the [original] patrol was alive and well. Then after that we met up with some other patrols, and then we were pulled out to bury Sergeant Ian 'Kiwi' Hunt.

Hunt, twenty-eight, had been killed in an exchange of fire with an SAS patrol near Teal Inlet, East Falkland, on 2 June. He had accidentally strayed into an area patrolled by the SAS and was the only SBS member who died during the Falklands War – an event made all the sadder because it was the result of a 'blue-on-blue' incident.

James and his men stayed in the Falklands until after the end of the war.

At various times, we were taken back to [HMS] *Fearless* for briefings and sent on other patrols right until the end of the war. Then

I went with my boss and another team to take the surrender at Pebble Island. Once the war had ended, we were given a choice of waiting for an available aircraft or going back on the ship we had come out on for a sort of decompression cruise to Ascension and then flying back from there.

In his previously mentioned book *First Into Action*, Duncan Falconer said of James:

> For those who really knew him, he was high up on the list of men you would want by your side. He showed a seemingly uncharacteristic coolness and determination under fire. He was very bright, and even though scared, no less than anyone else, he could be counted on to do the right thing.

James retired from the military with the rank of WO in late 1989. He joined the police, where he was placed in the Armed Response Unit. Once again, Falconer takes up the story, using the pseudonym of 'Luke' for James to protect his friend's identity:

> He was not in the force very long before he joined a section called in to help calm demonstrators who were trying to block the building of a motorway through some woodland. The situation turned nasty and at one point Luke found himself cornered by a dozen anarchists who were responsible for the increased tension between the demonstrators and the police. This group's only objective in life was to travel to demonstrations and incite trouble. By the time other police officers had arrived, the anarchists had beaten Luke to the ground, surrounded him and kicked him unconscious. It was obvious his career was over even before he went to hospital.

For some time, James, whose back was badly injured, could walk only with the aid of a cane. He later suffered from severe pain day and night, as well as PTSD. After leaving the police, he worked as manager of the Royal Marines Museum in Southsea, Portsmouth, retiring from that role in 2012.

Today, James, who is married with two grown-up sons, lives on the south coast of England. Reflecting on his role in the 1982 war, he said, 'I am very proud to have played a part in enabling us to regain the Falkland Islands.'

JOHN STUART PETTINGER

Service: Army

Final rank: Captain

FALKLANDS WAR DECORATION / DISTINCTION:

DISTINGUISHED CONDUCT MEDAL (DCM)

DATE OF BRAVERY: JUNE 1982

GAZETTED: 8 OCTOBER 1982

John Pettinger was decorated with the prestigious Distinguished Conduct Medal (DCM) while serving in the rank of Sergeant in the 3rd Battalion, the Parachute Regiment (3 PARA). The Commander of a patrol within 'D' (Patrol) Company, he distinguished himself several times when he and his men became the 'eyes and ears' of 3 PARA during eleven days of daring operations in and around the Mount Longdon area of East Falkland in the build-up to the final battles of the war. Completing no less than six close-target reconnaissance missions among enemy lines, Pettinger and his men obtained detailed information on enemy strength and locations prior to the final assault on Mount Longdon. Having 'ghosted' in and out of Argentine lines for so long, he then played an active role in the battle itself, killing at least three of the enemy.

John Stuart Pettinger was born on 16 August 1953 in Blackburn, Lancashire, the youngest of three children. The son of a chef, he attended Norden County Secondary School in Rishton. However, he did not enjoy his school days, preferring instead to embark on the 'university of life'. Pettinger effectively 'joined up' at Preston recruiting centre in the summer holidays, aged fourteen. It was 6 August 1968, and at the end of his interview, the recruiting officer realised he was not yet the required age of fifteen – so he simply 'solved' the problem by bringing the young Pettinger's birthday forward by a month to comply with regulations.

Within thirty days, Pettinger was a junior soldier in the Parachute Regiment. He spent two years serving with the Infantry Junior Leaders Battalion at Oswestry, Shropshire, after which he completed Pegasus Company ('P' Company), training and selection. He was posted to 3 PARA in early 1971. In an interview, he told me:

> I was initially due to serve with 2 PARA, however the under-eighteen rule had just been imposed for troops in Northern Ireland, which resulted in me getting posted to 3 PARA instead. During 1972, after a very arduous physical and mental selection phase in South Wales, I joined 'D' (Patrol) Company, 3 PARA (also known as 'Patrol Company'). I stayed with the company several years and returned as a Sergeant in 1981 after various postings, including numerous tours in Northern Ireland, both on the border and in Belfast ... and also as a Corporal instructing recruits at Browning Barracks, Aldershot, for two years during 1976–78, which was both enjoyable and fulfilling. Additionally, I had two tours in Malaya and attended the Jungle Warfare Instructor Course.

> In 1978, I attended the SAS selection and after a month of arduous training I had to withdraw due to injuries. However, instead of being RTU'd [returned to unit], which was the normal action for injuries, I was kept on at Hereford, helping out on the Training Wing, and was to await the next selection phase. After approximately a month, I was directed to attend the selection for what was

commonly known as 'The Det' or '14 Intelligence Company' and which now is officially named the Special Reconnaissance Regiment [SRR, part of the UK Special Forces]. I passed the difficult selection phase and was deployed as an operator for the next couple of years. Skills learnt from this work, I utilised and taught later on, both with Patrol Company and also in civilian life.

In 1981, Pettinger rejoined Patrol Company, 3 PARA, in Germany before taking part in training for those due to serve in Northern Ireland. However, the events of 2 April 1982 meant that 2 and 3 PARA were needed for a role 8,000 miles away. Pettinger takes up the story:

Political wrangling and logistic preparation held us back until 8 April, when we were to join SS *Canberra* [a requisitioned cruise liner] at Southampton. We sailed the next day, heading south. This was to be a long six-week voyage, where all basic skills were honed, blood given and fitness training continued. We also received several intelligence briefings and lectures and were able to conduct some map studying, still not knowing quite where we were going. Additionally, it included some time spent on Ascension Island where the Battalion practised beach landings from LCUs [landing craft utility], and we were able to test-fire and check our weapons, including the Battalion support weapons and sniper rifles.

The Company Order of Battle was organised, and Pettinger's patrol consisted of himself, Lance Corporal Mark 'Zip' Hunt as radio operator, Private Yanto Evans as gunner and Private Richard 'Dickie' Absolon as lead scout and sniper. During the afternoon of 19 May, the battalion cross-decked by LCU from SS *Canberra* onto HMS *Intrepid*, where conditions were cramped due to a surplus of men and equipment. Pettinger recalled one of the saddest days in SAS history: 'Later that day [19 May], a Sea King helicopter ditched astern of HMS *Intrepid* just before landing. Carrying members of 22 SAS, it had lost power and control. An incredibly sad night when we lost twenty-two men, including a couple of personal friends, before we had engaged the enemy.'

On the morning of 21 May, 3 PARA was transported by LCU and dropped a little short from land in San Carlos Bay. Pettinger recalled:

> I stepped off into waist-deep, freezing water. The Patrol Company undertook various tasks around the settlement, including putting an early warning protective screen around the Battalion whilst the bridgehead was being prepared. My task was to get as far north as possible to give the earliest warning of any Argentinian aircraft approaching at low level, using the valleys to avoid radar. I found a location approximately 12 miles north of San Carlos, on the high ground between Foul Bay and Concordia Bay. This proved a very difficult night move due to the trackless terrain, the possibility of enemy activity and the weight we carried; each man had approximately 140lb of kit and equipment. The weight in our four bergens included three radios, spare batteries, a hand generator, a change of clothes, seven days' stripped down GS [general service] rations, sleeping bag and poncho, extra GPMG [general-purpose machine gun] ammunition and all of the ancillary bits required, our webbing equipment with ammunition, bayonet, grenades and water, and we also had our various weapons. Over the next few days, from this location, we activated several 'Air Warning Red' by radio, allowing the Battalion to take cover from possible air attacks. We were also able to listen to the BBC World Service on our HF radio.

On 27 May, the battalion, along with Patrol Company HQ and other patrols, received orders to move east, cross-country towards

Teal Inlet 30 miles away. On 29 May, the battalion received the news that 2 PARA had attacked and secured Goose Green, although several soldiers had been killed, including the Commanding Officer, Lieutenant Colonel Herbert 'H' Jones. On 30 May, the battalion started the move further east towards Estancia House, another 20 miles away. The climate was brutal – biting winds, heavy rain and blizzard conditions – and the terrain was tough to negotiate. Once again, Pettinger takes up the story:

> Just before last light, the Battalion stopped in a lay-up area, where several patrols received orders to continue on to Estancia House and the surrounding areas to check for enemy and secure the location. My patrol's task was to escort four men from 9 Squadron Royal Engineers onto the western slopes of Mount Estancia, past and northeast of the settlement, where a local man had reported a minefield. This included crossing the tidal River Estancia and enduring atrocious sleet and blizzard conditions. No mines were found.
>
> The Battalion moved into the area by 1 June, and the companies were established in defensive positions in the mountains surrounding Estancia where the Battalion HQ made their base. That day, I led my patrol on a clearance patrol and reconnaissance further over Mount Estancia and onto Mount Vernet. We almost stumbled into an Argentinian position so stopped short to watch and listen before approaching very carefully, ready to attack it. Fortunately, it appeared to possibly be an Argentinian radio-relay station which had recently been abandoned in haste. A lot of equipment had been left, including radio logs, maps, vehicle batteries, tents, sleeping bags, clothing and much more. We gathered all of the paperwork together and returned it to the Battalion HQ for crucial intelligence, and I debriefed on the patrol work. A couple of days later, I noticed that some of that equipment – tents etc. – had been gathered and used around the Battalion.

The next day I was tasked with the first recce, or close target reconnaissance, onto Mount Longdon (approximately 12 miles away) to gain information about enemy positions and possible routes onto the mountain in preparation for the Battalion attack. We were very aware that a compromise during this patrol onto the enemy position could possibly alert the enemy to the Battalion's intentions, and our high 'prone to capture' situation was certainly not favourable.

The four of us moved out before last light to cover some of the ground in daylight, as just east of Estancia are areas of 'rivers of rocks' which are open expanses of bare, loose rock, some of which were car size and very difficult to cross even in daylight. At the same time, other patrols conducted similar recces on various areas forward of the Battalion location. I aimed for Murrell Bridge, which is about 3 miles short of Mount Longdon, to use it to cross the river. Tactically not very sound, but at that point we had no idea of the depth of the river, which we found out on later recces. This became our patrol's FRV [final rendezvous], to be used if we got split up. We approached in the darkness and spent time observing the bridge for any enemy movement. Our lead scout, Dickie Absolon, moved carefully forward to have a closer look and check for any booby-traps etc. All was clear, and we quickly crossed at the bridge at around 2200, moving further forward to a position by a shallow peat bank, crossing the Furze Bush stream, which was later to become the start line for the Battalion. This was approximately 600–800 metres short of the forward edge of the concave slopes of Mount Longdon, and where I left Zip and Yanto, making this our first RV, with the orders to open fire onto the mountain if they saw any form of firefight, as it could possibly be Dickie and I trying to extract after a compromise and hopefully they could divert some attention.

Dickie and I crawled forward and onto the edge of the western end of the rocky out-crops of Longdon, unaware of any possible minefields. I was astonished at the height of some of the rocks containing the defended position that was in some depth eastwards. We worked our way into the enemy positions and around to the north of the rocks, cautiously probing in where we could. Numerous enemy were seen and heard, often only a few metres away, and machine-gun and mortar positions were found and noted. The time on the position was forgotten and went very quickly, as I had told the other two patrol members that if we were not back by 0430 to report us missing and move back to the FRV at 0500 so that they would be clear before first light. I eventually checked my watch to see it was almost 0430; we were still on the enemy position having been there for about five hours.

I took the decision to place our weapons down by our sides and just walk off the position heading north – a tactic used in Northern Ireland years before. To our surprise and fright, we discovered we had walked through several occupied enemy trenches with men talking. Nobody stopped us. Once clear, we ran as fast as possible back westwards towards our first RV. Zip and Yanto had left, so we continued to move quickly back to the FRV. We caught up with them a short time later. We returned to the Battalion, and I gave my report and debrief to the CO, Lt Col. Hew Pike, before re-preparing our equipment, cleaning weapons and then getting a couple of hours' rest.

It became obvious that the CO was keen to move the Battalion forward and attack Longdon as soon as possible, as the Brigade plan was now to move without delay onto the hills and mountains surrounding Port Stanley, with 3 PARA to attack and capture Mount Longdon, 45 Commando to attack the mountain called Two Sisters and 42 Commando onto Mount Harriet.

A few hours later, we deployed again back towards Longdon for a further recce. Unknown to us, the Battalion later moved forward and was preparing to attack. We completed our recce like the first one, gathered further information of enemy positions and again walked off, this time avoiding the trenches. We linked up with Zip and Yanto, and I was informed of the Battalion move forward as Zip had received it by radio. We walked back very carefully, in fog, to the Battalion front line, where the soldiers were aware that in front of them somewhere was the enemy. We approached very cautiously to avoid a 'blue-on-blue' situation, and eventually we heard the noise of men digging shell scrapes and voices. We went to ground and shouted that we were approaching their front line, which worked – thankfully. However, there was to be a delay due to the arrival of General Moore taking command of Brigade operations. This delay at least gave us the chance to reassess the situation and conduct further patrols on and around Mount Longdon.

The Battalion moved back to the mountains around Estancia and we [Patrol Company] continued to conduct recces onto and around the area of Mount Longdon, gaining more information with each patrol. This intelligence gave us the ability to build a large earthen model of the mountain and enemy positions therein, which the CO and the companies could use to brief from. During this patrolling phase, two patrols had contact and a firefight with the enemy near Murrell Bridge, extracting without injuries.

Anti-tank mines had been found in an area west of Mount Longdon, although no mines or markings for mines were found in the areas to the north and north-west of Longdon, which on many occasions were the lines of our approach and exit from the mountain. Later we were to find out that there were scattered AP [anti-personnel] mines in this area.

On 11 June, 3 PARA started its advance onto Longdon to conduct a silent night attack, with the patrols marking the start line at Furze Bush stream. My task was to get 'B' Company across the start line then assist with casualties and POWs, but tactics and battles will always change once across the start line and into contact with the enemy.

After crossing the area of the start line, one of my patrols was to lead 6 Platoon to the western slopes of Longdon, and my patrol approached with 'B' Company HQ between 4 and 5 Platoon. It was a bright moonlit night, and we were on an open concave slope with very little cover, somewhere I had already been on numerous occasions. 'B' Company had almost made it silently to the forward edge of the enemy positions when a Section Commander stood on an AP mine. This explosion and the accompanying eerie scream were the start of what was to be a very hard night of close-quarter battle, followed by two days of occupation on Longdon under heavy enemy artillery and mortar fire.

Following that first mine explosion, the enemy opened fire at us in the open ground, where we took cover and returned fire. The sky turned red with tracer and chaos ensued. I managed to locate 5 Platoon Command and then 4 Platoon Command, showing them a centre axis to aim for amongst the rocks through the skyline that was now familiar to me, having sketched it previously.

The men had their initial orders to capture this mountain, which was now their focus. With enemy fire pouring down on us, the Platoons broke down to sections, half-sections and pairs, skirmishing forward with bayonets fixed and grenades ready. My patrol stayed with Company HQ, and we skirmished towards and onto the mountain. After an extremely hard, close-quarter, bloody fight, 'B' Company reached the top of the mountain and came to a standstill with many men killed and injured. They reorganised and prepared to continue the push further forward when it was decided that 'A' Company could now take up the fight.

Our own Naval Gunfire Support was employed onto the mountain within 50 metres of our position. I was tasked to locate 'A' Company and guide them forward and through 'B' Company position and onto the mountain. I left my patrol in cover on the top of the position and worked my way back down to familiar voices of 'A' Company, and then showed them the way up … 'A' Company then moved eastwards along the mountain [and] continued the fight through, finally securing the position approximately nine hours after crossing the start line. That night, seventeen men of 3 PARA were killed and many more injured. Many enemies were killed and injured.

A couple of days later, 13 June was also eventful. Pettinger again takes up the story:

'A' Company went 'firm' and started to reorganise themselves. I was tasked with clearing between the company areas on the mountain for any enemy stragglers. We came across some enemy in bunkers and tents, which gave us a few fraught moments, but without resistance, they were now POWs and were passed back through the Companies to an area at the north-west end of Longdon near our own regimental aid post (RAP). Immediately after this, our next task was to lead a Support Company group of a Milan detachment and two sustained fire gun groups to the forward edge of the position as quickly as possible. We collected the men and weapons and moved quickly along the northern edge of the position, still finding enemy stragglers.

A short while later, this task was cancelled, and the Support Company men returned to their original positions, while we dropped back through 'B' Company position. Longdon was being bombarded with artillery and mortar fire throughout the day, and we continued taking more casualties. The incoming artillery and mortars were constant and accurately being controlled by an enemy Observation Post on Mount Tumbledown immediately to our south. 3 PARA had six more soldiers killed and a number of others seriously wounded.

As a patrol, we had several remarkably close encounters with the enemy bombardment, being almost buried by one explosion and being blown off our feet with another; many more were too close for comfort. I decided that we would move off the mountain for a short period and collected another patrol as we headed west. We had been on the go for over two days and desperately needed to rest before we were required and re-tasked again. I led the men westwards about 600 metres to a group of rocks where we rested, cleaned weapons and had some food. During this time, the Battalion HQ was organising the evacuation of casualties and dead.

After a few hours, we received a radio message from the CO, who was on Longdon between 'A' and 'B' Companies, ordering us to attend a briefing. A short while later we arrived at the northwest corner of the position, where the RAP and some of Battalion HQ were based. Whilst stopped, I left the men together with other Patrol Company members and made my way towards the CO's position. This was quickly curtailed as a few seconds after leaving the men and about 10 metres from them, an artillery or mortar round landed amongst them. This was devastating, injuring most of those close by. Zip had turned to cover me and had his back to the explosion, which threw him to the ground. He was just winded; however Dickie had taken a large piece of shrapnel through his helmet and through his head. Unfortunately, he died a little while later. There were four or five other injuries from this explosion.

The brief from the CO was for us to locate and destroy the enemy mortars that were close to Wireless Ridge and firing accurately onto Longdon. We knew the artillery location was in Stanley as we had seen it before. My patrol was now just the two of us, so I gathered another patrol to assist, and after a discussion with a Senior NCO [Non-Commissioned Officer] in the Battalion Mortar Platoon, we moved forward of the Battalion and onto the western end of Wireless Ridge. Here, we could see many Argentinian troops, some very close to us and others heading off the mountains towards Stanley. Additionally, we could see the enemy artillery on the racecourse in

Stanley. However, the enemy mortars were out of sight to us. We were able to use a search and destroy method with our mortars, and after some time the enemy mortars stopped. Whether we hit them or they realised what was happening and left, we will never know.

During that period, I radioed many times to our artillery for a fire mission onto the enemy guns in Stanley, which were still highly active. Our guns were busy adjusting fire further onto Wireless Ridge for the pending 2 PARA attack, so we were not given the priority. Later that day, just before last light, we were eventually given the fire mission, which we used effectively against those enemy guns on the racecourse. Later, I sent the additional patrol back to the Battalion area and myself, Zip and one other stayed forward to watch the 2 PARA assault onto Wireless Ridge.

The next day [14 June], 3 PARA prepared to move through 2 PARA and attack Moody Brook and the racecourse. As orders were being given by the CO that afternoon, the shout came that the Argentinians had surrendered.

Pettinger's gallantry during eleven days of operations in the Mount Longdon area, including taking part in the assault, was recognised with the award of the DCM, one of five (one posthumous) awarded to the Parachute Regiment for the war. His comrade in his patrol, Private Dickie Absolon, was awarded the MM posthumously.

Pettinger's decoration was announced on 8 October 1982, and his citation stated:

Sergeant Pettinger is a Patrol Commander D (Patrol) Company 3rd Battalion The Parachute Regiment. On the nights of the 2nd/3rd June Sergeant Pettinger was Commander of one of a number of patrols tasked to gain information about enemy forces holding Mount Longdon.

Sergeant Pettinger's mission was to recce routes onto Mount

Longdon with the aim of placing a rifle company in the best possible position for a night assault later. This meant closing with the enemy who at times were only a few metres away in order to gain his information. This he did with great success on four occasions over the two nights, displaying a high standard of skill and coolness, knowing that capture would lead to the compromise of the battalion plans. The information gained led to him being able to produce accurate descriptions of routes onto the objective, detailed information on enemy strengths and locations, and on the night of 8 June to lead a platoon along the assault route in a rehearsal for the planned attack. Once again he closed with the enemy, gained further information, and cleared more routes, again with great coolness. On the night of 11th/12th June, Sergeant Pettinger acted as a guide for B Company for their part in the battalion night attack onto Mount Longdon and was able to place them in such a good starting position that the attack came as a complete surprise to the enemy. Once the battle had commenced he was a constant source of information and advice to the Company Commander, while acting with dash and determination during the many assaults against strong points on that night, killing at least three enemy. During the preparation for the attack on Mount Longdon Sergeant Pettinger completed six close target reconnaissances against the objective. He displayed the highest standards of professional skill, alertness, accuracy of reporting, coolness in the face of the enemy as well as courage during the actual assault.

After the Falklands War, Pettinger was promoted to Colour Sergeant. In 1983, he was posted to the Infantry Training Battle School at Brecon as an instructor on the Senior NCO Division. Towards the end of 1983, he returned to 3 PARA and back to Patrol Company as a Platoon Commander. Later, he became the Company Quarter Master Sergeant for Support Company. He was promoted to WO

Class 2 and Company Sergeant Major of 'B' Company in 3 PARA and later served as the Senior Permanent Staff Instructor (SPSI) with 10 PARA (TA) in north London for the period 1986–89.

In 1989, he joined 2 PARA for a further tour of Northern Ireland on the border. And in 1990, he became the Regimental Quarter Master Sergeant for the Logistic Battalion and was advised that he would eventually be promoted to WO Class 1 as the Regimental Sergeant Major (RSM) of 2 PARA. Earlier than expected, in November of 1990, an RSM post became available in Holland at the Support Unit for UK troops at Allied Forces Central Europe. With a pending move to 2 PARA, this was not something Pettinger wanted; however, his orders were to take the post. Starting in early 1991, he remained there for the next two years.

Pettinger finished his regular service in August 1993 and the next day joined the Non-Regular Permanent Staff with 10 Battalion, the Parachute Regiment (10 PARA TA) as a Company Quarter Master Sergeant. After some six years, because of defence cuts, 10 PARA was disbanded and Pettinger transferred to another TA unit of the local Royal Logistics Corps. This posting lasted for just over a year before he was commissioned as a Captain and became the permanent staff administration officer with 144 Parachute Medical Squadron in Hornsey, where he served for a further three years before finally retiring from the army after a total of thirty-six years' service.

During his time as SPSI with 10 PARA in north London, Pettinger learnt how to sail and started earning qualifications in the sport, which has allowed him to work in that field – all over the world – since retiring from the army. He has a string of sailing qualifications, including being a yachtmaster instructor and examiner. Today, Pettinger lives with his third wife in Norfolk. He has grown-up twin daughters by his late second wife and two granddaughters.

CHAPTER 4

THE AIR WAR

It would be a considerable understatement to say that fighting an air war 8,000 miles from home presented significant challenges. The task was made all the harder because the Argentine Air Force was fairly formidable and had the advantage of fighting its war from only 400 miles off its mainland.

As the Falklands crisis descended into war, Argentina possessed one of the largest and best-equipped air forces in Latin America – one that mounted a huge threat to the British forces heading to the South Atlantic. The threat was largely underestimated too by British military Commanders, due to a lack of up-to-date intelligence of the enemy. For example, intelligence from London wrongly stated that the enemy possessed only one Super Étendard aircraft capable of launching AM39 Exocet missiles, and only five of the weapons themselves. This vastly underestimated the Super Étendard / Exocet fire power at Argentina's disposal. The determination of the enemy air force had also been miscalculated: 'death before dishonour' was their motto and many pilots took this vow seriously.

The Falkland Islands were invaded on Friday 2 April. The previous day, the aircraft carriers HMS Hermes *and* Invincible *had been alerted because the invasion appeared imminent. And on the Friday, two squadrons of Sea Harriers met the carriers at Portsmouth – Lieutenant Commander Andrew Auld's 800 Squadron was assigned to* Hermes, *while Lieutenant Commander Nigel 'Sharkey' Ward's 801 Squadron was assigned to* Invincible.

A detachment from No. 1 Squadron, RAF was also embarked on Hermes. Indeed, the RAF played a significant part in 'Operation Corporate' to recover the Falklands, but because of the distances involved its role was limited. Due to the unusual circumstances, the Royal Navy's Fleet Air Arm was left to perform perhaps the key role in terms of the war in the air. The Fleet Air Arm's Sea Harriers – jet fighter, reconnaissance and air attack aircraft – in particular proved crucial to the campaign, while the Sea King helicopters provided both anti-submarine warfare cover and air lift. Further important contributions to the war in the air were provided by 656 Squadron, Army Air Corps, and 3 Commando Brigade Air Squadron, Royal Marines.

A total of 171 naval aircraft were eventually deployed to the South Atlantic, most permanently based aboard ships of the Royal Navy and the Royal Fleet Auxiliary, the latter of which provides logistical and operational support to the Royal Navy and Royal Marines. A major contribution to the air war came from the Royal Naval Air Station, Yeovilton, Somerset, which sent a total of around 120 Sea Harriers and helicopters, along with some 1,400 officers and men. Nine squadrons, three of them formed specifically for the campaign, went to war, and twelve men from the station lost their lives during the conflict.

On 25 April, the air war commenced when a British Wessex helicopter flying close to South Georgia dropped two 250lb depth charges next to the enemy submarine Santa Fe. It did not take long before more British helicopters were in action, as has already been detailed, and soon the Union flag was restored on the island.

The first air attack took place less than a week later on 1 May, when, at 4.23 a.m., a single RAF Vulcan bomber of 101 Squadron, Strike Command, attacked Port Stanley airfield shortly after Britain's decision to extend the maritime exclusion zone to a TEZ. The pilot of the elderly aircraft released twenty-one 1,000lb bombs from a height of around 10,000ft and from some 3 miles before the coast. Twenty bombs missed the runway, but one landed on the target, damaging *the Tarmac. The air war proper had begun, and it escalated later that very day.*

One primary role of the British aircraft and helicopters was to provide protection for our ships in the open sea and those close to the Falkland Islands, along with our troops once they had landed on the enemy-held territory. However, these aircraft were also used in offensive roles to target enemy positions, aircraft, ships and troops. Once again, this book seeks only to provide a snapshot of the incredible bravery displayed by pilots, air crew and support crew, rather than a comprehensive account of the air war in general.

Those wanting to know details of the air war and of the aircraft, weaponry and manpower involved should read books such as Rodney A. Burden et al.'s Falklands: The Air War *and Commander 'Sharkey' Ward's* Sea Harrier over the Falklands. *As previously mentioned, Ward commanded 801 Naval Air Squadron, HMS Invincible. He was also senior Sea Harrier adviser to the Command, flew more than sixty missions and was awarded the DSC. In his book, Ward revealed how the 801 pilots had to fight the enemy, exhaustion and hostile weather.*

In total, ten fixed-wing aircraft and twenty-five helicopters were lost to enemy action and accidents.

RODNEY VINCENT FREDERIKSEN

Service: Royal Navy

Final rank: Lieutenant Commander

FALKLANDS WAR DECORATION / DISTINCTION:

MENTIONED IN DESPATCHES (MID)

DATE OF BRAVERY: MAY 1982

GAZETTED: 8 OCTOBER 1982

Rodney 'Fred' Frederiksen had the distinction of leading the surprise attack on Goose Green airfield on the opening day of British operations to recapture the Falkland Islands, destroying or badly damaging at least three enemy aircraft. Furthermore, on 21 May, the Sea Harrier pilot shot down a Dagger single-seat fighter over West Falkland with a Sidewinder missile, and the following day strafed and wrecked an enemy patrol boat. He was Mentioned in Despatches for his relentless wartime bravery while serving in the Fleet Air Arm, Royal Navy, with 800 Naval Air Squadron. During a distinguished career, he was also twice awarded the Queen's Commendation for Valuable Services in the Air (QCVSA).

Rodney Vincent Frederiksen was born in South Shields, near Newcastle upon Tyne, on 7 April 1947. The son of a wireless officer in the Danish Merchant Navy who had moved to England, he was educated at St Aidan's Grammar School, Sunderland. He joined the Royal Navy in 1966, beginning his operational career in 1970 as a Sea Vixen pilot with 893 Naval Air Squadron on HMS *Hermes*. Transferring to 899 Squadron, Frederiksen, who was known by his comrades as 'Fred', flew the Phantom jet fighter-bomber from the aircraft carrier HMS *Eagle* in the early 1970s before attending the Central Flying School at RAF Little Rissington, Gloucestershire, in 1973. The following year he became a qualified flying instructor. In 1977, having been described in his flying assessment as the 'epitome of professionalism', Frederiksen was selected for No. 36 Fixed Wing Course at the Empire Test Pilots' School at Boscombe Down, Wiltshire. For the next five years, he was a test pilot at Boscombe Down. During this period his logbook records hundreds of hours flown on a variety of aircraft, including Hunters, Jaguars, Lightnings and Hawks. He was awarded his first QCVSA for this work in 1977.

His first Harrier flight came on 25 September 1978, and he logged a solo flight in a Sea Harrier on 2 May 1979. Flying Sea Harriers exclusively from June 1980 as part of 800 Naval Air Squadron, he was still testing at Boscombe Down when jump jets from his squadron were landing on *Hermes* on 4 April 1982, in preparation for the journey to the Falkland Islands.

Inveigling himself aboard, Frederiksen was welcomed by his fellow 800 Squadron pilots under Lieutenant Commander Andy Auld, and a month later he was in the thick of war. On 1 May 1982, *Hermes* entered the 200-mile TEZ that Britain had declared around the Falkland Islands and moved into a position 95 miles east-north-east of the capital Port Stanley, ready to launch all twelve of her Sea Harrier aircraft for attacks on Stanley Airport (nine aircraft) and Goose Green (three aircraft). Frederiksen, in Sea Harrier ZA191, led the latter group of three ('Tartan Section') off the *Hermes*' 'ski-jump' at 10.56 a.m., a mission later recounted by Jeffrey Ethell and Alfred Price in *Air War South Atlantic*:

> While the attack on Port Stanley airfield was in progress, Lieutenant Commander 'Fred' Frederiksen led his three Harriers southwards down Falkland Sound before running in to attack Goose Green airfield from the north-west. Approaching fast and very low, the raiders achieved almost complete surprise at their target. As the aircraft pulled up to begin their bombing runs one of the pilots saw the muzzle flashes of small arms fire aimed at them, but that was the sole reaction from the ground. The Sea Harriers released their bombs and were clear before the defenders could bring heavier weapons to bear. As the raiders swept in one of the Pucará [aircraft] had been preparing to take off, and the exploding cluster bombs wrecked the aircraft, killing the pilot and six ground crew.

By 11.55 a.m., 'Tartan Section' had landed back on *Hermes* unscathed. The safe return of all the Harriers of 800 Squadron gave rise to the memorable words uttered by BBC reporter Brian Hanrahan: 'I counted them all out and I counted them all back.'

Overall, the two attacks were considered highly successful with no losses on the British side, while a Sea Harrier photo reconnaissance flight later the same day apparently revealed five damaged Pucarás on the Goose Green airfield in addition to the one destroyed.

Over the next eighteen days, Frederiksen flew a further thirteen Combat Air Patrols from *Hermes* before the British landings in San Carlos Water on 21 May. The landings provoked a strong reaction from the Argentine Air Force, and so this became a day of fierce aerial combat, with an estimated ten enemy aircraft shot down. Unsurprisingly, it was also Frederiksen's busiest day of the war. On his first sortie that day, Frederiksen and Lieutenant Mike Hale of 800 Squadron gave chase to six Argentine Daggers (the Israeli version of the French Dassault Mirage 5 multi-role fighter) that had just attacked HM ships *Broadsword*, *Argonaut* and *Antrim* in San Carlos Sound with 1,000lb bombs. Hale later recalled to authors Ethell and Price:

> We picked them up visually as they were coming down the Lafonia side of the Sound, just over land at low level and running out at high speed. I was the nearer to them. I dropped in behind the left-hand man in their formation and got a good missile lock. The range was a bit on the high side but I decided to give it a try and launched a Sidewinder.

His missile exploded short of its intended victim and the two Sea Harriers, unable to close the range and short of fuel, broke off the chase and returned to the carrier.

That afternoon, however, on his second Combat Air Patrol of the day, Frederiksen had more success. Ethell and Price pick up the story:

> Lieutenant Commander 'Fred' Frederiksen and Lieutenant Andy

George of No. 800 Squadron were on patrol when one of the first of the new raiding forces came in: four Daggers of Grupo 6 led by Captain Horacio Gonzalez. The raiders had been seen on radar before they descended to low altitude west of the Falklands, however, and directed by [HMS] *Brilliant* Frederiksen and George headed west to intercept them. Meanwhile the low-flying raiders had headed south-east from Jason Island, and after making a landfall at King George Bay on West Falkland they swung on to a north-easterly heading to take them through a gap in the high ground towards their target.

As the Daggers crossed the coast Frederiksen, by then over Chartres Settlement at 2,500ft, caught sight of them three miles away to the right; at the time he thought the aircraft to be Skyhawks. 'I put Andy George into [a] one mile trail on me to keep an eye open for any escorts that might be behind them as we accelerated and I went in behind the left-hand element. Having checked there were no escorts, Andy went for the right-hand element. I went for the tail man in the left element; there was no sign that they had seen me...' [said Frederiksen]. The tail man in the left element was Lieutenant Hector Luna, who recalled: 'We were about four minutes from the target and flying very low; I could see the peaks of the mountains covered by cloud as we flew down the valley between them. And at that moment I saw a Sea Harrier turning above me. I tried to advise my leader but my radio malfunctioned. Then I looked in my mirror and saw a second Harrier behind me fire a missile – I could see the flame clearly.' The Sidewinder, fired by Frederiksen, struck the Dagger at the rear and Luna started to lose control. Instinctively he pulled on the stick to gain height before ejecting but, probably because the control surfaces on the rear of one of the wings had been damaged by the explosion, the fighter-bomber immediately lurched into a violent roll. Luna had no time to consider the matter further, he pulled the ejection-seat handle. A split second after the pilot emerged from his aircraft the Dagger smashed into the ground, and Luna could feel the blast of the impact. Immediately afterwards he was dumped on the ground hard, pieces of flaming wreckage falling around him. He had a dislocated arm and a sprained knee and so, after releasing his parachute, had to crawl clear of what, not many seconds earlier, had been a fighter-bomber.

Frederiksen saw the aircraft smash into the ground in front of him, and as it did so he came within gun range of the element leader and opened fire with his 30mm cannon, though without seeing any hits. Meanwhile the Daggers, hugging the ground as their pilots endeavoured to avoid the cloud-covered mountains, went into a turn to the left. Frederiksen immediately pulled right, away from the fighter-bomber he had been following: if he continued his attack he knew the right-hand element of the enemy force would swing round on to his tail. Once out of the potential trap he pulled left again and loosed off the rest of his cannon shells at the right-hand element. 'I was in a high G turn at very low altitude and I wouldn't claim any hits. The last I saw of them they were continuing their turn to the left, going into cloud' [Frederiksen said]. As the rest of the Daggers let down beneath cloud on the other side of the high ground it was clear one of their comrades was missing; at the time they thought Luna had flown into a hillside. Surprisingly, none of their pilots had seen the Sea Harriers. Shaken by the apparent sudden death of one of their number, the remainder pressed on grimly towards the target area.

The following day Frederiksen, once again paired with Lieutenant Hale, launched from *Hermes* at dawn for the first air patrol of the day. Approaching Goose Green, they sighted the coastguard patrol boat *Río Iguazú* on its way up Choiseul Sound carrying field guns and ammunition to reinforce the Argentine defences. After getting permission from their control ship, the pair dived on the boat, strafed it with 30mm cannon and left it burning. Later, it was seen aground among the kelp in Button Bay, still burning, having been abandoned by its crew.

Frederiksen eventually completed more hours on air defence than any other pilot flying from *Hermes*, and he undertook a remarkable fifty-five Combat Air Patrols during the war as well as bombing missions over Goose Green and Port Stanley. For his services in the South Atlantic he was Mentioned in Despatches in *The London Gazette* of 8 October 1982. His unpublished recommendation stated:

> Lieutenant Commander Frederiksen has played a key role in the battle of the Falkland Isles. On 1st May 1982, he led an attack on the airstrip at Goose Green settlement, which was fiercely defended by heavy anti-aircraft ground fire and subsequently resulted in the loss of two Harriers. He flew over fifty operational missions and a greater number of hours on air defence than any other pilot on H.M.S. *Hermes*. In one sortie he destroyed one Skyhawk and aggressively engaged the second aircraft until his missiles and guns were expended. Lieutenant Commander Frederiksen's courage and cheerful determination in conditions of great stress have been an excellent example to all the aircrew and are in the highest traditions of the Service. He is highly commended for his contribution to Operation Corporate.

Frederiksen was also the subject of an original oil-on-canvas painting by artist Jack Froelich, depicting the moment the pilot launched his Sidewinder air-to-air missile to bring down the Argentine jet above San Carlos Water on 21 May 1982. The artist's work was cleverly called, 'Is this a Dagger which I see before me?'

After the Falklands War, Frederiksen returned to Boscombe Down, flight testing an updated Sea Harrier armed with the Sea Eagle air-to-surface missile. From 1985 until 1988 he commanded 800 Naval Air Squadron, flying from the carrier HMS *Illustrious*. On one occasion, he was reprimanded after faulty navigation equipment took him close to the Russian city of Murmansk, a scrape that earned him the nickname 'Red Fred'. In 1988, he passed the Naval Staff course, but he disliked the desk-bound environment and the following year he joined British Aerospace in order to continue flying, working as a test pilot at Dunsfold Airfield, Surrey. There, he test-flew improved versions of the Harrier until, when armed with the latest advanced medium-range air-to-air missile, it became Britain's most effective air-defence fighter. Remaining in the role until 1994, his second QCVSA was gazetted in June of that year. Between 1995 and 1997, Frederiksen was based in Dabolim, Goa, where he helped to train Indian naval pilots to fly their Harriers and later also trained Indonesian pilots to fly Hawks. He took up his last job in 2003, teaching on the simulator at 208 Squadron, RAF Valley, Wales. For a time, his family home was in Anglesey, and he later moved to Leicestershire.

Frederiksen, a heavy smoker, fell ill in his early sixties and he lived his final days in a care home in Spalding, Lincolnshire, where he was looked after by a cousin. He died on 27 September 2009, aged sixty-two. His funeral, on 9 October 2009, was marked by a flypast followed by a cremation at Boston Crematorium. Frederiksen had three grown-up daughters, and he is remembered fondly for his passion for flying, which he passed on to many other young would-be pilots. He was a popular leader who commanded respect, but he was also great fun to be with when raising a glass at the bar.

JEFFREY WILLIAM GLOVER

Service: Royal Air Force

Final rank: Squadron Leader

FALKLANDS WAR DECORATION / DISTINCTION: **N/A**

DATE OF BRAVERY: N/A

GAZETTED: N/A

Jeff Glover was the only British pilot to be taken as a POW by the Argentines after his Harrier jet was shot down over West Falkland. Having ejected from his aircraft, he received serious injuries and was then held as a captive for seven weeks until well after the end of the war. Later, in a distinguished RAF career, he was awarded the QCVSA and went on to fly with the world-famous Red Arrows aerobatics team.

Jeffrey William Glover, the son of a school headmaster, was born in St Helens, Lancashire, on 2 April 1954. An only child, he was educated at Cowley School, where Maurice Clifton, his former headmaster, remembered him as 'one of the most gifted pupils ever to pass through my hands in forty-two years of teaching'. He added, 'He was a very pleasant, outgoing lad who made his mark at the school by winning a scholarship to Oxford and an RAF cadetship. Later he won Cowley its only "blue" for soccer.'

Glover gained a BA (Hons) degree in engineering sciences after three years at St Catherine's College, Oxford, but according to his tutor, Dr Don Schultz, he was best known for his service as a keen pilot in the University Air Squadron. 'He was a chap who knew exactly what he wanted to do and how to go about it,' he said.

From 1976 to 1977, Glover attended RAF College Cranwell in Lincolnshire, where he won the Battle of Britain Trophy for best aerobatics pilot. The following year, at RAF Valley on the island of Anglesey in north Wales, he came top of his course in advanced flying training on Gnat jets. Next, he trained at RAF Leeming in Yorkshire before returning to RAF Valley to be a qualified flying instructor on the Hawk, while also winning the aerobatics trophy.

While based at RAF Leeming, he met his first wife, Dee, with the couple marrying in February 1981, just fourteen months before the start of the Falklands War. In fact, Argentina invaded the Falkland Islands on Glover's twenty-eighth birthday. By this point, Glover had spent two more years at RAF Valley as a Hawk instructor, with training in 1981 at the Harrier Operational Conversion Unit, where he won all but one of the course prizes. After that, in the run-up to the Falklands War, he served as a Harrier pilot with No. 1 (Fighter) Squadron at RAF Wittering on the Cambridgeshire / Northamptonshire border.

In an interview at his home town of Stamford, Lincolnshire, Glover recalled that he had been on an intended one-month training course at the German Air Force base Jever on the day the Falklands were invaded. Two weeks into his course, he was recalled to RAF Wittering as the possibility of war loomed. 'The squadron had been put on a footing for possible deployment,' he said.

At this point, Glover was serving in the rank of Flight Lieutenant. 'There was a feeling of excitement because this was what we had been trained for,' he said. Eventually, No. 1 Squadron deployed nine pilots and six Harrier jets to the South Atlantic. Glover flew one of the aircraft from RAF St Mawgan in Cornwall to Ascension Island – a journey of nearly nine hours that required mid-air refuelling en route. After that flight, Glover and his fellow pilots travelled on towards the Falklands on MV *Norland* while the aircraft went on board the SS *Atlantic Conveyor*. Glover continues the story:

Eventually we cross-decked to the *Atlantic Conveyor* and the six Harriers vertically took off and landed on HMS *Hermes*. As one of the junior pilots, I did not fly one of the planes; instead I was one of the three pilots helicoptered onto *Hermes*. I think we arrived on 18 May, and for the next couple of days we flew three practice sorties to familiarise ourselves with flight deck operations. I was teamed up with the Boss, Wing Commander [later Air Chief Marshal, Chief of the Air Staff] Peter Squire, as a flight of two aircraft.

On the morning of 21 May 1982, Glover took part in his first wartime mission – but things did not go to plan:

It was the squadron's second mission of the day. The Wing Commander and I were to get airborne, liaise with HMS *Antrim*, which was controlling the missions, and await targeting information. We took off at around 8 a.m. local time – it was a beautiful day, not a cloud in the sky. I just wanted to perform to the best of my ability, and not let the side down. The *Hermes* was less than 200 miles to the north-east of the Falklands. I lined up behind the Boss on the carrier. We each had two cluster bomb units and guns loaded. He selected full power and four seconds later I too went to full power, chased him down the flight deck and left the end of the ski jump at 120 knots – nearly 140mph. I then took 35 degrees of nozzle to be partially wing-borne and jet-borne. We started to climb to around 25,000ft but the Boss could not retract his under-carriage. He had to abort his mission because of the problem... leaving yours truly on his own to complete the mission.

I then spoke to HMS *Antrim* over the radio, and I was given targets in the Port Howard area of West Falkland. I was given 'lat and long' [latitude and longitude] references to the target. My only navigational aids were an E2C compass, accurate to about 20 degrees, and my stopwatch. The Inertial Navigation System fitted to the RAF Harriers was inoperative whilst deployed on the carrier since the inertial platforms could not stabilise on the rolling deck.

My aim was to drop both my cluster bombs on the target. I then went down from 25,000ft to low level – around 200ft. I flew up the coastline on the east side of West Falkland and entered the Port Howard Harbour area doing around 480 knots. I identified a jetty on the map and set off on what I hoped was about 355 degrees looking for targets – ground troops – but didn't see any. I flew through the target area without dropping and continued at low level for a minute before climbing back up to 25,000ft. It was still a glorious day – blue skies. At this point, I had seen no enemy planes and had not been shot at from the ground. So far, so good, except I had not dropped my bombs.

I then spoke to HMS *Antrim* again and said, 'No targets seen. What should I do?' They said 'stand-by' and about a minute later I said I could go back to the target area and this time take photographs because my aircraft had a port-facing oblique camera for reconnaissance purposes. *Antrim* agreed this plan, so I now set about returning to the target area. I was going to approach from a different direction. I then let down from around 20,000ft over land and dropped down to 200ft for about four minutes, approaching the Port Howard area from land, not sea, this time. I was flying at 535 knots. Once I identified the jetty area, I went into a hard turn to the left, rolled out at 510 knots and pressed the camera button. Then I felt and heard 'bang, bang, bang'. The aircraft then entered a maximum-rate roll to the right – the roll taking no more than a second but it was as if it was happening in slow time. I had three separate thoughts: the first was 'I cannot control the roll with this control column', the second was 'that sea is awfully close' and the third was 'I have to time my ejection right'. After the aircraft had gone through 320 degrees, I looked down and saw my right hand pull the ejection seat handle. I then heard a metallic bang and I lost consciousness. I woke up about 4ft under water, sunny-side up, and flapped to the surface and saw the sun again. In fact, I had been hit by a Blowpipe missile that had been fired from the ground by an Argentinian. The missile had hit and taken off half of my right wing, which is why I had done a hard roll to the right. The reason I blacked out was that normally you try to pull the ejector handle with both hands but, because it happened so fast, my left hand was still on the throttle so, as I ejected, my left arm went into a whiplash movement at around 600mph, and I lost consciousness. After I ejected, my parachute opened and I dropped into the freezing sea.

So, I was in the water in my protective immersion suit, and after what seemed like five minutes of being in shock, I started to think about getting into my self-inflating dinghy, which was attached to me by two quick-release clips. At some point, I realised that I couldn't see out of my left eye – this was because my helmet had flown off during the ejection, which shouldn't have happened. The end of the oxygen hose, which got separated from my oxygen mask as the helmet flew off, had bashed into my mouth causing some damage. My left side was also completely incapacitated from various injuries. I then heard voices and looked around. There was a little rowing boat with some Argentinian troops in it, holding rifles. In my stupidity, I reached for my RAF-issue pistol but, thankfully, I had mistakenly left it on the *Hermes* and did not have it with me. The soldiers pulled me out of the water and I was from then on, for the next fifty days, a POW.

Glover was then rowed ashore from the position he had dropped into the water, some 200 metres from land. He was taken as a passenger on a motorbike to the Port Howard Social Club, which had been converted into a medical centre by the invading force. Glover's injuries amounted to a deep cut to his mouth and top lip, severe bruising to the left side of his face, a broken left arm, a broken left shoulder blade and a broken left collar bone. 'I was a bit of a mess. I was feeling a bit sorry for myself, but I was glad to be alive,' Glover said with understatement. After his immersion suit was cut off him, he was asked his name, rank and serial number, all of which he provided. His dog tags confirmed this information. Glover's left arm was put in a loose sling, and he was then given an injection so that he went to sleep. When he woke up, there was a huge commotion and a lot of screaming – two young Argentine conscripts had been outside the perimeter after curfew hours and they had both been shot by their own forces as they approached in the dusk light.

The next day Glover, by now wearing olive-green fatigues, was flown to Goose Green by helicopter, but beforehand he was asked if he wanted to meet the man who had shot him down. Glover recalled, 'I said, "OK," and I was then introduced to Lieutenant Sergio Fernandez. We shook hands and I said, "Good effort," which used to be a bit of a catchphrase of mine.'

Later, Glover was flown by Chinook helicopter, fast and at low level to avoid possible RAF Sea Harrier attacks, from Goose Green to Port Stanley. Eventually, after more medical treatment, on 25 May Glover was taken in a Hercules transport plane to Comodoro Rivadavia, a city and military base on the Argentine mainland. Also on board were four or five Argentine pilots who had been shot down by the British but survived.

Immediately after Glover's plane was downed, however, it was unclear to the British military whether he had been killed or taken as a POW. For a whole week his wife did not know whether he was alive or dead, but eventually word reached her from the Ministry of Defence that he was alive – but being held captive. Dee Glover, then twenty-five, said back in 1982:

I had a week not knowing where he was or whether he was alive or dead. I always felt that he was alive, and prayed I was right. I have no details about how he was shot or what happened, just that it was over the Falklands. I aged twenty years in the time from when he was shot down to when I heard about him.

As the war continued, Argentina used Glover as a propaganda tool. He was – falsely – quoted in newspapers in Buenos Aires as saying, 'My people are wrong, and that is dangerous. Our forces are suffering the effects of the Argentine offensive. Their morale is deteriorating due to the confusion caused by air attacks.'

Glover told me that he was never aggressively interrogated or mistreated by the enemy, but it was a tough fifty days with his future uncertain the whole time, even after the Argentine surrender:

After a night at Comodoro Rivadavia, a Mirage pilot came to my room, gave me a bottle of wine, shook my hand and said he had respect for a fellow aviator. After a couple of nights, I was flown north. I was told I was going to Buenos Aires but in fact ended up at Chamical Air Base, which was in the middle of nowhere but from where I could see the Andes. I was held there for the next five and a half weeks. For the first week, I was locked in a room and not allowed out, but then an International Red Cross man pitched up.

I was initially suspicious of him but then I warmed to him when he started taking measurements of the size of my room [to try to get Glover a larger room]. I warmed to him even more when he left me 200 cigarettes because I was a smoker back then. I was also able to write a letter to my wife of no more than twenty-five words, which he said he would deliver. I just wrote I was OK, I was missing her and for her not to worry. There is not a lot you can write in twenty-five words! That first week of isolation was pretty painful and I was getting a bit down, so it was a major boost when this Red Cross man turned up. I knew too that the outside world knew where I was and my conditions improved after his visit. For example, I was allowed to exercise in a courtyard for two hours a day. A fortnight later the Red Cross representative came back with another box of 200 fags, which then got pinched by the guards during my exercise break and that really pissed me off.

Glover said that initially his guards were cocky towards him, but after three and a half weeks their attitude changed: 'I knew we had won the war even though they never told me. I could tell they had lost because they were so much less cocky.' Glover said that he spent time reading books delivered by the International Red Cross, and for the most part his spirits were not too low. He was also given a copy of the Geneva Convention so he could understand his legal rights and a set of air-mail envelopes to write an agreed one letter a week.

At the end of his time in captivity he was flown to Buenos Aires, but before leaving Chamical the head guard handed him all the letters he had written home – none of which had been sent as agreed. 'That annoyed me, of course,' Glover said. In Buenos Aires, there was a one-day delay before he was flown in a military plane to Montevideo, the capital of Uruguay, where he was given his freedom on 8 July 1982. Glover was formally handed over to a representative of the British ambassador and taken to the embassy for a celebration lunch including 'quite a few gin and tonics'. Glover recalled, 'After lunch, the ambassador said, "Do you want to ring home?" and I said, "Ah, yes, OK." So I was able to speak to my wife and tell her all was well.' Glover flew back to Gatwick via Brazil on two passenger flights and almost immediately after putting on his 'No. 1' RAF uniform had to attend a press conference with his wife at the request of the MoD.

After Glover returned home, there was initially some media speculation that he might not fly again. 'It took me seven months before I could fly solo again. It was eventually discovered that I had had a paranoic reaction to isolation and captivity. My problems were more mental than physical,' he said.

In early September 1982, Glover attended a dinner in honour of the former Marshal of the RAF Sir Arthur 'Bomber' Harris, the legendary Commander-in-Chief of Bomber Command. The event at the Guildhall in the City of London was also attended by the equally legendary Second World War fighter pilot Sir Douglas Bader and bomber pilot Leonard Cheshire. Sadly, however, on the way home from the dinner, Bader suffered a heart attack and died, aged seventy-two.

Glover was awarded the QCVSA on 31 December 1985 while still in the rank of Flight Lieutenant. In February 1988, then aged thirty-three and a father of two young children, he became a member of the world-famous Red Arrows aerobatics team. By then in the rank of Squadron Leader, he said it had been a lifelong ambition to fly with the Red Arrows. His appointment to the team was, however, tinged with some sadness: he took over as 'Red 8', the position held by Flight Lieutenant Neil MacLachlan, who was killed in an air crash while conducting a practice flight from RAF Scampton in Lincolnshire. Glover's previous job had been as OC of the Advanced Squadron of the Examining Wing of the Central Flying School at RAF Scampton. While a member of the Red Arrows team he was photographed for *Hello!* magazine sitting next to the Queen Mother when she visited the Red Arrows as part of their twenty-fifth anniversary celebrations in 1989.

Upon his retirement from the RAF in December 1996, Glover received a warm letter of congratulation from Air Vice-Marshal

David Hurrell in which the Air OC offered his 'deep appreciation and gratitude' for his service.

> You have clearly given varied and rewarding service as an aviator in the strike attack role, as a flight instructor, a display pilot and finally, adding variety to your logbook, by flying in the air transport and air-to-air refuelling roles. I hope this wide ranging experience in operational, display and instructional flying proves valuable in your future endeavours. Your record shows that you have maintained the highest professional standards and contributed significantly during tours ... your brilliance in the air, amiable nature and, latterly, golfing prowess, will be sorely missed by all who have worked with you.

After retiring from the RAF, Glover became a commercial pilot, finally retiring in 2019, aged sixty-five. Just five years ago, while working for the Qatari royal family, he found himself in Buenos Aires for twelve days and decided to look up the man who had shot him down some thirty years earlier, now retired Major General Sergio Fernandez.

> He had tracked me down about ten years after the war and we had swapped emails. But this time we went out for dinner, and it was only then that he told me that I had been in the sea after being shot down for *forty* minutes, when I had always thought it was for about five minutes. We had a great evening. He speaks good English and he was, and is, a smashing chap.

Glover, who has three grandchildren, now lives with his second wife, Angela, in Stamford. Reflecting on his role in the war nearly four decades ago, he said, 'At the time, as a POW in 1982, I thought I had let the side down and lost one of our six planes [from his squadron]. But, nearly forty years on, I have got over it.'

JEFFREY PETER NIBLETT

Service: Royal Marines

Final rank: Captain

FALKLANDS WAR DECORATION / DISTINCTION:

DISTINGUISHED FLYING CROSS (DFC)

DATES OF BRAVERY: 28–29 MAY 1982

GAZETTED: 8 OCTOBER 1982

Jeff Niblett was awarded the DFC for outstanding bravery while serving as a helicopter pilot with 3 Commando Brigade Air Squadron, Royal Marines. It was the first ever DFC awarded to a Royal Marine. In one incident, he was leading a pair of Scout helicopters seeking to evacuate a casualty – no lesser man than Colonel 'H' Jones VC – during the battle for Darwin and Goose Green. Not only did Colonel 'H' perish, but so too did the pilot in the accompanying helicopter, shot down by one of two Argentine Pucará aircraft that attacked them. The pilot was Lieutenant Richard Nunn of the Royal Marines, who received a posthumous DFC.

Jeffrey Peter Niblett was born in Aldershot, Hampshire, on 26 September 1949. The younger son of a businessman and his wife, he completed his education at Farnborough Grammar School aged eighteen. In the same year, he gained his private pilot licence through a Royal Naval Flying Scholarship while serving in the Combined Cadet Force. After leaving school and failing RAF aircrew selection, Niblett worked locally in a variety of manual jobs that allowed him to continue flying, attend the Eskdale outward bound course and travel widely in Europe. During this time he met the son of a family friend who was serving as a Royal Marines officer.

It was this chance meeting that led to Niblett's application for a commission in the Royal Marines, which was successful in

September 1970, just days before his twenty-first birthday. A year later, Niblett completed training and was appointed as a Troop Commander with 45 Commando, with whom he did two tours of duty in Northern Ireland. In June 1975, Niblett was awarded his army pilot's 'wings', followed by a Royal Naval Gazelle conversion course and a deployment to the Mediterranean for a NATO exercise. In October 1975, he converted to the Royal Naval Wessex V helicopter, and the following year he was awarded the Hallam Trophy as the top pilot completing Commando operational flying training that year. A further flying tour followed in August 1979, with a conversion course to the Scout helicopter and appointment to 3 Commando Brigade Air Squadron, based at Plymouth, as OC, Brunei Flight, the brigade anti-tank flight.

After completing his final winter deployment in Norway in March 1982, Niblett was due to attend the qualified helicopter instructor course at RAF Shawbury, Shropshire. However, the day before he was due to leave the squadron, Argentina invaded the Falkland Islands and instead he began preparing for deployment with the Task Force.

Niblett, by then a Captain, kept a diary throughout the whole of his deployment detailing events as they unfolded and highlighting the challenges and demands placed on aircrew flying in support of the Task Force units, particularly following the troop landings on 21 May. The extreme dangers faced by all crews became apparent within the first hour, when two Gazelle reconnaissance helicopters from the squadron were shot down by enemy ground fire, with the loss of three crew. Once deployed ashore, Niblett's flight provided support wherever it was required throughout the beachhead, as tasked by the Commando Brigade. At the end of the first week, Niblett flew in support of the breakout by 2 PARA and their subsequent assault on Darwin and Goose Green. It was during this operation that he repeatedly showed such great courage that he was awarded the DFC. His decoration is exceptional for two reasons: it was until 2006 one of only two DFCs ever awarded to a Royal Marine, and it is one of just nine DFCs awarded during the Falklands War. Of the five awarded to crews operating with the ground forces, four were given to Scout helicopter pilots.

The citation for his DFC, announced on 8 October 1982, stated:

During the attack on Darwin and Goose Green, Captain Niblett led a section of two Scout helicopters, supplying ammunition and evacuating casualties for two days, often in the thick of battle and under enemy fire. During one mission both Scouts were attacked by Argentine Pucará aircraft. The helicopters evaded the first attack but one was subsequently shot down. However, with quite exceptional flying skill and superb teamwork with his aircrewman, Captain Niblett evaded three further cannon and rocket attacks, safely completing the mission. He then resolutely continued support and casualty evacuation operations until well after dark.

His courage, leadership and flying skills were also demonstrated in an incident when he evacuated a seriously wounded Marine from Mount Challenger, flying in dark and misty conditions over most hazardous terrain. Captain Niblett proved himself an outstanding Flight Commander and pilot. The superb support that his flight as a whole gave to the landing force reflects his exemplary and dedicated service.

However, what the citation failed to reveal was the identity of the casualty whom the two lightly built and unarmed Scouts had been going to collect on 28 May 1982: Lieutenant Colonel Herbert 'H' Jones, the Commanding Officer of 2 PARA, who was famously awarded a posthumous VC.

In an interview at his home in Norfolk, Niblett told me:

I was commanding a section of two Scouts, flown by myself and

Lieutenant Richard Nunn, attached in direct support of 2 PARA during the battle for Darwin and Goose Green. Throughout the morning [of 28 May 1982] we had flown over three and a half hours ferrying ammunition forward to the battalion mortar lines and front-line troops and returning to our Forward Operating Base at Camilla Creek House with casualties, both our own forces and enemy troops. Enemy action included artillery fire on and close to our landing points throughout the morning.

While at Camilla and part way through loading further ammunition for the front line with rotors running, I heard the radio call on the battalion command net saying that 'H' [Jones] had been shot: 'Sunray [the radio call sign for the Commanding Officer] is down.' At this stage, additional casualties were mentioned but no exact details. On hearing the call, I immediately radioed Lieutenant Nunn and ordered that the ammo was offloaded and replaced with stretchers, which was done. Less than a minute from the original call, we were airborne and heading south towards the Darwin area where 'H' had been shot. I led the pair, and within a minute or so of lifting a pair of Pucarás appeared directly ahead of us, descending from the very low cloud base and crossing ahead of us at approximately 500 metres range. The weather had remained overcast all day, with low cloud at about 150–200ft but with good visibility underneath and no precipitation.

On seeing the enemy aircraft I ordered a break, which we achieved – one aircraft to the right and the other to the left. The Pucarás had seen us and turned towards us, and when they saw our break they took one of us each. At very low level and high speed, we manoeuvred hard and fast to escape their attack. Quite early on Lieutenant Nunn and I crossed paths flying in opposite directions, and that was the last time I saw his aircraft before he was shot down. The Pucará attacking me engaged us with cannon, machine-gun and rocket salvos, trying unsuccessfully to down us with successive passes. The Pucará flew at relatively low speed and was extremely agile, which is not something we had previously encountered...

After two or three attacks on my aircraft, my attacker was joined by the second Pucará, which had obviously broken away from attacking Lieutenant Nunn. At this stage we were unaware that he had been shot down. Both Pucarás then continued to attack me in successive passes, and after perhaps two or three more attacks when I was flying at extremely low level, I found myself close to Camilla Creek House where ground troops were able to engage the enemy aircraft with small arms and drive them off. Throughout all the engagements, my air gunner, Sergeant John Glaze, was positioned in the back of the Scout and was giving me a running commentary on the Pucarás' attacks, which I was able to respond to. The ground we were flying over was very exposed with no cover whatsoever, and the low cloud base had kept the enemy aircraft close to our operating height.

The closest [we came] to being hit was a salvo of rocket fire which passed ahead and behind my aircraft, simultaneously throwing large amounts of dirt and soil in the air as a result of the explosions. It was during this attack that I recall instinctively reaching down to the control panel and operating the windscreen wipers to clear the windscreen and offer better vision. Other attacks by cannon and machine gun were equally close, but luckily the aircraft suffered no material damage. Following the breaking off of the enemy aircraft, I immediately found a safe area to land near the Camilla Creek defences, made my fastest ever shutdown and dived into the nearest trench with Sergeant Glaze. I had been lucky during my two or three minutes under attack: I was so at one with the aircraft after nearly three years that it was like a second skin. I could fly it to its limits and at times we had been literally inches off the ground.

On hearing of the loss of the second Scout, Niblett was called forward by one of the squadron Gazelles to where Nunn's helicopter had crashed after the pilot had been shot and killed during the attempted evasion. Nunn's air gunner, Sergeant Bill Belcher, was seriously injured and had lost part of a leg but had been thrown out of the Scout when it impacted the ground. It was obvious that nothing could be done for Nunn, but Belcher was given immediate first aid and then loaded onto Niblett's aircraft to be flown to the hospital at Ajax Bay for immediate surgery. The next day, Niblett returned to recover Nunn's body from the crash scene. Nunn was buried at Ajax Bay alongside the other casualties from Goose Green the following day. It later emerged that one of the Argentine Pucarás that had attacked the two Scouts flew into a mountain on its return trip, killing the pilot, Lieutenant Miguel Giménez, whose remains were not discovered for another four years.

Niblett also recalled how, on 3 June 1982, he had been involved in another rescue:

The weather at first light was particularly bad and had prevented helo [helicopter] support to the front line. A call was received in Brigade requesting an urgent casevac [casualty evacuation] for a Marine who had lost a foot in a minefield explosion during an overnight reconnaissance patrol. The injury was such that they could not move the casualty themselves and a helo casevac was the only safe option in the circumstances, as speed was important. I elected to accept the mission and, with Sergeant Glaze, departed Teal Inlet in a slow hover taxi in poor visibility, once again following the only set of telephone wires which the map showed led towards the area we needed to reach some 15km away. On the first attempt, the weather closed in completely and we were unable to climb onto the higher ground, and instead diverted to pick up another casualty from a nearer unit who we returned to the Field Dressing Station at Teal. We immediately made a second attempt with similar results, and on the third attempt we finally succeeded in reaching the mountainous area where 42 Commando was operating. After a quick brief on the ground we continued to move forward, still in very poor visibility, and eventually we located the casualty, loaded him on board and returned him to Teal Inlet for treatment. All in all, a very testing but satisfying sortie carried out in almost impossible weather conditions. Luckily, the Marine concerned recovered well.

Niblett only learnt of his gallantry award when back in Britain – on the morning of 8 October 1982, when it was announced in *The London Gazette*. He was called to see his squadron CO Major Peter Cameron and was 'dumbfounded' but proud to discover the news. Between 1983 and 1995, Niblett completed further staff and flying tours in the Royal Marines.

However, in 1987, he realised that he was suffering from the effects of PTSD as a result of his experiences in the Falklands. Niblett has spoken honestly and movingly about his battle with PTSD – which eventually cost him his first marriage, from which he has a son – in a book, *The Scars of War*. He told the book's author, Hugh McManners, how life had been difficult in the five years after the Falklands War and how he was burdened by the loss of comrades, particularly Nunn. 'When you lose someone close to you, someone you like very much, you feel anger at the safeness of the normal world, turning against people and the environment in which you once felt comfortable. You come to distrust and resent authority,' he said. It was not until Niblett read a newspaper article about a survey on post-Falklands trauma, conducted by Royal Navy psychiatrist Surgeon Commander (later Surgeon Captain) Morgan O'Connell, that he realised he had all the symptoms of someone with PTSD.

For the first time, he addressed the issue that led to his removal from the Royal Naval Staff College at Greenwich and had several sessions with O'Connell. Eventually, Niblett made a return trip to the Falkland Islands to relive incidents that had troubled him and to visit Nunn's grave to pay his final respects. However, a recurrence of his health problems associated with PTSD resulted in Niblett retiring early from the Royal Marines in 1995, aged forty-five.

After ending his military service, Niblett worked initially as a Ministry of Defence civil servant and then with his local health authority. After finally retiring in early 2002, aged fifty-two, he moved to France with his second wife, Mary, and they lived in Brittany for eight years. Eleven years ago, in 2010, the couple returned to Britain, and they now live happily on a smallholding near King's Lynn, Norfolk, with their three horses, eight chickens, five cats and dog.

Prior to the publication of this book, Niblett asked me to add a personal postscript to his write-up. He wrote:

> As the years pass and we approach the fortieth anniversary of the conflict, I think it is so important to recognise the incredible dedication of all the squadron ground crews, in particular the aircraft maintainers. Without their skill and total professionalism we, as aircrew who were fortunate to be recognised for our contribution to the success of the campaign, could not have achieved what we did. Their contribution was vital and for so long barely recognised but equally deserving of praise.

WILLIAM CHRISTOPHER O'BRIEN

Service: Royal Marines / Army / Royal Naval Reserve
Final rank: Lieutenant Commander (Royal Naval Reserve)
FALKLANDS WAR DECORATION / DISTINCTION:
DISTINGUISHED FLYING MEDAL (DFM)
DATES OF BRAVERY: MAY / JUNE 1982
GAZETTED: 8 OCTOBER 1982

William 'Uncle Bill' O'Brien, whose military career spanned thirty-eight remarkable years, is the only Royal Marine ever to have been awarded the Distinguished Flying Medal (DFM); no other Marine will in future receive the decoration because it is no longer awarded. Furthermore, O'Brien has the distinction of being awarded the only DFM of the Falklands War. He has enjoyed a long and varied military career that included, as well as his Falklands exploits, serving on the streets of Belfast, in the mountains of northern Iraq and in the most recent conflict in Afghanistan. During a tour of duty in Afghanistan from 2009 to 2010, O'Brien became both the only reservist pilot to fly front-line combat missions and the oldest Apache pilot to fly on operations, celebrating his fifty-fifth birthday in Helmand Province – hence his affectionate nickname of 'Uncle Bill'.

William Christopher O'Brien was born in Romford, Essex, on 16 November 1954. He was the son of two Irish car factory workers living in Coventry, where he attended Caludon Castle School, Wyken. He left school at sixteen and after a brief period working in the same factory as his parents, enlisted in the Royal Marines in 1972, aged seventeen. On completion of basic training, he was awarded the 'King's Badge' as the best all-round member of his recruit troop, 29 King's Squad. He was initially posted to 41 Commando, based in Malta, and then volunteered to join 42 Commando on a tour of Northern Ireland. He was promoted to Corporal and after completing an Arctic survival instructors' course became part of the cadre set up to train 42 Commando in Arctic warfare techniques for the first time.

Between 1974 and 1978 and at the height of The Troubles, O'Brien completed three tours of Northern Ireland. In 1978, he qualified as an air gunner with 3 Commando Brigade Air Squadron, and he then completed his fourth tour of Northern Ireland. His career changed direction after he successfully applied for pilot training as a result of the mentoring and guidance he received from many members of the squadron. O'Brien gained his pilot 'wings' in 1981 and was awarded the Bob Bowles Trophy as the best student on his course. After being posted to Montfortabeek Flight 45 Commando Group, Royal Marines, he completed his fifth and final tour of Northern Ireland.

After the outbreak of the Falklands War in 1982, it was with this unit that O'Brien found himself deployed to the South Atlantic to play his part in helping to regain the British territory as part of 'Operation Corporate'. In the war zone, O'Brien flew one of Montfortabeek Flight's three Gazelle helicopters in direct support of 2 PARA at Goose Green, and then, at one time or another, most of the other units involved in the conflict.

His DFM for courage during the Falklands War was announced on 8 October 1982, when his citation stated:

During the attack on Darwin and Goose Green Sergeant O'Brien piloted a Gazelle helicopter of M Flight, 3 Commando Brigade Air Squadron. For two days his helicopter conducted supply and casualty evacuation operations, often under enemy fire. With his Flight Commander, he also took part in seventeen night flying sorties to evacuate wounded personnel and resupply vital ammunition.

At times these sorties necessitated flying forward to company lines in the heat of battle and in appalling weather. The conspicuous gallantry and cool professionalism displayed on all these occasions was superb and Sergeant O'Brien made an outstanding contribution. His expertise and competence as a pilot has been widely admired and recognised.

In an interview at his home in Somerset, O'Brien told me how he and his fellow helicopter pilots had on the voyage down to the Falklands trained themselves to use the then new and fairly rudimentary night-vision goggles (known at the time as passive night goggles). He also said he felt a strong sense of responsibility for the troops on the ground, regardless of the threats posed by Argentinian air and land forces, which shot down a number of Royal Marine helicopters:

> I felt a huge obligation to the infantry because I knew what it was like to be running short of ammunition, to be wet, dirty, bone tired, hungry and thoroughly frightened. These were the same men with whom, up until just a few years earlier, I would have been sharing the trenches. So I felt a huge affinity towards them and felt I had to go the extra mile to discharge my responsibility.

O'Brien added:

> I landed one time at Goose Green during a mortar barrage. I could see the plumes of smoke and explosions and could feel a slight con-cussion through the airframe, but I felt detached in my own space – because the helicopter was so noisy you couldn't hear the battle unfolding. I really thrived on the intensity of it, the test if you like, and frankly missed it when I returned to Britain after the war.

O'Brien heard the news of his gallantry medal while back in Brit-ain undergoing a senior command course, required for promotion from Corporal to Substantive Sergeant (he had been an acting Sergeant during the Falklands campaign). He was 'very pleased' to discover he was being awarded the DFM and soon afterwards, along with his wife Helen and their two daughters, found himself at an investiture at Buckingham Palace. O'Brien received his medal from the Queen, who mentioned during their brief chat that her son Prince Andrew had also flown helicopters during the war. As O'Brien was leaving Buckingham Palace, Lieutenant General Sir

Steuart Pringle, then Commandant General of the Royal Marines, stopped his staff car at the gates in order to shake him by the hand.

O'Brien was at pains to tell me that he had done no more than many other courageous helicopter pilots from the squadron who were doing 'very much the same thing and I want to acknowledge that'. He noted that there was a more general citation for 3 Commando Brigade Air Squadron for their contribution to the war effort. Dated 14 June 1982, it read:

> From the first landings in San Carlos Water on 21 May until the Argentine surrender 3 Commando Brigade Air Squadron RM (Major CP Cameron) supported the landing forces often under appalling conditions, by day and night, and in the early stages, were frequently attacked by Argentine fighter and ground attack aircraft. During the initial landings and in the course of the attack on Darwin and Goose Green the Squadron lost three aircraft to enemy action together with four aircrew killed and two wounded. The Squadron was involved in every major ground battle during the campaign in a variety of roles; reconnaissance, liaison, the movement of ammunition to the front line and the recovery of casualties from the forward positions. All these were undertaken in a variety of weather conditions, sometimes at night and often under fire. Its six Scout and nine Gazelle helicopters flew a total of 2,110 hours in just over three weeks reflecting a remarkable rate of serviceability and flying. The skill and courage of the aircrew backed by the skill and devotion to duty of the ground support enabled the Squadron to make a significant contribution to the defeat of the Argentine ground forces and their surrender on June 14.

Next, O'Brien qualified on Lynx helicopters, and in 1984 he became a qualified helicopter instructor, being awarded the Westland Trophy as the best student on his course. O'Brien was commissioned into the Royal Marines in 1985. Still serving with 3 Commando Brigade Air Squadron, he took part in 'Operation Haven' in southern Turkey and northern Iraq at the time of the First Gulf War – his first experience of working with and observing the US Apache attack helicopters in action.

He became the Lynx Flight Commander of 3 Commando Brigade Air Squadron and then served as the first Royal Marines officer on Army Flying Standards, the group responsible for maintaining the highest standards of flying in the army. In 1999, he had another change of career direction, transferring with the rank of Major to the Army Air Corps (AAC) in order to fly Apaches. 'I had wanted to fly attack helicopters for as long as I could remember and so I took the opportunity when it was offered,' he said. O'Brien was posted to America, where he became a qualified Apache pilot at Fort Rucker, Alabama, in 1999. On his return to the UK, he was posted to the Attack Helicopter Training Unit (which later became 673 Squadron Army School of Aviation).

In 2003, O'Brien became the senior flying instructor of the newly formed Air Manoeuvre Training Advisory Team, responsible for delivering 'conversion to role' (effectively combat skills training) to the Field Army, enabling the first combat-ready AAC Apache Regiment, 9 Regiment AAC, at Dishforth in Yorkshire. In 2005, at the age of fifty, O'Brien retired from the military but was then employed by a private company as its first civilian qualified helicopter instructor, flying with 673 Squadron. In 2008, O'Brien was commissioned into the Royal Naval Reserve and volunteered for service in Afghanistan.

Although his wife suggested it might have been 'a midlife crisis', O'Brien insists his reasons for wanting to serve in the war zone were straightforward:

I had never been on operations in an Apache. I was training Apache pilots to fly but I was also a gunnery instructor involved in pre-deployment training for Afghanistan. In order better to understand their requirements, I thought I should experience operations in Afghanistan for myself. Once I was there, I again felt a huge, almost parental, responsibility to the troops on the ground.

O'Brien was deployed with 663 Squadron, based at Camp Bastion, on 4 September 2009 – a week before the eighth anniversary of 9/11. Christened 'Uncle Bill' by his more youthful comrades, O'Brien found himself alongside many of the pilots he had trained, none of whom had even been born when he was awarded his green beret (presented to those who complete the tough qualifying course to become a Royal Marine). O'Brien's operational duties ended in January 2010, when he was fifty-five, and he then briefly returned to his duties as a flying instructor with 673 Squadron.

O'Brien finally retired in December 2010. In July that year, he received a Personal Commendation from then Commander Joint Helicopter Command, Rear Admiral Tony Johnstone-Burt. The lengthy citation was an affectionate testimonial to an extraordinary career:

Mr O'Brien is a civilian Qualified Helicopter Instructor currently serving in 673 (Attack Helicopter Training) Squadron in Middle Wallop and is ultimately responsible for the training of future Apache pilots during a period of surge to meet expanding operational output. A former officer in the Royal Marines, Mr O'Brien is a quiet and unassuming man whose faithful service, tireless dedication and devotion to duty is an inspiration to everyone with whom he comes into contact.

After a service flying career that spanned service on Op Corporate in the Falklands to early conversion onto the Apache, Mr O'Brien retired and joined Aviation Training International Limited in late 2005 as a civilian flying instructor. Since that time he has trained many students on Conversion to Type courses. Not satisfied with this, he recently volunteered to reinstate his commission as a reservist in the Fleet Air Arm and then deploy on a four-month tour to Afghanistan as an Apache Aircraft Commander in the rank of Lieutenant Commander – this despite being aged fifty-five and a Grandfather to boot!

During this tour he served in support of numerous high intensity operations, overcoming adversity in the face of many challenging aviation situations. His sustained commitment and self sacrifice in a highly charged operational environment proved legendary. Although his deployment attracted considerable media attention Mr O'Brien remained humble and modest throughout. His Commanding Officer described him as an 'exceptional officer, aviator and role model'. He does not seek any public recognition for his contribution and would be highly embarrassed by any award.

Mr O'Brien remains passionate about aviation and imparting knowledge to his students who, in turn, hold him in high regard. He is a gentle giant of a man who has given much to the benefit of others. For his exceptional and loyal service, and the totality of his commitment, Mr O'Brien is awarded the Commander Joint Helicopter Command's Personal Commendation.

The award could hardly have been delivered in more unusual circumstances. Shortly after retiring from the military for the second time, O'Brien was walking with friends on Dartmoor, Devon. After stopping for lunch at The Plume of Feathers Inn in Princetown, the group heard the sound of a helicopter. The aircraft landed behind the pub and its crew came into the bar to hand over the award to its recipient.

'I couldn't have been more surprised; clearly someone in the party had colluded in the delivery arrangements. That's mates for you!' O'Brien told me. A married man with three children and five grandchildren, O'Brien is enjoying his retirement at his home in Somerset.

CHAPTER 5

THE SAS OFFENSIVE

Chapter 3 examined the role of the SAS and other Special Forces units in carrying out reconnaissance duties in the build-up to war. Before that, Chapter 2 dealt with the involvement of 'D' Squadron, SAS and SBS members in 'Operation Paraquet', the retaking of the British islands of South Georgia.

This chapter examines, through individual stories, the role of the SAS as an offensive unit. This was, of course, the very reason that The Regiment had been formed four decades earlier – to carry out hit-and-run raids in North Africa, and later in mainland Europe during the Second World War. As detailed in the introduction to Chapter 3, both 'D' and 'G' Squadrons were quickly deployed to the South Atlantic in the spring of 1982, with their SAS leaders keen for them to have a role if diplomacy failed and war loomed.

Once the fighting began, the role for the SAS was always going to be to attack specific targets rather than to take part in the major battles – a role better suited to the Parachute Regiment and other units. Surprise has always been a key element of Special Forces assaults, enabling a small, well-trained, highly equipped force to do great damage to a larger force or a major target. In many ways, the attack by forty-five men from 'D' Squadron on the airstrip on Pebble Island on 14 May 1982 was a quintessential SAS raid. Lifted by helicopter onto the small island off the north coast of West Falkland, they destroyed eleven enemy winged aircraft / helicopters in minutes. Even more significantly, they denied the enemy the further use of the airfield and, for all this damage, suffered just one minor casualty.

However, just five days after this success, the SAS suffered a terrible tragedy, one entirely unrelated to any enemy action. While cross-decking, transporting men and equipment from HMS Hermes *to HMS* Intrepid *over a distance of around half a mile, a Sea King helicopter crashed into the sea. Of the thirty men on board, only nine survived, by scrambling out into the freezing sea. Of the twenty-two fatalities, eighteen were SAS members. General Peter de la Billière, the Director of the SAS, was woken with news of the disaster at his London flat. 'Accentuated by the hour, this was a savage blow: I did not immediately have the names of the men who had been killed, but it was a certain fact that I had known many of them, and to a small regiment this was an immense loss,' he later wrote in his autobiography* Looking for Trouble. *A bird strike was suspected of causing the disaster, as the helicopter had been circling before landing on the second ship when its engines cut out.*

Despite the huge loss, the SAS was soon back in the heat of the action. On 21 May, as the main British landings took place at San Carlos, the SAS carried out diversionary attacks in the areas around the Argentine-held settlement of Darwin and the nearby Goose Green air strip. The attack from 'D' Squadron on the Argentine positions prevented the enemy from targeting the landing British troops. Intelligence gathered after the war discovered that the Argentine forces believed they were under assault from at least a battalion-sized formation – in fact, the attacking force numbered just sixty.

Unsurprisingly given the ferocity of the war, there were other setbacks for the SAS other than the Sea King helicopter crash. Notably, on 10 June the Argentines spotted an SAS patrol on Port Howard, West Falkland – a position overlooking Falkland Sound. In the gun battle that followed, the Patrol Commander, Captain John Hamilton, was shot and killed and a second SAS member captured. Hamilton, who had led the successful attack on Pebble Island and was a hugely popular officer, was later awarded a posthumous Military Cross (MC). He had tried to shoot his way out of the situation and bravely gave covering fire for his companion.

The bravery of men from the SAS and SBS continued right up to the end of the war. For example, on 13 June, the SAS along with men from the SBS attempted to carry out a diversionary amphibious raid on Port Stanley Harbour. The attack was intended to coincide with 2 PARA's assault on Wireless Ridge. The plan was that four rigid raiding craft, carrying a troop from 'D' Squadron along with six SBS men, would travel quickly across the harbour and attack the oil storage facilities. However, the assault party was spotted and came under such heavy fire that the raiders withdrew – fortunately without any fatalities. The next day, the SAS's task was a more welcome one: Lieutenant Colonel Michael Rose, the Commanding Officer of 22 SAS, flew by helicopter into Port Stanley to help negotiate the terms of the Argentine surrender.

This chapter also examines one of the biggest controversies of the war in terms of the SAS's involvement in it: the decision to deploy an SAS team to the Argentine mainland – initially a reconnaissance team and then a larger assault team. The aim was to use a third SAS unit – 'B' Squadron – to attack the Río Grande air base with the hope of destroying the deadly French-made Exocet missiles and the aircraft used to fly them towards their targets. However, after the initial reconnaissance, codenamed 'Operation Plum Duff', the larger mission, codename 'Operation Mikado', was aborted. The decision to attempt, and later call off, the operation led to huge tensions within the SAS, particularly in 'B' Squadron, and the dismissal of one senior officer for his reservations over the wisdom of the mission. To this day there is a lively debate over whether the whole mission was inspired, or sheer madness.

ANDREW LEGG

Service: Army (SAS)

Final rank: Captain

FALKLANDS WAR DECORATION / DISTINCTION: **N/A**

DATE OF BRAVERY: N/A

GAZETTED: N/A

Andy Legg commanded what was arguably the most audacious mission of the entire war. His SAS team was sent to infiltrate Argentine airfields and destroy enemy aircraft and Exocet missiles destined for British ships. However, after various setbacks and suspected detection, his 'suicide mission' was eventually aborted and, as a result, no gallantry medals were awarded for their actions.

Little is known about Legg's early life, but he graduated from Reading University in 1976 with an MSc in applied mathematics. In March 1977, he joined the Royal Hampshire Regiment in Northern Ireland via a direct entry course from the Royal Military Academy, Sandhurst. Legg was determined to join the SAS and passed its tough selection course in 1978, only to be told he had to do a second tour in Northern Ireland. In August 1980, Legg passed the SAS selection course a second time (he was forced to take it again due to a change of training personnel), and in January 1981 he joined 'B' Squadron as a Troop Commander. He then served with the SAS in Oman, in Northern Ireland and as part of the UK's anti-terrorist team.

In April 1982, a few days after the Argentine invasion of the Falklands, Legg was ordered to report to the SAS base in Hereford. At the start of the war, Legg was twenty-eight years old and a Captain in 'B' Squadron. He was described by one source as 'an unconventional officer who was popular with his men'.

The briefing for the mission came at 8 a.m. the next day: Legg was told there would be an undercover SAS operation by 'B' Squadron to remove the threat of enemy jets stationed at Río Grande on Tierra del Fuego, off the southern tip of Argentina, 400 miles from the Falklands. The Argentine Super Étendard jets carried Exocet missiles and posed a serious threat to the Royal Navy Task Force and the 5,000 troops heading for the islands.

The task for Legg and his men was to destroy the jets, and their mission would be called 'Operation Mikado'. It had echoes of some of the early missions in North Africa in the days and weeks immediately after the formation of the SAS in 1941. Then, some of the so-called 'SAS Originals', including daring men like Blair 'Paddy' Mayne, destroyed hundreds of enemy planes during hit-and-run raids. 'Operation Mikado' was also partly inspired by 'Operation Entebbe', the counter-terrorist raid by the Israeli Defense Forces in Uganda on 4 July 1976, which ended in the successful rescue of 102 of the 106 hostages still being held after their aircraft was hijacked.

The plan for the 1982 raid, just six years after Entebbe, was that two C-130 Hercules transport planes, with a total of around sixty men on board, would make a low-level approach over the sea at night and land stealthily at Río Grande. After a hurried landing, Land Rovers armed with heavy machine guns would burst onto the airfield. The Land Rovers would then fan out, destroy the planes and kill the pilots in their accommodation blocks. Once again, this would chime with the efforts of the earliest SAS soldiers, who were instructed that it was easier to replace a plane than a trained pilot. Paddy Mayne in particular was ruthless when it came to carrying out these orders: no enemy pilot was spared. Once their mission in southern Argentina was over, the squadron would then split into small groups and make their way to the border with Chile – on the basis that the two Hercules planes would have already had to take off again immediately after delivering the men and their vehicles.

The plan had been sanctioned by Mrs Thatcher and her War Cabinet, and the SAS men were not invited to debate the pros and cons of their mission. However, there were, perhaps inevitably, plenty of raised eyebrows. In particular, it was known that Argentina had sophisticated radar systems: how would it be possible to land two fully laden RAF planes without being detected?

The next few days were spent training for the mission at day and night: there were night and long-distance forced marches in Wales, hours spent on the rifle ranges, night-navigation exercises, night-ambush drills and parachute drops. At Wick Airport in the north of Scotland after a heavy snowfall, the SAS men practised low-level approaches and landings by night to test the feasibility of flying in low off the sea without being picked up on radar. So, as both 'D' and 'G' Squadrons were sent to the South Atlantic, 'B' Squadron was held back... but for how long?

On 14 May 1982, a week before British troops were due to land on the Falklands, Legg and his men met with Brigadier (later General) Peter de la Billière for their final briefing in the operations centre at Hereford HQ. At the time, de la Billière was the most decorated soldier in the British Army and hugely respected both inside and outside The Regiment. In an article for *The Times*, Legg claimed that it was de la Billière who personally informed him that the mission had changed: instead of a full-scale attack on Río Grande, Legg would be leading a nine-man patrol on a search-and-destroy mission to Río Grande codenamed 'Operation Plum Duff'.

'Operation Plum Duff' was intended as a recce mission for 'Operation Mikado'. Legg and his men were under no illusions about the difficulty of their mission, and much of the detail was still under consideration. When one of the SAS men asked about the method of insertion into Argentina, de la Billière apparently told him: 'We think you will be using a submarine, but we could be using a fast frigate and a patrol boat, or we could use a helicopter. Tomorrow you will be taken to Ascension Island and then flown down to the South Atlantic, where you will parachute into the sea.'

According to Legg, he then asked, 'If we are going into Argentina on a helicopter one way, what happens when they find that helicopter? You cannot just get rid of it. It is pretty large.' According to Legg once more, de la Billière basically replied, 'It is not your concern.' In fact, Legg's concerns grew and grew. He was particularly worried that intelligence on the strength and positions of the Argentine forces on the mainland was in short supply. As a result, Legg and his men were short on confidence too. By the time they reached Ascension Island, there were growing fears that they were on a 'one-way trip'. As well as complaining of little intelligence, they complained that they had few maps, no aerial photographs of Río Grande and little idea of any enemy forces. 'It was going to be a wing-and-a-prayer job,' Legg later insisted.

In his article for *The Times* published on 3 May 2018, Legg said that after another ten hours flying down over the South Atlantic, he and his men made a rendezvous with RFA *Fort Austin* off the Falklands and parachuted fully loaded into the sea with all their kit. He said the men had hoped to be fished out of the sea swiftly in a small boat, but it was in fact twenty minutes before they were found and taken to HMS *Invincible*. The next day, the men were told that they were going into Argentina aboard a stripped-down Sea King helicopter, which would then be abandoned and blown up by the crew. Furthermore, according to Legg, the men had food for only three days, because as well as taking their normal kit, weapons and ammunition, they had lots of explosives. 'We'd been issued with one-man tents, but because of all the extra stuff we didn't have room for the tent poles,' Legg wrote.

When they came to depart, the SAS took off from HMS *Invincible* in darkness, and Legg could soon see the lights of an oil rig. Near the Argentine coast, the navigator apparently told Legg that the aircraft had been detected on the enemy radar, so the plane started to fly at low level through the fog. During the flight, the Royal Marines pilot and the navigator were using night-vision goggles. After a further fifteen minutes, according to Legg's account, the men reached the drop-off point north-east of Río Grande airbase on the island of Tierra del Fuego. Legg wrote how one of the patrol had disembarked from the aircraft and was standing alone on Argentine soil when the party saw lights and a flare going off. 'We were clearly compromised, so we hauled him and his kit back on board and headed for the secondary drop-off point, flying at low level,' Legg wrote.

Legg described how, as the flight headed towards the border with Chile, the visibility was poor and the aircraft had to gain altitude to 2,000ft – a height at which the plane could be picked up on radar. There and then, the decision was taken to continue into Chile and land as close to the border as possible. Legg said that the intention was then to cross back into Argentina and continue the mission. He added that, after landing, the SAS men immediately headed back towards Argentina across fairly rough ground. As their adventure continued the crew chose a position close to Punta Arenas, Chile, to destroy their helicopter in the sea by blowing it up with demolition charges.

According to Legg, the party established a lying-up position, attempted to work out exactly where they were and made contact with their SAS base at Hereford using a sophisticated satellite phone borrowed from US Special Forces. Once they got through to Hereford, Legg was asked for his wife's name as proof that they were not being held at gunpoint by the enemy. Legg gave her correct name and they said: 'Right, carry on – get some eyes on the ground.'

Legg described the conditions in southern Chile, close to the Argentine border, as 'bloody awful' and much colder than he and his men had expected. By this point, one of the party was 'quite ill', having got exceptionally cold from spending so long in the sea the previous day. The man received medication and was allowed to get some rest as they got closer to the border.

However, by the third day, the party was running out of rations and so they talked to Hereford again over the satellite phone. At this point, according to Legg, the party was told to move west to a position from where, once they could provide a precise location, they could be picked up. But the batteries ran out on the satellite phone and they could not arrange a pick-up. Legg wrote, 'We could probably manage for six days on three days' rations, but could not hold out for ever. Operation Plum Duff was running out of time.'

Legg took the decision to go with another SAS man to try to get help, leaving the rest of the party behind. They walked for several hours along a road until a Toyota pick-up truck came along. The driver gave the pair a lift and dropped them off at a small town called Porvenir, where they stood out as they were dressed in uniform and carrying 9mm pistols. Next, the men, who were carrying both US dollars and Argentine currency, booked into a local guest house from where Legg phoned the British Embassy in Punta Arenas. He explained their predicament but claimed his request for active assistance fell on deaf ears.

As Legg and his comrades wandered around Porvenir at dark, he said that 'something unbelievable happened'. He noticed a four-wheel-drive vehicle and looked through a restaurant window to see three other SAS men inside. Legg said he had no information to suggest other SAS were in southern Chile, let alone in this small 'shanty town'. Using their vehicle, Legg collected the rest of his party and all their kit, and then they 'holed up' in a safe house. By this point, Hereford knew their whereabouts.

In his article, Legg insisted that he and his men still hoped to get into Argentina and finish the operation, but they were flown on a small Chilean Air Force plane to Santiago. They remained in the Chilean capital in a safe house, a spacious bungalow, for a week, waiting to see what Hereford would ask them to do next. By this point they were in civilian clothes, but they spent their time cleaning their weapons and resting. 'Our expectation was that we were going to be sent back south,' he wrote.

Then, one morning they were ordered back to Hereford, travelling on a civilian flight in borrowed civilian clothes while their kit was moved back on a different flight. Each SAS man was given a passport shortly before they got on the plane, and they were deliberately spread around the aircraft so they did not talk to each other. The flight went to São Paulo in Brazil, then to Lisbon in Portugal and on to London. On arrival, they did not have to go through passport control.

Legg wrote, 'The next day, at HQ, I discovered that my squadron boss had been dismissed after saying that Operation Mikado was not simply foolhardy, but downright unachievable.' Legg said that many members of 'B' Squadron held the same view. Legg wrote that an Intelligence Corps officer attached to the SAS came and said: 'Just calm down and deal with it. Keep your mouth shut because the stakes are so high on this.' According to Legg, the Intelligence Corps source later told him that they subsequently discovered the Argentine Air Force was not actually keeping their planes on the Río Grande airfield at all; they were stationed on runways on the country's huge estancias, or cattle ranches, which had their own airfields.

Legg noted that de la Billière later blamed 'B' Squadron for the whole episode. 'I was dismayed to find that the attitude of this unit remained lukewarm,' de la Billière wrote in his autobiography. Speaking of 'Operation Mikado' and the dismissal of a senior officer, the General said, 'I had to do what I thought was right for all the people whose lives were going to be at stake.' However, he declined to provide a detailed account of the failed mission.

Legg's behaviour on the mission was later the subject of an internal army investigation. 'Even though the board of inquiry exonerated me, I felt I was being blamed for something,' he wrote. Legg left the SAS of his own volition the year after the war ended, meaning he only served for six years in the army, three of them in the SAS. He felt that his once promising career was the price paid for the failed mission and the controversy around it. To some in the SAS, 'Operation Mikado' became known as 'Operation Certain Death'.

In his article for *The Times*, Legg concluded: 'Today I have moved on, but I've still got my demons ... Who dares wins [the SAS motto], but proper planning, reliable information and back-up always help.' After leaving the SAS, Legg worked for a time as a maths teacher. Today a father of four, he lives in the south of England, and he declined to be interviewed for this book.

HENRY McCALLION GOW
Service: Army (SAS)
Final rank: Corporal
FALKLANDS WAR DECORATION / DISTINCTION: **N/A**
DATE OF BRAVERY: N/A
GAZETTED: N/A

Harry Gow has enjoyed an eventful and at times brutal existence, with violence never far away in both his personal and professional life. He left school at sixteen after the toughest of childhoods and went on to serve in both the South African Special Forces and the SAS before obtaining a law degree from Leeds Metropolitan University and becoming a barrister. Although Gow ultimately played only a walk-on part in recapturing the Falklands, he has some remarkable stories to tell about the 1982 war. He also provides another fascinating insight into the secretive and controversial 'Operation Mikado'.

Henry McCallion Gow, who was always known as 'Harry', was born on 26 January 1953 in a tough working-class area of Glasgow, the eldest of five children born to his mother Mary. His father, Allan, was a small-time Glasgow gangster, and domestic violence in their household was commonplace. Gow's grandfather, Henry McCallion, served in the First World War and was awarded the MM for bravery with the Argyll and Sutherland Highlanders at the Battle of Ypres. By the age of eleven, Gow had attended twelve different schools both in Glasgow and in cities in the north of England, where his family had briefly relocated. For part of his childhood, he was brought up by his maternal grandmother. In his own words: 'I was dragged kicking and screaming through a time that only resembled childhood into a premature adulthood.' He left school at sixteen – by which point he had attended some twenty schools – with no qualifications but an abundance of physical and mental scars that would remain with him for life.

Aged seventeen, he joined the army, enlisting into the Parachute Regiment after hearing that its members were 'the toughest in the army'. After taking a train to Aldershot, Hampshire, home of the Paras, he did not see any member of his family for the next four years. He passed the brutal training course and received his 'wings', or coveted red beret. On 2 January 1971, still only seventeen, he joined 2 PARA and would serve with the regiment for seven years. Within four months of joining 2 PARA, he was on his first tour to Northern Ireland – it would prove to be the first of no less than seven tours to the province during The Troubles, but he found them increasingly wearing. 'I was sick and tired of being treated as a moving target [for terrorists] in Northern Ireland, and I wanted to get some real combat experience,' Gow told me.

On 5 May 1977, he was officially discharged from the Parachute Regiment in the rank of Corporal, having already lined himself up an interview with the South African Defence Force. He landed in Pretoria on 6 May 1977. 'I don't intend to die for anybody, but I am quite willing to risk my life for South Africa,' he had said during his interview, and the job was soon his. He soon embarked on Special Forces training and served in South Africa for two and a half years with the South African Special Forces Brigade, known locally as the 'Recces'.

In late 1979, Gow was back in the UK and preparing to rejoin the army in order to undergo challenging SAS training, first on the Brecon Beacons and later in the Belize jungle. He was soon a fully badged member of the SAS, first serving as a trooper in 'A' Squadron in Northern Ireland, and later in 'B' Squadron after the break-up of his first marriage. During his time in the SAS, he undertook three deployments in Northern Ireland, his old stomping ground from his days with the Paras.

In the early spring of 1982, there was growing speculation that Argentina might try to invade the Falkland Islands. Gow's immediate response echoed that of the majority of other British servicemen: 'Where the hell are the Falklands?' Most people in Britain, including senior politicians, were initially dismissive that the tensions would lead to war and instead Gow and other members of 'B' Squadron were preparing to fly to 'Flintlock', an annual exercise held in Germany. All that changed on 2 April 1982, when a Troop Sergeant appeared in the NAAFI at Hereford and announced: 'The Argentinians have landed an invasion force on the Falklands. It looks like war.' 'D' Squadron was the stand-by squadron and had already been deployed; 'B' Squadron was originally the next in line, and its members were hopeful of seeing action until it was revealed that 'G' Squadron had jumped ahead of them in the queue. Was it possible that three squadrons might be deployed?

In his autobiography *Killing Zone*, written under the pseudonym Harry McCallion and first published in 1995, Gow details how tough the training became for 'B' Squadron's possible role in the Falklands War:

> Boy did we train. Never before in my military career had I gone into such a continuous spate of prolonged and intense preparation. We spent hours practising four-man drills, troop drills and attacks, and squadron drills and attacks. We shot every weapon in the armoury and when we had done that we got new weapons, American M202s, four-barrelled rocket launchers and 60mm assault mortars. Our normal day started at 0700 and we worked until 2200.
>
> We got daily briefings from the Intelligence Corps, those green-bereted wonders. They went into some detail but almost always ended with the warning that in their opinion the whole thing would be settled politically before any landing by British troops. They were giving the same view only days before the shooting started. These stalwarts failed to realize that the Argentinian junta had staked its very existence on this invasion, and Maggie Thatcher would never

back down. I sometimes wonder what the 'intelligence' in Intelligence Corps stood for.

We trained hard, night and day, but in our heart of hearts none of us really believed that we would be deployed. Between 10 and 26 April 1982 elements of D Squadron assisted in the retaking of South Georgia. I was on guard duty on the 21st, the night two helicopters crashed on Fortuna Glacier. The initial reports were conflicting: men missing, then hurt, then dead, then missing again. It was with great relief at the end of the night that we heard that, thanks to the heroic efforts of an RAF pilot, all our men had been evacuated safely.

With the retaking of South Georgia our Task Force was within striking distance of the Falklands and none of us expected a long campaign to recapture the islands. This was not going to be B Squadron's war.

However, as tensions escalated, it emerged that 'B' Squadron was being held in reserve for a Special Forces operation. Its soldiers soon learnt the details of the daring mission codenamed 'Operation Mikado': its aim was to attack the home base of Argentina's five Super Étendard striker fighters at Río Grande, Tierra del Fuego, destroying the aircraft, their Exocet missiles and killing their pilots. The details of the mission are revealed in this book's write-up on Captain Andy Legg. Gow, then aged twenty-nine, was not chosen for the nine-man recce mission led by Legg. However, he was allocated a key role in the main 'Operation Mikado' attack. Once again he takes up the story in his autobiography:

The next morning Boss M [the CO of 'B' Squadron – full name withheld for security reasons] told us that it had been decided that B Squadron would train for an assault on the Argentinian mainland, to attack and destroy the Super Étendards at source. Training would begin immediately. We would have about two weeks to prepare for the operation. We were already at a peak of training but this new phase would concentrate on the specific tactics to be employed on the proposed raid. The operation was in essence very simple. It was envisaged that two Hercules C130s would carry the Squadron in ... Once deployed on the ground the Squadron would fan out, destroying the Étendards and any Exocets we could find.

As detailed planning was impossible because we didn't know what we would encounter on the ground, our training concentrated on deploying from our aircraft as fast as possible in the few vital seconds after we landed. My task was to assault the officers' mess and kill every pilot there. If everything went to plan, we would hit them so fast they would be unable to react.

For the next week B Squadron began to assault airfields from northern Scotland to the Midlands and beyond. We practised low flying, combat loading and airfield assaults until we could do it blindfolded. Anyone who's never had the pleasure of low-level flying in a Hercules cannot imagine what it's like. Do it once and you'll never wonder again why sick people's faces are painted green in children's cartoons.

As our training intensified, divisions began to appear in the Squadron. From the start there had been those who'd been opposed to the operation. Most outspoken of these was my own troop staff sergeant, Jakey V. [full name also withheld for security reasons]. He made no secret of the fact that he believed the operation was ill-conceived and would lead inevitably to the destruction of the entire Squadron. Jakey's views were shared by a large number of the older hands.

While the nine-man recce was under way, opposition to 'Operation

Mikado' grew within 'B' Squadron, but one night in mid-May the men were told the job was on and they were to report for duty at 5 a.m. the next morning. In his autobiography, Gow described the scene as the men gathered to deploy on their mission:

We made our way to the interest room where the rest of the Squadron had assembled. Boss M, a tall man with thinning light-brown hair, drew himself up to his full height and delivered a stirring speech, 'Only one unit stands between the Task Force and hundreds of casualties. That unit is B Squadron, 22 SAS. We're going in, with help on the ground if possible, blind if not, but we're going in. Our country is at war and we're needed. I know none of you will let me down.' I felt the short hairs rise on the back of my neck; I took a series of short, sharp breaths. At that moment I would have led a charge against the devil in hell with a bucket of water.

We were told to make our way to the armoury to collect our weapons. I looked around for Jakey, but couldn't find him. I walked outside and bumped into the Director [Peter de la Billière] heading towards our Squadron office.

'Is your boss in?'

'Yes.'

'Is he alone?'

I nodded.

'Good,' he replied and brushed past me.

The news began to circulate that Jakey had RTUd [returned to unit] himself, believing the job was a suicide mission. He'd submitted his resignation to the OC the previous night when he'd been told the job was on. So well-respected was Jakey that the news came like a thunderbolt to us all. Groups stopped to discuss the situation. One was addressed by a senior sergeant.

'I think Jakey's right and we should support him by offering to resign also.'

Bob T. spoke up angrily. 'What you're suggesting is mutiny. I'll have none of it.'

There was a murmur of agreement. Even when this debate was going on, a fresh shock was delivered. Boss M had been sacked. When Jakey had announced his resignation the OC had in turn voiced his own doubts. The Director had sacked him that very morning. There hadn't been a shot fired against us in anger and already we were shell-shocked. The only good news was that Ian Crooke – Crooky as we all called him – the regimental second in command was taking over as Squadron commander. He was a no-nonsense, well-respected soldier.

All this absorbed each man's thoughts as we prepared to leave. Normally at this time the Squadron is a boisterous crowd shouting jokes and making noisy conversation. On board our bus not a word was spoken as the engines started and as we drove through the camp's gates I stared at the passing streets and wondered, as I'm sure each man did, if we'd ever see Hereford again.

Gow told me that he was always on the side of those who *did* want to carry out the daring mission. 'I was gung-ho and ready to go. There was a war on and I was up for it,' he said.

In his autobiography Gow described what happened next:

We deployed to Ascension Island, landing in the early hours of the morning. We were all tired and most of us were asleep long before our heads hit the pillow. The next morning we set off to our Squadron office, situated in a large tent some hundred metres from our bashas [shelters], to receive our first impromptu briefing. The gloom of the previous day had gone and the Squadron was its usual self, full of banter. Crooky ducked out from under the tent. One look at his face told me something was terribly wrong.

'Gentlemen, it is my sad duty to inform you that the Regiment [SAS] has suffered its largest casualties since the Second World War. A Sea King has crashed while cross-decking troops. There are twenty fatalities. I will now read out the confirmed casualty toll...' And so the list went on, each name bringing to mind a familiar face we would never see again.

'This news is a blow to us all. Any words I say will only be superficial,' Crooky added. 'There will be no more training this morning. Each of you have this time to come to terms with it.' We made our way silently back to the bashas. Not a word was spoken. It was like a funeral march, and in a way it was.

The next week was one of the most difficult of my life. The operation was on, only to be postponed for twelve, twenty-four or forty-eight hours. One moment we would be sitting in vehicles ready to drive to the airfield, the next the job was cancelled yet again. When I joined the Paras, I was told the story of Arnhem [the famous Second World War battle] in graphic detail. What particularly fascinated me was that, after a month of postponements, the Division had gone in, despite warnings from the Dutch Resistance that two Panzer Divisions were in the area. Now, all these years later, I understood. It wouldn't have mattered to me if the entire Argentinian Air Force was waiting just over the horizon. I just wanted to go. To get the thing over with, one way or another...

At 0600 [the next day] those who could stomach it ate breakfast. We crowded on to the trucks once again, then drove to the airfield. We loaded the aircraft for the assault, then each of us went to his pre-arranged position. After all the false starts, I felt calm and at ease now that we were ready to go. I'd never been afraid of death. Sometimes I'd even chased it. I wondered whether this was one of those times. On the faces of my comrades I saw a mixture of emotions: excitement on the faces of the younger ones, grim determination on the others.

A Land Rover appeared with several RAF personnel. Crooky was called off the aircraft – I thought to be given last-minute instructions. Then the engines slowly died. The job was cancelled, permanently. The RAF had discovered that the Argentinians had deployed a new radar on a boat just off the coast. The airfield we would be attacking would have too great a warning of our approach. We unloaded and made our way back to the bashas.

A lot has been said inside Special Forces circles about B Squadron and the operation that never was, and much of it has been derogatory. But, when the chips were down, when they told us to go, every man went, even those who thought we were doomed.

Crooke, the squadron CO, was keen for 'B' Squadron to assist the other two SAS squadrons already on the Falklands, and the training of the men continued on Ascension Island. In his autobiography Gow wrote:

The war was reaching its climax and still we hadn't been called forward. Then a new task beckoned: the airport at Port Stanley. The high command wanted it taken as part of the final assault. B Squadron had been trained for it. Hastily we rearranged ourselves for a combat parachute deployment. Once on the Task Force, the actual assault would go in by helicopter. We were to leave in three days – no ifs or buts. Two C130s plus refuelling aircraft were laid on. This time we would go.

Bob T., the legendary Fijian Tak, myself and several others decided to get drunk and we did so gloriously. At about three in the morning, twelve hours before the off, we were seated outside our basha and running short of beer. As the junior man present, I was dispatched to a nearby RAF basha to drum up some reserves. I returned with a goodly supply and a four-man RAF escort...

We were sober by 1400 when we loaded on to two Hercules. We would be jumping in dry suits because of the temperature of the water we would be landing in. Our equipment would be dropped in containers after us. The flight across was as eventful as the rest. One of our refuelling aircraft could not make the RV and had to turn back, meaning we lost half the Squadron, which also had to return. We kept going and the pilot, with some persuasion from Crooky, made our refuelling point. I could feel the butterflies start to flutter in my stomach. There was no turning back now.

The lights were dimmed, the rear door slowly opened. We shuffled up to the tailgate, the red light came on, we tensed, then the green. As I stepped out into the cold air I looked below me. I could see several ships and one to my right which had been badly damaged by a missile attack on its bow. I think it was the *Gloucester*, which had been hit by a land-based Exocet the previous night. Fast-moving inflatables were dotted between them, waiting to pluck us up, and I had no sooner hit the water than a hand grasped me and I was pulled aboard. We raced to a nearby frigate where I heard the sound of the Hercules coming in to drop our fighting equipment.

Over half the parachutes didn't open, a lot of precious equipment went to the bottom of the sea. It didn't matter to me. I didn't care where my equipment was. I was in the war, that was all that mattered. I turned towards the islands and pointed a dark finger in the direction of the enemy. 'You don't know what's coming,' I whispered.

Gow and his comrades from 'B' Squadron who had landed in the bitterly cold sea went below deck to get some dry clothing and a hot drink. They were told that in four hours' time they would be moved to HMS *Hermes* to prepare for their assault. Gow continues the story in his autobiography:

We were told to get some sleep. I managed to scrounge a bunk from a friendly sailor. Two hours later I was woken by a loudspeaker message: 'A white flag has been raised over Port Stanley. The war is over!'

I fervently hoped the message was wrong but within an hour it had been established that the Argentinians had surrendered. To say I was disappointed was an understatement. I had come so close to the action in a full-blown war and the opportunity to fight for my country, only to have the chance snatched from my grasp at the very last minute. I was almost inconsolable and prowled about the ship unable to come to terms with the situation. The frustrations of the last few months boiled up inside me. All those weeks with the prospect of violent actions and almost certain death hanging over us had taken their toll. Each of us had steeled himself for a mission of no return and now it had ended in anticlimax. A cascade of pent-up emotions went through me: anger, depression and perhaps, although I didn't recognize it then, relief. I found a quiet corner and for the first time in years had a good cry.

Within hours, Gow was in Port Stanley surveying a scene of joy and despair – the British servicemen were jubilant, but many of the enemy soldiers were frightened teenagers and by then POWs who 'staggered around, hollow-eyed, dirty and hungry'. Gow described an argument in which he intervened:

I heard raised voices and turned. Two Argentinian officers were arguing with a young Scots Guard lance corporal, to whom they refused to give their side-arms. I drifted over to stand a few feet behind the Guardsman. I wore no beret and was dressed in an SAS combat smock, jungle camouflaged trousers and a Royal Navy blue pullover. My hair was long, the wind blowing it behind me. I had a 48-hour beard and a thick, black, drooping moustache. The Argentinian Captain looked over the lance corporal's shoulder and our eyes met. In his I read arrogance and the bitter anger of defeat. What he saw in mine I don't know but his eyes suddenly widened as he glanced down at the weapon I was carrying: an American M203 equipped with a 40mm grenade launcher, the standard weapon of the SAS. I slipped off the safety-catch. Moving very slowly he handed over his automatic pistol without resistance.

Over the next few days the anger of young Argentine recruits towards their often bullying officers became apparent. Gow recalled:

Two days later [after the surrender] Argentinian other ranks attacked the officers' holding area and burnt it down. They were only dispersed when a platoon of 2 PARA, bayonets fixed, moved in to quell the disturbance.

Boat Troop [Gow's troop] stayed on the Falklands for six weeks after the war in case of an Argentinian counter-attack and were billeted in one of the few B&Bs on the island, the Ross Guest House. We spent the time visiting outlying farms where we were treated like VIPs. A cow would be slaughtered and we would be treated to an impromptu banquet.

We heard terrible stories of how the Argentinian officers had treated their men. On one occasion a lad of no more than seventeen had come to one of the farms to beg for food. He had been chased into a nearby peat shed, and when he refused to come out, an officer had thrown in a grenade. The farmer showed me where they had buried him. We made a note so that the grave could be located and the unknown soldier's body returned to his motherland.

Gow and his colleagues eventually returned to Britain on two flights: the first on a Hercules to Ascension Island, then a second flight with the 2nd Scots Guards and on to a heroes' welcome. A red carpet was laid out and a piper was playing 'Scotland the Brave' when they arrived. The Guards were able to enjoy a return in the spotlight, but as usual the SAS men had to remain in the shadows and discreetly return to Hereford. Gow's account of divisions within 'B' Squadron and the open hostility towards 'Operation Mikado' have been confirmed by several other sources.

As for Gow, he remained in the SAS until 1985 when he made another significant career switch, again leaving the army in the rank of Corporal. Although a Roman Catholic by birth, Gow had changed his faith while serving with the Paras in Northern Ireland to Church of Scotland. He applied for and was accepted into the Royal Ulster Constabulary (RUC). 'More than anything else the RUC offered me the chance to continue my own private little war with the IRA,' Gow wrote in his autobiography. In fact, while he was still training his RUC base came under a major mortar attack from IRA terrorists. Gow went to the aid of injured RUC men in the burning building and was later highly commended for his bravery. Gow and his friend, who was also highly commended for his courage, are believed to be the only RUC men in history to be so commended while still training. Gow then served in the RUC for five years until 1990.

His time in the RUC was ended by the serious injuries he received in a near-fatal car crash on the outskirts of Belfast. In the collision with another car, his head was thrown through the windscreen and the muscles in his back were torn to shreds. He was unable to walk properly for three years, meaning his RUC career was over and he returned to Hereford. Remarkably, without any qualifications and while recuperating, he decided to become a lawyer. First, he obtained a law degree and then was eventually called to the Bar in October 1995. Since then, he has worked as a barrister from his chambers in Liverpool. He also has a Master's degree in international relations from the University of East Anglia.

Gow, who lives in the north-west of England, has been married twice and had twin boys from his marriage to his late second wife, although one of his sons died from a heart attack. His remarkable and varied life perhaps epitomises the motto of the SAS: 'Who dares wins'.

SIDNEY ALBERT IVOR DAVIDSON
Service: Army (SAS)
Final rank: Sergeant
FALKLANDS WAR DECORATION / DISTINCTION: **N/A**
DATE OF BRAVERY: N/A
GAZETTED: N/A

Sidney Davidson fought in the SAS with great distinction during the early actions of the Falklands War. Serving with 'D' Squadron, 22 SAS Regiment, he played an important role in the capture of South Georgia from the Argentines and later in the raid on Pebble Island. Tragically, he was one of those killed on 19 May 1982 when the Sea King helicopter crashed into the sea while cross-decking off the Falkland Islands. The accident resulted in the largest single loss of life to the SAS since the Second World War, as eighteen of its serving members perished.

Sidney Albert Ivor Davidson, known by family and friends as 'Sid', was born on 18 November 1947 and spent part of his child-hood growing up in Chepstow, Gwent. He joined the Parachute Regiment in 1970 and then passed SAS selection in 1973, serving in Dhofar, Saudi Arabia (during 'Operation Storm'), and in Northern Ireland.

In early April 1982, military Commanders were asked to come up with a plan to remove the Argentines from South Georgia and the Falkland Islands. It was soon decided the first task would be to retake South Georgia, surrendered on 3 April following a heroic defence by twenty-two Royal Marines led by Lieutenant Keith Mills (as detailed earlier in this book). As well as providing a significant morale-booster, taking South Georgia would have major strategic advantages, notably that it could provide a secure base – beyond the reach of the Argentine Air Force – from which to assault the Falkland Islands. Such a move would also give the Task Force more time to gather intelligence and establish air superiority. 'Operation Paraquet' involved a force of SAS, SBS and Royal Marines, who were tasked with removing the Argentines led by the notorious Lieutenant Commander Alfredo Astiz. On 14 April, Major Guy Sheridan, Royal Marines, was ordered to plan covert surveillance of Leith and Grytviken to determine the strength and position of enemy forces. This would be carried out by patrols from the SAS and SBS and an initial photographic reconnaissance would be undertaken by air from Ascension Island. Fifteen men from Mountain Troop, 'D' Squadron, on board HMS *Endurance* were tasked with helicoptering onto the Fortuna Glacier to the north of Leith and then moving via Husvik and Stromness to the outskirts of Leith, where they could carry out the recce. The two SBS members on board *Antrim* were tasked with a similar recce operation of Grytviken. Once the SAS men, under Captain John Hamilton, landed on South Georgia on the night of 21 April, they were met with horrendous weather – temperatures of -27 degrees, a driving snowstorm and winds gusting to 70 knots – in which they could not move. Frostbite or worse was such a possibility that they asked to be extracted the next day. However, when three helicopters came to remove them from the glacier, one crashed in the white-out conditions and landed on its side. Fortunately, there were no serious casualties and all the men eventually made it off the glacier in the two remaining helicopters. Lieutenant Commander Ian Stanley, one of the helicopter pilots, was awarded the DSO for his heroics. On 23 April, during a lull in the blizzard, members of Mountain Troop were landed a second time and on this occasion were able to carry out the recce.

On 25 April, the Argentine submarine *Santa Fe* had come under attack and been hit before limping into Grytviken, and it was therefore decided to bring forward the main attack. Major Sheridan and thirty SAS men, including Sergeant Davidson, went ashore and set up tactical headquarters at Hestesletten before advancing along Brown Mountain. Sheridan ordered an advance, with more troops landing and ships entering into Cumberland East Bay. However, the enemy raised three white flags at King Edward Cove, and at 5.15 p.m. the enemy's Grytviken garrison formally surrendered.

Major (later Lieutenant-General Sir) Cedric Delves was in command of the SAS party when they witnessed the surrender – at which point the enemy had not suffered a single fatality. Davidson was in his party too, and Delves described him as 'a thoroughly amiable, mild-natured Mountain Troop man, with a smattering of Spanish, or so he assured me'. On 26 April, the enemy position at Leith, where Astiz himself was positioned, also surrendered. In Delves's words, 'It was all over,' and South Georgia was back in British hands. In fact, a message from Rear Admiral Sandy Woodward on 25 April had read: 'Be pleased to inform Her Majesty that the White Ensign flies alongside the Union Flag in Grytviken, South Georgia. God save the Queen.' Later that evening, John Nott, the Defence Secretary, had read out a statement saying South Georgia had been recaptured and Mrs Thatcher told reporters to 'rejoice at that news and congratulate our forces and the marines'.

Incidentally, Davidson is clearly visible in the famous 'D'

Squadron photograph taken soon after the capture of South Georgia. Furthermore, at one point, the SAS had unknowingly advanced through a minefield in which one soldier accidentally set off an anti-personnel mine, sending himself high into the air and leaving him dazed and slightly injured from shrapnel. In the aftermath, Davidson helped to settle the injured soldier and carried him to safety before extraction.

As stated earlier, Davidson was also involved in the raid on Pebble Island, one of the smaller Falkland Islands lying north of West Falkland. Delves sets the scene in his book *Across an Angry Sea*:

> The intelligence referred to a small group of engineers and marines at Pebble Island, little else. We had been searching for this sort of thing: an isolated enemy detachment to attack. We didn't mind what it was, exactly, provided its destruction or damage seized the imagination of the occupying force as a whole, precipitating anxiety. It shouldn't be too big. I had in mind an enemy facility of about sixty, at most, a number that we could overwhelm by the surprise and ferocity of our attack. The filed information suggested a small garrison of that size, up to no good, doing something interesting.

Delves consulted Roger Edwards, a pilot married, back in Britain, to a native of the Falklands called Norma. With his intimate knowledge of the islands, he had somehow become attached to 'D' Squadron. Edwards was convinced that Pebble Island, which had a small airstrip, was likely to be used as a radar site. It seemed the perfect target but Delves was wary: the destroyer HMS *Sheffield* had been hit and foundered on 4 May. 'A dramatic failure coming hard on the heels of *Sheffield* would be awful. It might even damage national morale, erode the public's will to see things through,' he later wrote.

In the end, however, the hit-and-run raid – typical of the type carried out by the SAS during the Second World War – was carefully prepared, initially through ground reconnaissance, and skilfully executed. During the night of 14–15 May, Sea King helicopters departed from HMS *Hermes* with some forty-five heavily armed members of 'D' Squadron on board. HMS *Glamorgan* would be in direct support with her guns. Their prime targets were the eleven enemy aircraft the recce team had identified on the airstrip. Despite winds of up to force eight, Delves decided to press on with the attack. 'We owed it to everyone to give it our best shot,' he said. 'We would go noisy with an illuminating round from the mortar.'

Mountain Troop was tasked with the destruction of the Argentine aircraft while the remaining personnel acted as a protection force, securing approaches to the airstrip and forming an operational reserve. The raiders attacked their targets with explosive charges, mortar bombs and light anti-tank weapons, as well as small arms and grenade launchers. When instructed, *Glamorgan* began shelling the Argentine positions on the airfield using high-explosive rounds, hitting the ammunition dump and fuel stores. The raiders, including Davidson, departed on the same Sea King helicopters that had brought them to the island – and returned to a hearty, triumphant breakfast on *Hermes*. The enemy had put up little resistance and the SAS took only two minor casualties, one with shrapnel wounds to his leg. Six Pucará ground-attack aircraft, four Turbo Mentor light-attack aircraft and one Skyvan transport plane had been destroyed in some forty-five minutes of controlled violence, along with an ammunition and fuel dump. Delves said:

Certainly for the entire Task Force it came as a timely, reassuring shot in the arm. We might have taken a knock or two, *Sheffield* notably, but mostly the hits continued to go the other way. We were more than getting the measure of our opponent. Our professionalism would seem to have us coming out on top.

However, just four days later, disaster struck. On Wednesday 19 May 1982, when the 846 Squadron RAF Sea King 4 helicopter being used to cross-deck men from HMS *Hermes* to HMS *Intrepid* ditched into the sea. The helicopter dropped from a low altitude and then turned and partly submerged. The aircraft quickly filled with water as some of its windows smashed on impact with the sea. Eighteen men from 'G' and 'D' Squadrons were among the twenty-two dead. However, eight men, including the two pilots, were rescued from the icy waters. Some blamed a bird strike; others suspected engine failure. Davidson, who was aged thirty-four, was one of those killed. He left a widow, Elizabeth, and three stepchildren. One former comrade said of Davidson: 'He was outstanding from day one, a soldier's soldier.'

Many years after the crash, Mick Williams described the scenes that day when he was serving with the SAS, aged twenty-one. In a newspaper interview, Williams, who went on to suffer from PTSD as a result of his terrifying experiences, said:

We were due to cross-deck from HMS *Hermes* to HMS *Intrepid*. I remember how still the water was before we took off and how many of us there were on the Sea King. I sat down, with my back to a porthole, but my arms were so tight against my sides I couldn't put my seatbelt on. The engine struggled with the additional weight – it seemed as likely to drill a hole in the ship as to take off. As we climbed, I became drowsy.

He believed that the helicopter hit a large bird, possibly an albatross:

I didn't hear the bird get sucked into the engine. Instead, I woke when the helicopter hit the water. The Sea King had already tilted on its side and I was at the bottom of a heap of bodies. I had been thrown backwards and swallowed mouthfuls of water. It was strangely calm and surreal in this cocoon of blackness and muffled sound. Then everyone's survival instinct kicked in. Men who had been SAS soldiers together for years fought each other, desperately trying to reach a tiny air pocket.

Guys were standing on top of me, their boots digging into my chest. So I pulled them down, grappled with them, my best mates, guys I loved, we all wanted to live. If I had died maybe some of them would have lived. I think about little else. My life since the accident has been consumed by this dilemma of conscience. I don't know how I pulled myself out of the Sea King. My next memory is when I bobbed up on to the surface. My fingers, arms and legs were numb. I couldn't inflate my lifejacket. Then other people started appearing. Their cries for help echoed across the bay. We swam together and clung to each other. There was a group of about seven of us. We shouted out other people's names but there was no reply. I remember this guy next to me saying he wanted to sleep. He and I knew if he went to sleep he would never wake up. The guy next to me was now floating face down in the water. Knowing he was dead, I held on to his body to keep myself upright. I wish I could erase that memory but I know I never will.

After what seemed an eternity, a boat from HMS *Brilliant* arrived to haul him and the remaining survivors aboard. Williams said:

The medics put me under a mountain of blankets and gave me

morphine. I shouted people's names, guys who had gone down with the helicopter. Then I began to feel this overwhelming sense of guilt that I had survived and my best friends Mick and Paul had not. I did not feel I deserved to live.

Because he was numb with cold, Williams was initially unaware that he had a punctured lung and shattered ribs.

Comrades of the eighteen SAS and four other dead had little or no time to grieve – they had a war to fight. A memorial service was held at St Mary's Parish Church in Chepstow in late May 1982. Davidson's widow, then forty, said, 'But for that accident he would never have died – he knew too much about how to live.' The couple had married seven years earlier in 1975.

I can reveal too that the Prince of Wales also thought about the widows and fatherless children of the dead SAS men in the wake of the helicopter crash. On 26 May 1982, he sent this telegram to 22 SAS Regiment:

For Commanding Officer. Could you please convey my very deepest sympathy to the wives and families of the members of the SAS Regiment who lost their lives in that tragic helicopter crash. I have the most profound admiration for the dedicated courage displayed by these men but at the same time I can imagine the terrible strain that this puts on their families. Perhaps there is some small compensation in the fact that their country is enormously proud of them.

One unidentified widow wrote a moving letter to 22 SAS Regiment in which she said:

As an SAS wife whose husband died in the unfortunate helicopter accident last week I wish to pay tribute to all the men of the SAS for their courage and dedication they put in, not only the job in hand, but the tremendous build-up and effort they exert in their training.

Most of all I would like to praise the wives of the Regiment who, for security reasons, never know where their husbands are, who endure long periods of being on their own, of coping with the family problems, of their patience and understanding when grief comes to others, and the comradeship they provide each other in days of need and distress.

Last but not least, I wish to pay my deepest respect to my own husband who gave me so much support, understanding, and I hope that the courage he showed will help sustain me in the years ahead.

Later in 1982 and beyond, at a series of memorial services, the families, friends and comrades of the men paid their respects to those who had died in such tragic circumstances. In particular, there was a service of remembrance for 22 SAS Regiment at Hereford Cathedral on 14 November 1982 – Remembrance Sunday. In the wake of the Falklands War, an SAS memorial window was created at St Martin's Parish Church, Hereford, and this was formally unveiled at a dedication service on 19 May 1983 – the first anniversary of the tragic helicopter crash.

PETER RATCLIFFE

Service: Army (SAS)

Final Rank: Major

FALKLANDS WAR DECORATION / DISTINCTION:

MENTIONED IN DESPATCHES (MID)

DATE OF BRAVERY: JUNE 1982

GAZETTED: 8 OCTOBER 1982

OTHER DECORATIONS / DISTINCTIONS:

DISTINGUISHED CONDUCT MEDAL (DCM)

Peter 'Billy' Ratcliffe was decorated with the DCM for courage during the First Gulf War. However, he had already displayed great bravery almost a decade earlier during the Falklands War as part of his work for an undercover SAS patrol. This prolonged gallantry under the most brutal of wartime conditions resulted in him being Mentioned in Despatches.

Ratcliffe was born into a working-class family in Salford, Greater Manchester, in 1951. He was the second of five children and the son of a bread delivery man who had served in the Royal Navy during the Second World War and a Roman Catholic mother. The passionate young Manchester United supporter was a rebellious youngster and left home at sixteen. He initially worked as an apprentice plasterer in Preston, Lancashire, but became disillusioned with his job. He enlisted in the army in January 1970. Later that year, he joined the 1st Battalion, the Parachute Regiment, having passed out as the top recruit of his intake. It was while serving with the Paras that he was given the nickname 'Salford Billy', later abbreviated to just 'Billy'.

Ratcliffe served with the Paras in Northern Ireland before, in 1972, applying for SAS selection, which he passed at the first attempt. Over the next twenty-five years, he served with The Regiment in Oman, Northern Ireland, the Falklands and the Middle East – as well as mainland Britain.

On 5 April 1982, three days after Argentina had invaded the Falkland Islands, the SAS was on its way to war. Ratcliffe, by then a Sergeant, was among those flown to the war zone. At the time, he had been stationed in Birmingham on a two-year posting to 23 SAS, one of The Regiment's two Territorial Army units, as a staff instructor. However, as a supposed Spanish speaker (he later admitted that he was anything but fluent), he was sent to join 'D' Squadron when it flew on a VC-10 to Ascension Island. 'There were eighty men aboard the flight to Ascension, sixty SAS and twenty support staff. In a sense it was a flight into the unknown because we didn't know at the time that we were off to a real scrap,' Ratcliffe later wrote in his autobiography, *Eye of the Storm: Twenty-five Years in Action with the SAS*.

Later, once the Task Force had caught up, the squadron was split among three warships. Ratcliffe went on board HMS *Plymouth* for what turned out to be a ten-day voyage to South Georgia. Members of 'D' Squadron ate, drank beers and played cards en route to South Georgia, very much aware that the temperatures were dropping and the sea was getting rougher as they sailed further south. Ratcliffe wrote:

> On 21 April we came in sight of South Georgia and its attendant icebergs, and that day our formal orders came to retake the island from its illegal occupiers, using whatever force was necessary to do the job. D Squadron, 22 SAS, was to get the first close look at the enemy in the Falklands War.

After some skirmishes, including an attack by British helicopters on an Argentine submarine, the British attacked the enemy force on South Georgia. 'D' Squadron was tasked with the assault on Grytviken, supported by the SBS and the gunfire from two destroyers, *Antrim* and *Plymouth*. At 2.45 p.m. on 25 April, the attack began with a naval bombardment, directed by a Wasp helicopter, while Lynx and Wessex helicopters were ferrying the assault party ashore on the outskirts of Grytviken. As has been detailed previously, the enemy soon surrendered without putting up a fight. As the Union flag was hoisted to replace the blue-and-white Argentine flag, Ratcliffe looked towards Grytviken from the deck of the *Plymouth*, wishing he had seen some action.

Ratcliffe wrote, 'Although recapturing South Georgia had proved no big deal in the end, it had been accomplished without the loss of a single British life ... It had also achieved one very important objective: Britain now had a safe haven for the liner *QE2*, then making her way south with the Task Force.' Rather than be at greater risk from submarine and air attack on the open seas, the *QE2* could anchor in South Georgia's Stromness Bay.

Shortly after the capture of South Georgia, Ratcliffe and his comrades from 'D' Squadron were transferred by helicopter, nine men per journey, from HMS *Plymouth* to HMS *Antrim*. On board, the men watched a video of Margaret Thatcher outside No. 10 telling the nation, 'Rejoice, just rejoice. South Georgia has just been liberated.' However, within two days, they again switched ship by helicopter, this time to HMS *Brilliant*, a Type-22 frigate. Within another twenty-four hours, they cross-decked again, this time to HMS *Hermes*, the aircraft carrier and also flagship of the Task Force. At this point, the SAS men had to sit and wait: the Task Force was still some three weeks away from launching their offensive aimed at liberating the Falklands.

However, on 2 May they heard the news that the *Belgrano* had been hit by a torpedo and sunk. Just two days later, HMS *Sheffield* was struck by an Exocet missile, eventually forcing the Captain and her crew to abandon ship. She was the first Royal Navy ship lost to enemy action since the Second World War.

By mid-May, 'D' and 'G' Squadrons, plus their mountains of weaponry, ammunition and other kit, were cross-decking yet again, this time from *Hermes* to HMS *Intrepid*, an assault ship equipped for amphibious warfare. However, as related earlier, one of the Sea King helicopters transporting the SAS soldiers crashed into the sea and sunk. Twenty-two men, including eighteen men from 'D' and 'G' Squadrons, were killed while the others scrambled to safety. 'As

the stricken helicopter slowly slipped beneath the waves, the survivors could only think of their mates on the inside of the aircraft.
It was a horrible way to die, and it affected us all pretty deeply,'
Ratcliffe wrote. News of the tragedy was held back by the Ministry
of Defence for several days so as not to damage public morale back
home.

On board *Intrepid*, Ratcliffe was told that he was being appointed as the Troop Sergeant of Mountain Troop, which, following
the helicopter accident, was just eight-strong under the command
of Captain John Hamilton. The troop was to be put ashore at
Darwin some twenty-four hours before the main landings at Port
San Carlos. The purpose of the Darwin landings was to make the
enemy believe that the invasion was taking place from close to
Darwin rather than the main beachhead.

After the landing, 'D' Squadron put down a lot of fire – from
mortars, Milan AT missiles, general-purpose machine guns and
small arms. The enemy below apparently believed they were being
attacked by a full battalion – 600 men rather than the forty or so
highly trained SAS men who were in fact firing down on them. As
Ratcliffe noted, 'Since this had been the purpose of our raid from
the first, we had obviously achieved what we'd set out to do.'

The diversion tactic was short-lived, as in the early hours of
21 May 3 PARA and 42 Commando, Royal Marines, had come
ashore in landing craft launched from San Carlos Water, thereafter taking up positions at Port San Carlos. To the south, 2 PARA
and 40 and 45 Commandos had safely landed at San Carlos Water.
Meanwhile, 'D' Squadron had used their time on the island well,
'tabbing' (a tactical advance into battle) some 20 miles with full kit
as they watched enemy Skyhawks and Mirages bomb and strafe
the British ships in San Carlos Water, with HMS *Ardent* among
those hit and badly damaged.

On 28 May, which saw the start of the two-day battle for Goose Green, Ratcliffe and his Mountain Troop were situated south of Mount Kent, but there was not enough cover to hide all eight men. So they split up, with Captain John Hamilton taking three men and Ratcliffe taking the other three. On 30 May, from their position to the south of Mount Kent, Ratcliffe observed a four-man Argentine patrol advancing towards the observation post (OP) that he and his three men had been using. They allowed the enemy to come within 100 metres of their position before opening fire with their M16 rifles. Three enemy soldiers were hit, one left screaming in pain. Within moments, they had hoisted a white flag from behind the boulder where they were hiding – the young, teenage conscripts were not badly wounded, but they were all terrified as they were taken as POWs. As plans were finalised for the final push towards Port Stanley, Ratcliffe and his troop were brought back to HMS *Intrepid*.

Next, on 5 June, Ratcliffe was tasked with the mission of establishing an OP at Fox Bay, on the south-east coast of enemy-occupied West Falkland. His comrade, Captain John Hamilton, was to establish a similar position some 12 miles to the north-east on the same coast. Once again, each of the two teams was just four-strong, and they were dropped off by a Sea King helicopter at their respective locations. Carrying 90lb packs, Ratcliffe's team inadvertently strayed onto a grass airfield at Fox Bay and were forced to lie low in a marsh and dig into a sloping bank.

When it was light, they found themselves just 200 yards from the enemy and right on the edge of their forward position. 'And the beauty of it was that they had no idea we were there,' Ratcliffe wrote.

I thought, Hell, a few more feet and we would have been sharing their trenches … From the OP we had a clear view of Fox Bay. The area was bristling with enemy soldiers and their gear. They were at least a battalion strong – perhaps as many as 1,000 men – supported by artillery pieces and plenty of vehicles.

All this information and more was being regularly radioed back to HMS *Intrepid*. The team remained there for five days until Ratcliffe decided it was becoming too dangerous and their job had been completed. 'We left, as we had come, like thieves in the night,' Ratcliffe wrote.

They moved further away but were still able to send radio reports on the enemy's positions and strength. In turn, they heard over the radio that Captain Hamilton had been killed while carrying out a similar observational role at Port Howard – they later learnt he had been discovered by the enemy and was shot dead while trying to escape. Another member of the four-man team had been captured when he ran out of ammunition. Hamilton was later awarded a posthumous MC – his bravery had enabled the other two men in his team to escape. His comrade was the only British soldier to be captured during the war.

On 12 June, with Ratcliffe's seven-day mission up and their food supplies virtually gone, his team received a radio message: 'Stay in your location. Helicopter arrival to be advised soon.' It was to be another five days, however, before the unit – by now frozen and hungry – were picked up by a Sea King helicopter. On 14 June, Ratcliffe and his men learnt over their radio that the Argentine forces on East Falkland had surrendered just before the final push on Port Stanley. The team was finally picked up on 17 June.

Ratcliffe's then confidential recommendation for a Mention in Despatches spelt out the key role he and his men had played:

The acquisition of detailed intelligence on enemy strengths and dispositions was considered a prerequisite for any Squadron direct action operations. Sgt Ratcliffe was tasked to gather such information on the Argentine garrison at Fox Bay, in the West Falklands.

At the time of his insertion, the enemy were considerably aware of the threat posed by our surveillance. Their tactics to eliminate this threat included counter patrolling and radio signal direction finding. Despite this Sgt Ratcliffe at times sited his observation post within 600 yards of the enemy's forward positions. His information was exhaustive and accurate. This necessitated lengthy radio transmissions. Heedless of the dangers this posed, he nevertheless persisted in the regular passage of his intelligence. Because of changed circumstances his patrol duration was extended by some three days. This he achieved on reduced material support with no denigration of efficiency. The quality of the patrol's intelligence was outstanding. Previously acquired intelligence was confirmed and a great deal of new intelligence added. Had an attack been required to be mounted on Fox Bay there is little doubt that the patrol's contribution would have proved vital.

Throughout the campaign, Sgt Ratcliffe has performed with dedicated thoroughness. He saw action during diversionary attacks prior to the main amphibious landings and again on advance force operations in the Mount Kent area. He has acted as 2IC [second-in-command] to the Mountain Troop since the helicopter crash of 21 May inflicted 50 per cent casualties on that troop. He set about the task of rebuilding the troop and was largely responsible for the rebuilding of their operational effectiveness and confidence. Altogether Sgt Ratcliffe's performance has been exemplary. I strongly recommend his endeavours be suitably recognised.

By 28 June, with the war won, Ratcliffe was back in the UK and preparing to train for a squash tournament; he had begun his journey home from Port Stanley via Ascension Island only two days earlier.

On 8 October, he was Mentioned in Despatches for his command of the SAS undercover patrol. Three days earlier, after learning the news privately, the Prince of Wales, Colonel-in-Chief of the Parachute Regiment, sent Ratcliffe a telegram that read: 'Having heard of your Mention in Despatches I wanted to send you my warmest congratulations. I have immense admiration for the way in which you carried out your duty in such conditions and upheld the gallant traditions of the Regiment. Charles.'

After the Falklands War, Ratcliffe's career in the SAS went from strength to strength. As previously stated, he was awarded the DCM for bravery behind enemy lines during the First Gulf War. In 1992, Ratcliffe was commissioned to the rank of Captain and went to Germany on detachment for six months. He then spent two years as a Quarter Master with 21 SAS, based in London, followed by a further two years with 23 SAS, based in Birmingham. He left the army in November 1997 as a training Major. Three years later, he published his account of his life and army career.

Ratcliffe is in no doubt that his time in the army, especially his years in the Special Forces, was the making of him. In his book, he wrote:

Thirty years ago, no one would have figured me for a soldier. At the time, I was a scarcely educated, often dishonest, streetwise kid from a poverty-stricken slum home – in the end, a broken home – in the depressed industrial north-west of England. Almost without prospects, I joined the army for all the wrong reasons: to get away from a miserable dead-end existence as a manual labourer, and because I had been thwarted in my efforts to emigrate to Australia. I owe to my Regiments – first the Parachute Regiment, then, for twenty-five years, the Special Air Service Regiment – the fact that I am not still a manual labourer in a dead-end job, or even worse, in prison. I owe a great deal more than that, however, most of which I could not put into words, and all of it priceless ... What I do know is that I gained from the SAS a sense of self-worth and confidence while soldiering with the best in any army, anywhere in the world.

Ratcliffe, who has two grown-up daughters, married again in 2015. He and his wife live on a golf estate in South Africa.

FRANK COLLINS

Service: Army (SAS)

Final rank: Corporal

FALKLANDS WAR DECORATION / DISTINCTION: **N/A**

DATE OF BRAVERY: N/A

GAZETTED: N/A

Frank Collins enjoyed a distinguished career in the SAS during which he served all over the world. He also had the distinction of being the first SAS man through the roof of the Iranian Embassy during the siege of 1980. Like Harry Gow, his SAS comrade, Collins's hopes of seeing frontline action were frustrated by the Argentine surrender, but he nevertheless took part in a fascinating episode of the war.

Collins, one of five children, was born in Newcastle upon Tyne on 5 November 1956, the son of a hard-drinking ship's carpenter. His family moved to Whitley Bay when he was a youngster. As a schoolboy at Whitley Bay Grammar School, Collins had wanted to be a soldier and joined the Army Cadet Force. Later, he joined the Royal Corps of Signals, aged sixteen. He failed a fitness test to join the Parachute Regiment but then, aged nineteen, switched his ambitions to joining the SAS after a Troop Sergeant told him: 'The SAS is the cream of the British Army. The elite. They are highly trained, mate, to a degree you can't imagine. Shooting, demolitions, medicine, hostage rescue, jungle warfare... proper soldiering, the best.'

After his failure to join the Paras, Collins's comrades mocked his chances of joining The Regiment. However, this time he trained hard – running 10 miles each night with an 80lb rucksack on his back. He was accepted into the SAS Signals just as Prime Minister Harold Wilson announced he was sending the SAS to Northern Ireland in retaliation for the Kingsmill massacre by the Provisional IRA in 1976. The IRA responded by issuing posters of Wilson and Merlyn Rees, Northern Ireland Secretary, holding pistols and looking menacing. The posters read: 'SAS – State Authorized Slaughter. An SAS man will dance with your daughter, deliver milk, drive your taxi. Trust no one. Talk to no one.'

After training in Hereford, Collins completed two tours of Northern Ireland as a member of the SAS Signals. By this point, he was determined to become a fully-fledged member of the SAS – not just a signaller – and he resumed his brutal training regime. It paid off: in December 1978, aged twenty-two, he was 'badged'. Collins later wrote of his thoughts at that time in his autobiography, *Baptism of Fire*: 'I've made it. I am in the Regiment. The undistinguished, unpromoted boy signaller from apprentice college has joined the cream of the British Army. No one is more surprised than me. I know I'm still me, I don't feel any different. But the uniform says I am different.'

As stated, in May 1980 Collins was part of the SAS team at the Iranian Embassy siege – and the following year he got married and was back serving with distinction in Northern Ireland. When the Falklands War broke out, Collins and some of his SAS colleagues were close to completing a tour of Belize. Soon they returned to Britain, keen to see action in the South Atlantic. With the nation in the grip of what he called 'Falklands fever', Collins takes up the story about his own involvement in his autobiography. Incidentally what follows are oblique references to both 'Operation Mikado' and 'Operation Plum Duff', as highlighted in previous write-ups in this chapter:

> Only the counter-terrorist team will remain in Hereford. Most of the rest of the Regiment are already out in the South Atlantic. We learn about our mission. It has been masterminded by the Regiment's brigadier, Peter de la Billière, and it is daring to the point of recklessness. Not that we care about that. Claire [Collins's wife] would care but, of course, I can't tell her about it.
>
> The squadron commander is relieved of his command and a highly respected senior NCO resigns because they both say this is a suicide mission. It's a brave gesture but nevertheless we take off from RAF Lyneham [Wiltshire], the 'Ride of the Valkyries' playing over the intercom, then 'Bat Out of Hell', then 'Cool for Cats'. The music adds to the mood of sheer excitement. It seems to me, and to most of us that what is happening is the pinnacle of our careers. We spend our lives training, until we are arguably the most highly skilled soldiers in the world. But our skills are seldom used in real conflict. Here, at last, is a war and we have to test our courage and ability. The odds are stacked heavily against us and that's how we like it.
>
> It's a long flight to Ascension Island, where we refuel. Before we can take off again we are told there's a delay. Then we're told the job's been put on hold. The RAF, who stood to lose an aircraft and crew, is relieved. We're disappointed and, if we're honest, a bit relieved. We're stuck on Ascension Island now. The job gets changed,

delayed, changed again and delayed. As the scenario keeps changing we put in the appropriate training, practising on the Ascension
Island airfield. We're frustrated and relieve our feelings with heavy
firing.

The attack that had been planned – the precise details of which
were never disclosed – was eventually completely called off, resulting in further disappointment. 'So here we are with a war on,
stuck miles away on a lump of lava with nothing to do but top
up our suntans,' Collins wrote. However, 'B' Squadron then learnt
they were flying to the Falkland Islands to support 'D' Squadron,
meaning its members were again convinced that they would see
action. Soon they were in two Hercules C130 transport planes,
knowing they had to parachute into the sea with their kit and be
picked up by ships in the sea.

Collins wrote:

> The flight is thirteen hours long. We sprawl around on the canvas
> seats and sling our hammocks up to get some sleep. Sometimes we
> climb up to the flight deck and watch what's going on there: occa-
> sionally the co-pilot lets us fly the plane. We all have a go. Sitting
> in the back we feel the C130, known as Fat Albert, suddenly keel to
> the left and then the right. That means one of our boys is having
> fun at the wheel.

However, their mission was again called off because of severe problems suffered by the plane in front of them:

> Finally, the plane loses altitude. By shoving our heads in the port-
> holes, we see our ships far beneath us. We're ready in our wetsuits,
> our fins tied to the side of our legs, all our equipment packed and

ready to go. We have had P minus 20, P minus 15, P minus 10. We can't see the other plane but we know it's ahead of us. We circle. We circle again. We're ready to go but suddenly we're gaining height and flying off. Flying back in the direction we came from.

Moments later the jump master appeared, waving his hands. 'It's off, no jump. Sit down,' he said. With its crew disappointed yet again, the plane returned to Ascension Island, where they learnt why the jump was aborted. Those who jumped from the first plane lost all their kit: bergens, weapons, personal belongings went to the bottom of the South Atlantic because the riggers had made an error with the parachutes and the weight they were carrying. But the setback was a temporary one – the men were told they would be taking off again in six hours' time. Once again, the flight to the war zone was straightforward and again the men prepared to leap into an icy sea with their equipment. Collins wrote:

> We circle a final time. We're ready to jump. But we're starting to gain altitude. We're heading back to Ascension Island. Word gets passed from man to man. The war's over. The Argentinians have surrendered. I look around at the others. This is the worst news we've had in a long time. So, the Argies heard we were coming and decided it wasn't worth fighting any more, we conclude. We all get gongs just for being there. It's a campaign medal and I can't help thinking I didn't do much to deserve it. And yet, preparing to carry out that mission is still the most exciting thing that's happened to me.

Collins left the army in 1989 to pursue a career in the security industry. At different times, he worked for Mohamed al-Fayed, the owner of Harrods, and Sir Ralph Halpern, the head of the Burton group. However, he tired of this and instead embarked on

a three-year course to be ordained as a Church of England minis-
ter. After qualifying, he became the curate of St Peter's Church in
Hereford – home to the SAS – and its daughter church, St James's.
In 1995, Collins rejoined the army as a chaplain to the Parachute
Regiment, earning the nickname 'Padre Two Zero'.

Collins's autobiography closed with the words:

> It's difficult to end a book about your life when life keeps rolling
> on. I want a lot more to happen to me, but my route so far has
> been so unpredictable that I can't even try to guess what's next. I
> just trust in God to show me the path.

But Collins's life did not keep rolling on. The Ministry of Defence
took a dim view of his book for its insights into the SAS. Collins
was forced to give up his role as army chaplain shortly before the
book was first published in 1997.

The following year, on 16 June 1998, Collins took his own life
and was found in his fume-filled car in a friend's garage in Stock-
bridge, Hampshire. He had been calmly reading Leo Tolstoy's *War
and Peace* as he died, and he left a suicide note titled 'The Final
Chapter' on his laptop. Collins, who was just forty-one when he
died, left a widow and four children under sixteen. At his inquest
in September 1998, his widow said that leaving the army had made
him deeply upset and he regretted writing his autobiography.
Later, Claire Collins revealed that her late husband had been bat-
tling PTSD for years.

CHAPTER 6

DARWIN AND GOOSE GREEN

British military Commanders knew from early on in the Falklands War that the Argentine invaders could not be defeated by air and sea power alone: a land assault would be needed if there was to be a swift and decisive victory. It was for this reason that so many troops were despatched to the South Atlantic so soon after the invasion of the islands. In mid-April, Brigadier (later Major General) Julian Thompson, who commanded 3 Commando Brigade, had told the naval staff, 'I can tell you immediately what beaches are suitable for landing the brigade but until I know what enemy are on them, I can't tell you which one I would choose.' By mid-May, however, reconnaissance missions by the SAS and SBS, as detailed in Chapter 3, had provided a great deal of intelligence on enemy positions on East and West Falklands.

So, after Thompson had made his choice of suitable landing points, in the early hours of 21 May the British Amphibious Task Group mounted 'Operation Sutton', the amphibious landings on beaches around San Carlos Water, on the west coast of East Falkland facing Falkland Sound. In simple terms, this was, in the words of the orders to 3 Brigade Commando, 'an operation for a landing with a view to the repossession of the Falkland Islands'. Some 4,000 men from 3 Commando Brigade were put ashore, notably members of 2 and 3 PARA and 40 and 45 Commando Royal Marines. The enemy was undoubtedly surprised by the choice of landing location: a pre-war study by the Argentine Navy had concluded that San Carlos Water was an 'impossible' site for a successful landing. After the landings, the priority for the British was to protect its troops and to ensure that the men could remain on East Falkland in order to advance and, eventually, be reinforced with more troops.

By dawn the next day, the British forces had established a secure beachhead from which to conduct offensive operations. Thompson's intention was to capture Darwin, a small settlement on the east side of East Falkland, and Goose Green, another small settlement close to Darwin and also on the Choiseul Sound, before turning towards Port Stanley. With the British troops on the ground, the Argentine planes began their regular night-bombing campaign using British-made Canberra aircraft. This campaign continued until the very last day of the war on 14 June. The trials and tribulations faced by the British Navy and RAF during this time, from late May to mid-June, are detailed in Chapters 2 and 4.

This chapter, however, concentrates on the early battles of the land war. From 28–29 May, 2 PARA, a force of approximately 500 men with naval gunfire support from HMS Arrow and artillery support from 8 Commando Battery, Royal Artillery, approached and attacked Darwin and Goose Green. The positions were held by the Argentine 12th Infantry Regiment, and the battle for both positions is usually referred to as the Battle of Goose Green. After a tough struggle that lasted all night and into the next day, the British won a hard-fought victory. During the battle, seventeen British and forty-seven Argentine soldiers were killed. In addition, 961 Argentine servicemen were taken prisoner.

In fact, the BBC jumped the gun and announced the taking of Goose Green on the BBC World Service before it had actually happened. It was during the height of the fighting that Lieutenant Colonel Herbert 'H' Jones, the Commanding Officer of 2 PARA, was killed while charging into the well-defended Argentine positions. He was posthumously awarded the Victoria Cross (VC).

I do not own the Jones VC, which is the sole reason he does not have his own write-up in this chapter. Over the past four decades, there have been various attempts to portray Jones as reckless with both his own life and those of his men. Others have claimed that he should not have been in the position he was (on the front line) when he was killed. All I can say is that the men from 2 PARA who I have spoken to do not share the view that his leadership and judgement were poor. Far from it, they see him as an inspirational leader. Perhaps like many great senior officers before him, including the legendary SAS hero Lieutenant Colonel Blair 'Paddy' Mayne, Jones was simply not prepared to ask his men to do what he would not do himself. The line between being highly reckless and being outstandingly brave is sometimes a thin one, but I believe that it was entirely appropriate for Jones's valour to be rewarded with a posthumous VC, Britain and the Commonwealth's most prestigious award for gallantry in the presence of the enemy.

Rather than level any criticism at Jones, I prefer to echo the assessment and sentiments of Mark Adkin in his book, Goose Green: A Battle Is Fought to Be Won. *The author wrote, 'Colonel "H"'s gallantry as such did not win the battle for Goose Green but his leadership of 2 PARA during the year he had been in command, and in the days and hours prior to his being shot, did. The Commanding Officer had imbued his battalion with his dedication, with his spirit, with his belief that, given the necessary will, anything was possible. He led by example. He set extremely high standards, and his battalion reflected this, particularly at platoon and section level. Colonel "H" had made 2 PARA into what it was at Goose Green – a first rate fighting force.'*

Once again, this book is not an attempt to give a blow-by-blow account of this ferocious battle. This task has been achieved already by Adkin and other military historians. As Adkin points out, as well as being the first battle of the land war, it was also the longest, the hardest fought, the most controversial and the most important to win. He also notes that what began as a raid turned into a vicious, fourteen-hour struggle in which 2 PARA – outnumbered, exhausted, forced to attack across open ground in daylight and with inadequate fire support – almost lost the action.

This chapter does, however, seek to provide an insight into the exceptional bravery displayed by members of the British Armed Forces during the heavy fighting that spanned 28–29 May. The result of the battle meant that 'the maroon machine' – as the Parachute Regiment is known – had passed its first test with flying colours. As Max Hastings and Simon Jenkins wrote in their book The Battle for the Falklands, *'2 PARA had brought about the collapse of an enemy force more than treble its own. They buried Argentine dead and took 1,200 prisoners of war. It was an extraordinary triumph, its conclusion a great tribute to Major [Chris] Keeble's handling of a desperate situation.' Keeble had taken over the temporary command of 2 PARA after Jones had been fatally hit.*

With the sizeable Argentine force at Goose Green out of the way, British forces were soon able to break out of the San Carlos beachhead. However, in the build-up to the Battle of Goose Green on 27 May, the troops of 2 PARA had not been the only men on the march. The men of 45 Commando and 3 PARA had started a 'loaded march' or 'tab' across East Falkland towards the coastal settlement of Teal Inlet, from where they would soon have their own battle to fight.

STEPHEN THOMAS ILLINGSWORTH

Service: Army

Final rank: Private

FALKLANDS WAR DECORATION / DISTINCTION:

DISTINGUISHED CONDUCT MEDAL (DCM)

DATE OF BRAVERY: 28 MAY 1982

GAZETTED: 8 OCTOBER 1982

Stephen Illingsworth showed such incredible courage in two incidents on the same day that he was recommended for a posthumous VC. In the event, he narrowly failed to become only the third member of the Armed Forces – and the Parachute Regiment – to be awarded the VC for gallantry during the 1982 war. Instead, he was decorated with a posthumous DCM.

Stephen Illingsworth was born on 25 April 1962 in Edlington, Yorkshire, the son of Gordon and Joyce Illingsworth. He was educated at Edlington Comprehensive School, which lies in the metropolitan borough of Doncaster. He joined the army aged eighteen and was enlisted into the Parachute Regiment. It was the perfect job for Illingsworth as he loved parachuting, sometimes going for recreational jumps after already having completed training jumps earlier the same day.

When the Falkland Islands were invaded, Illingsworth was serving in 5 Platoon, 'B' Company, 2 PARA, one of the two battalions from the regiment selected to go and win back the islands from the Argentine invaders. Soon after setting sail on the MV *Norland* on 26 April 1982, the day after Illingsworth's twentieth birthday, his mother wrote to him saying that she would rather have a son who was a 'live coward than a dead hero'.

However, Illingsworth, who was known to comrades as 'Illie' or Steve, was excited by the prospect of seeing action and putting his years of training into practice. Even as a boy, he had always wanted to be at the centre of the action and as a soldier his attitude was no different. He wrote to his father shortly before he went into battle, saying, 'Don't worry about me dad, I'm trained to do this job.'

His big test came on 28 May 1982, during heavy fighting at the Battle of Goose Green. As dawn broke, 'B' Company was pinned down on a forward slope by an Argentine position at Boca House. The citation for Illingsworth's decoration tells the story of his courage over the next few hours:

In the early hours of 28 May 1982, the 2nd Battalion, The Parachute Regiment launched an attack on the enemy positions in the area of the Darwin and Goose Green settlements on the Island of East Falkland. The enemy were thought to be entrenched in battalion strength. In the event, their numbers were far greater and fierce fighting ensued all day.

Private Illingsworth was a member of 5 Platoon, which was the depth platoon in B Company's advance. At one point the advance came under heavy and accurate enemy fire, and OC B Company attacked the enemy position with his leading platoons, leaving 5 Platoon to provide covering fire. Dawn was growing stronger and it became clear that 5 Platoon was in fact exposed on a long forward slope without protection and very vulnerable to increasingly heavy enemy machine gun and rifle fire. Its position became untenable and it was ordered to withdraw back over the crest. It was during this manoeuvre that one of their number was hit in the back.

Private Illingsworth, who had already reached comparative safety himself, immediately rushed forward in full view and fire of the enemy, accompanied by another soldier, to help their wounded comrade. In an effort to locate the wound they removed his weapon and webbing equipment, and having administered First Aid, dragged the soldier back over the crest line, despite a hail of enemy fire which miraculously missed them. Once in a position of safety, Private Illingsworth continued to tend the injured man's wounds.

The fire fight continued intensively, and 5 Platoon began to run short of ammunition. Remembering that he had left the webbing equipment, with ammunition in it, lying on the exposed forward slope, Private Illingsworth decided to go forward alone to collect it. Disregarding the enemy fire, which was still extremely heavy, he broke cover and advanced once again down the forward slope. As he did so he was killed.

In these two acts of supreme courage Private Illingsworth showed a complete disregard for his own safety, and a total dedication to others. Whilst his action in coming to the help of a wounded soldier may have been almost instinctive on seeing the plight of a comrade, his move forward to collect much-needed ammunition for his be-leagured [*sic*] platoon was a display of coolly-calculated courage and heroism of the very highest order.

The Prince of Wales, who had been appointed Colonel-in-Chief of the Parachute Regiment five years before the Falklands War, sent a telegram to Illingsworth's family on the day his posthumous deco-ration was announced. It read:

> Having heard the news of your son's award I just wanted to say how deeply moved and inspired I had been to read the account of his quite extraordinary gallantry. This country's history is enriched by the heroism of men such as your son, even though that may be small compensation for the loss of someone who meant so much. This comes with renewed and deepest sympathy. Charles.

At the time Illingsworth's decoration was made public, Major General Jeremy Moore of the Royal Marines, who had command-ed the British land forces during the war, wrote to Illingsworth's father, saying:

> I do hope my writing to you will not add to the burden of grief that the loss of your son has brought. However, I feel duty bound to write on behalf of all those who served with me in the Falk-land Islands to express our admiration for the bravery displayed by your son.
>
> His was a marvellous performance of courage and leadership

which inspired all around him. We are delighted that his exploits have been made public by the award of a Distinguished Conduct Medal. You, your family and his Regiment have every right to be very proud indeed.

Illingsworth's body was eventually repatriated back to the UK, and he was buried with full military honours at Aldershot Military Cemetery in Hampshire. He was laid to rest alongside many of his former comrades from 2 and 3 PARA – the so-called 'Class of 82' – who fell in battle. At Edlington Comprehensive School, pupils have competed each year for the 'Stephen Illingsworth Memorial Cup' and a road, Illingsworth Road, was named after him in the Falklands. Furthermore, when Mike Curtis, a former paratrooper and SAS soldier, wrote his book, *Close Quarter Battle*, he dedicated the book to Illingsworth's memory.

It was, however, not until 2005 that it emerged Illingsworth had in fact been 'strongly recommended' for a posthumous VC rather than the DCM. The revelation led to controversy and suggestions that he had been unfairly deprived of such a prestigious honour. The decision may have been prompted by fears that the VC would be 'cheapened' if too many were handed out and also concerns that the Paras were being given preferential treatment over other regiments.

Illingsworth was strongly recommended for the VC by Lieutenant General Sir Richard Trant, the Land Forces Deputy to the Commander of the Task Force, and Admiral Sir John Fieldhouse, the overall Commander of the Task Force. Trant said in his recommendation: 'For his outstanding courage, his dedication to others and his total disregard for his own safety, Pte Illingsworth is strongly recommended for the award of a posthumous Victoria Cross.'

Admiral Fieldhouse wrote: 'Pte Illingsworth's heroic acts of total disregard for his own safety were in the highest traditions of his regiment. He was an inspiration to others and is strongly recommended for the posthumous award of the Victoria Cross.'

The facts had never emerged before, and Illingsworth's mother disclosed in March 2005 that she had been asked not to talk publicly about the details of the gallantry award back in 1982: 'It was explained to me by Major [John] Crosland, Steve's company commander, but I was asked never to discuss it. It was so like him to look out for others and to put himself at risk to help his mates.'

In passing on the recommendation to the VC Committee, a specially appointed Ministry of Defence panel that decides whether such an award is justified, Lieutenant General Sir Roland Guy, then military secretary to the army, wrote,

> Illingsworth's actions were heroic and selfless and must have been carried out in the full knowledge of what he was risking.
>
> To save a wounded comrade under fire and then immediately to attempt to recover his ammunition epitomises the very best of soldierly qualities. However, brave though he was, his action does not match the standard of action by Jones and McKay.

Furthermore, Guy also wrote that there will 'inevitably be great public interest over whether the award is in any way being cheapened if an excessive number are awarded'. These newly discovered documents, some of which were redacted, hint that senior Royal Navy personnel were resentful about the number of VCs and other medals being directed to the Paras.

In an interview with her local paper the *Sheffield Telegraph* in 2007, Joyce Illingsworth said about her son's death:

> We were so proud. He was a right character. I didn't like the

thought of him going but he was excited about it. He had to be where there was adventure. He couldn't just sit behind a desk or something like that. He liked to be where the action was.

He wanted to be a paratrooper. He wanted to be in the elite. From a kid he wanted to jump out of an aeroplane. He used to come home on leave and then he used to go off to Bridlington to jump out of a plane even though that was his job. He just loved the thrill of parachuting.

People said it would be over in two to three weeks and we knew it would take two to three weeks for him to get there on the boat so we hoped it might be over before he got there.

No one wants their children to go before them. I said in my letters to him I would rather have a son who was a live coward than a dead hero. I never got to say goodbye or anything.

GARY DAVID BINGLEY
Service: Army
Final rank: Lance Corporal
FALKLANDS WAR DECORATION / DISTINCTION:
MILITARY MEDAL (MM)
DATE OF BRAVERY: 28 MAY 1982
GAZETTED: 8 OCTOBER 1982

Gary Bingley was decorated for an outstanding act of bravery that typified the attitude of the Parachute Regiment in battle. While tackling a well-entrenched enemy position in the area of Goose Green, East Falkland, he and his men came under heavy fire. As the Section Commander, Bingley was determined to lead from the front – and such gallantry cost him his life, with his MM being awarded posthumously.

Gary David Bingley was born on 28 February 1958 in Muswell Hill, north London, the eldest of five children. As a lifelong supporter of Tottenham Hotspur FC, he went through his army career saying he had been born in Tottenham – a minor inaccuracy that was even reported on his death certificate. As a teenager, he had more success on the football pitch than in the classroom. After deciding against further education, he enlisted in the Infantry Junior Leaders Battalion at Shorncliffe, Kent, passing out of Inkerman 'P' Company in October 1975, aged seventeen.

Having gained his regimental wings, Bingley, who was known by comrades and friends as 'Gaz', served a tour of duty with 2 PARA in Northern Ireland in 1977, at the height of The Troubles. During some 'R&R' (rest and recuperation) from the tour, he met his future wife, Jay, on 28 February 1977, his seventeenth birthday. Bingley, who was a quick thinker with a good sense of humour, was typically decisive when it came to his new relationship. Despite having spent only three weeks with her over a period of four months, he proposed to her in a letter at the start of a two-year posting to Berlin, Germany. She accepted and they were married in Taunton, Somerset, on 9 July 1977. Their daughter, Zoe, was born the following year. While based in Berlin, he continued to play football to a high standard, representing the battalion in the Combined Services XI.

Next came another tour of duty in Northern Ireland, this time in 1979 when his unit was based at Ballykinler, Co. Down. He narrowly missed being attacked at Warrenpoint on 27 August 1979, in what proved to be the deadliest terror attack on the army during The Troubles. The IRA ambushed an army convoy, killing eighteen soldiers and wounding more than twenty. Bingley would normally have been with the ambushed party but had remained at the barracks due to being 'out on a job' the previous day.

Having returned to Aldershot in 1981, Bingley, who was always popular with his comrades, served in 'A', 'B' and 'D' Companies, 2 PARA. The battalion was expecting to tour Belize in 1982, but in response to events in the South Atlantic the tour of Central America was cancelled and 2 PARA was chosen as one of the units to sail to retake the Falkland Islands. Most men were up for the challenge of a major conflict, including Bingley who, after a week's training, boarded the MV *Norland* on 26 April 1982, telling his wife: 'I've waited six years for this.' Another man completely up for the challenge was the previously mentioned CO of 2 PARA, Colonel Herbert 'H' Jones, who was on holiday in France when news of the impending deployment broke. He rushed back to England, ready to head to the war zone immediately. His second-in-command was Major Chris Keeble.

Bingley was Platoon Leader, 11 Platoon, 'D' Company, and on the 21-day voyage to the war zone he was enthusiastic about the intensive training on board. His immediate Commander was Major (later Lieutenant Colonel) Phil Neame, who later said in Max Arthur's book *Above All, Courage*:

I got my Company to prepare in the finest detail so that everyone was minutely ready for every eventuality. I think the biggest loss of confidence occurs when you are caught on the hop. The object therefore was to try to reach the stage where we had the reassurance we had talked through every situation, which could only help morale.

I couldn't very well tell them what it was like because I didn't know myself. All I could do was to try to anticipate the difficult areas beyond the military textbook and to try to get across to the platoon commanders and, through them, the whole way down, what I was expecting of them and what I was likely to do in certain situations. Then at least my behaviour and actions would be predictable and expected, and we'd all be working along the same lines.

I was also concerned about how much kit we should take ashore. I spent days trying to pare it down to essentials. 'H' even declared that to reduce weight we wouldn't take bayonets as we were going to win the war through firepower. I thought, 'That's all right until things go wrong.' So I managed to persuade them that we should take them as tin openers. He didn't normally brook arguments but that rather appealed to him.

The other thing I found myself lumbered with was Sports Day. I must admit it was quite a good day really ...We were a bit limited for space but I set up a tug-of-war which got everyone on the top deck cheering away ... As we went further south I had to organise a second Sports Day and by then the weather was getting a little rougher and H took one look at the steeplechase and slippery decks and the force five winds and decided that we were likely to lose more men on a repeat performance of that than going up against the Argentinians!

The men landed at Ajax Bay, codenamed Red Beach, on East Falkland on 21 May, and it was not long before 2 PARA took up their positions on Sussex Mountain. It was a treacherous march carrying heavy bergens; the soldiers had to look down constantly to avoid breaking their ankles and towards the air, at times, to avoid the enemy air force. Occasionally, they took shots at enemy aircraft that were coming in low to bomb British ships.

There were also conflicting orders and priorities involving the various services. On 24 May, 'D' Company had set off on an 11-mile tab towards Camilla Creek House, which was in enemy hands, only to be ordered to turn around soon afterwards because of the lack of air support. As Colonel 'H' apparently put it: 'I've waited twenty years for this and now some fucking Marine has cancelled it.'

As the waiting continued, the weather deteriorated. After six days of torrential rain and in the wind and the cold, twenty-seven men had to be evacuated, twelve of them with trench foot. On the evening of 26 May, the remaining fit soldiers from 2 PARA – all 450 of them – made their way towards Camilla Creek House for a second time, again weighed down by weapons, ammunition and other equipment, and again led by 'D' Company. By 3 a.m., the objective had been taken and the men grabbed a few hours' sleep. However, by morning they awoke to discover they were in a vulnerable position. Next came the unfortunate announcement on the BBC World Service that 2 PARA was within 5 miles of Darwin. It was a move that left many Commanders, notably Colonel 'H', incandescent with rage. 'H' even penned a letter saying that if any man was killed as a result of the blunder, the Ministry of Defence should sue the BBC. On the ground, the men of 2 PARA were ordered to spread out amidst growing fears of an attack from land, sea or air (the enemy particularly favoured the use of helicopters). That afternoon 'C' Company engaged and captured an Argentine Land Rover with three enemy soldiers in it. One of the captured soldiers, an officer, helpfully confirmed that their Darwin garrison was on high alert and preparing for an attack.

That afternoon, officers from 2 PARA gathered to plan their attack. Once again Major Phil Neame takes up the story:

After the BBC's message we were dispersed all around the house [Camilla Creek] with nothing to do but think about tomorrow. I had a long look at my map. What I saw was not particularly re-assuring. A long, narrow isthmus [narrow strip of land] with little chance to manoeuvre and the Argies knew we were coming. A frontal attack against an alerted enemy.

Intelligence on the enemy was imprecise. It was known they had at least three rifle companies and that Darwin Hill was defended by at least sixteen trenches, with more near Darwin and Boca House. Their plan was relatively simple but less easy to pull off: to advance 14km in fourteen hours to seal a key victory for the British forces.

In the early hours of 28 May, 2 PARA began their assault. After an initial brief contact involving men from 'B' Company, 'D' Company followed shortly behind, with Bingley at the head of 11 Platoon. During that night and into the next day, the ferocity of the firefights against a well dug-in enemy intensified. Some time after daybreak, 'D' Company realised they had pressed on further towards Darwin Ridge than their comrades, including Colonel 'H'. Soon the CO had identified a target he wanted 'D' Company to attack and destroy. Once again, Neame continues the story:

By then we were ahead of the other two companies. We dimly saw a position on the skyline ahead of us which offered no opposition at all. We just went into a frontal assault which was the first time I'd been in action in all my life. It all seemed to be going well, when suddenly two machine guns opened up on us from the right. Up until then I had thought, 'if this is war, it's all dead easy'.

But now we were suddenly really caught flat-footed. There was already one platoon clearing the position in front of us, the platoon on my right was completely pinned down by two machine guns and the difficulty was getting any troops available to manoeuvre around and actually assault the position.

Lieutenant Shaun Webster, in charge of 10 Platoon, also described the heat of battle: 'There was suddenly a huge racket and tracer started flying everywhere. We took cover and returned fire. I can remember thinking how strange that they should let us get so close because we must have been 30–40 metres away.'

In the mayhem, both Bingley and Private 'Baz' Grayling had shown great courage in attacking one of the machine-gun posts head on. The citation for Bingley's posthumous MM takes up the story:

> Throughout 28th May 1982, the 2nd Battalion The Parachute Regiment were engaged in fierce fighting to take well entrenched enemy positions in the area of the Goose Green settlement on the Island of East Falkland. Lance Corporal Bingley was a Section Commander.
>
> During the battle his section came under fire at close quarters from two enemy machine-gun posts. To destroy the enemy positions he led his section in the assault and whilst leading was fatally wounded.
>
> His heroic action enabled his company to continue their advance and was significantly instrumental in defeating the enemy.

Neame told how there had been four casualties at that early stage of the battle:

> One of those killed was Corporal Bingley who was very brave. He'd gone to ground not really knowing quite where these machine guns were and found himself virtually overlooking the position. He and Grayling just went in and did an immediate assault and the two of them took the five-strong position between them. But Bingley was killed in the process and Grayling slightly injured. It was the sort of

immediate get-up-and-go and flair that really got us out of a very sticky situation.

Lance Corporal Bill Bentley, whose own story is also told in these pages, was the person who brought in Bingley's body from the battlefield:

As daylight approached, we started to search for those of 'D' Company still missing. Padre Cooper called me over, he had found Gaz Bingley. Gaz had been shot through the head. I helped padre carry Gaz back to the RAP [regimental aid post] in a poncho. I will never forget that short walk, his head kept banging against my knee … it was a moving moment for everyone.

Gaz was the first of our dead to be recovered. The story of the last minutes of his life had already reached us through Baz Grayling. They had been making a frontal charge on an Argie machine-gun post. Grayling was hit at close range in his water bottle; it exploded shattering his hip. As Grayling collapsed, still firing, they silenced the M. G. [machine gun]. But as luck would have it the last few rounds squeezed off by the Argie gunner ripped through Gaz Bingley's head, killing him instantly.

Bentley later added of Bingley: 'He was a grand lad, we enjoyed many a laugh together. May he rest in peace.'

Bingley was aged twenty-four when he died. Corporal Tom Harley said later:

I was Gaz's section commander on the fateful day of 28th May 1982. We had been fighting through a position when Gaz said he was moving forward to the high ground to try and locate where the enemy fire was coming from, as he reached the crest he just about fell into their bunker, within a split second he was engaging with the enemy in a close quarter fire. He and his No. 2 Baz Grayling destroyed the position killing the enemy. It was one of the most heroic deeds I have ever seen.

Another comrade of Bingley's said, 'Gaz set the tone for how we fought our war. His bravery and determination showed us the way forward and showed the Argies what they were up against. A true airborne warrior.'

In his book *Goose Green*, Mark Adkin summarised the importance of victory for the British:

> Nothing succeeds like success, or depresses like failure. For Britain a win at Goose Green was even more essential than [for] the Argentines. Consider for a moment the consequences of a 2 PARA defeat coming on top of a week in which the Royal Navy had been hammered by the Argentine Air Force, losing four ships and having five badly damaged. Apart from the inevitable slump in the Task Force's morale and the dismay at home, it would seem to the world that Britain's launching of Operation Corporate was a ghastly and expensive mistake.

Bingley's body was eventually repatriated, and he was buried at Aldershot Military Cemetery, Hampshire. His widow, Jay, said, 'Always missed, never forgotten. My husband and my best friend.'

In 2017, his widow travelled to the Falklands to mark the thirty-fifth anniversary of the war. She retraced her late husband's footsteps from Sussex Mountain to Goose Green via Camilla Creek and went to the spot where Bingley fell. In honour of both 2 PARA and 3 PARA, she then tabbed over Mount Longdon and onto Port Stanley, completing the journey Bingley had intended to make. During the visit, in support of both the Falklands Veterans Foundation and Combat Stress, she also visited the Goose Green Memorial.

MARTIN WILLIAM LESTER BENTLEY
Service: Army
Final rank: Staff Sergeant
FALKLANDS WAR DECORATION / DISTINCTION:
MILITARY MEDAL (MM)
DATES OF BRAVERY: 28–29 MAY 1982
GAZETTED: 8 NOVEMBER 1982

Bill Bentley was decorated with the MM for outstanding bravery while serving as a combat medic at the Battle of Goose Green. At the height of the fighting, he made his way to a forward slope to help a seriously wounded comrade. Seeing the extent of the injuries, Bentley amputated the man's badly tattered leg using a Swiss Army knife, despite facing accurate enemy machine-gun and rifle fire.

The son of a bus conductor and one of ten children, Bentley was born in the north-west of England in 1955. After moving to Chorlton-cum-Hardy, Greater Manchester, in 1960, he was educated at Chorlton Park Primary School and nearby Wilbraham Technical High School. In April 1970, when still only fifteen, he joined the Junior Leaders Regiment of the Royal Armoured Corps as a boy soldier. He became a keen and talented sportsman and was awarded his regimental colours for cross-country skiing and represented the regiment at the national judo championships. By the summer of 1972 he achieved the rank of Junior Squadron Sergeant Major, and in August was chosen as 'best soldier passing out to a Cavalry Regiment'. He subsequently passed out as a trooper in the 14th/20th King's Hussars, where he was again awarded his regimental colours for cross-country skiing. From 1973 to 1976 Bentley was attached to the Parachute Squadron of the Royal Armoured Corps and during this time his postings included Malaya, Sharjah, Cyprus, Norway, Germany and Northern Ireland. His skiing and shooting skills were such that he was selected for the national biathlon squad.

Of his time in Cyprus, during the 1974 conflict between Greece and Turkey, Bentley wrote:

> Under the command of [then] Lt. Rod Hine, I was involved in the evacuation of Archbishop Makarios from Paphos. Later we were cut off behind the Turkish lines, in Kyrenia for ca. [approximately] one month, we were the last group to be brought out. Later still, I was the driver of one of two armoured escort vehicles which brought Rauf Denktasch [the senior Turkish Cypriot politician] into the Ledra Palace Hotel, Nicosia to sign the 'cessations of hostilities' agreement.

In 1976–77, Bentley was attached to 22 SAS, where he completed the selection course and all other training, but not seeing eye to eye with some of the training staff, he opted to return to the 14th/20th King's Hussars. In 1978, he was a divisional white-water canoeing champion while serving in the BAOR before completing another tour of Northern Ireland. He left the army in 1979, only to re-enlist later the same year with 2 PARA, with whom he conducted yet a further tour of Northern Ireland and later became a regimental medical assistant. Still supremely fit, Bentley represented his new regiment in the Northern Ireland judo championships and also came eighth in the international Mourne Mountain Marathon in Co. Down. Also a keen climber, while on R&R from Northern Ireland Bentley did a solo winter ascent of Jbel Toubkal, North Africa's highest mountain. Later, while on exercise in Kenya as a member of a 2 PARA team, he climbed Mount Kenya's five highest peaks and circumnavigated the entire massif.

During the Falklands War, Bentley – a member of the regimental aid post – served as a combat medic carrying out a dangerous role which involved spending a great deal of time in and around the battlefield. Captain Steve Hughes, the medical officer for 2 PARA, kept a diary throughout the conflict, extracts of which appear in Max Arthur's book *Above All, Courage*. Some of the accounts provide a fascinating insight into the role that Bentley and others performed during the Battle of Goose Green. Hughes wrote on 27 May 1982: 'The CO outlined a six-phase battalion plan to take the Goose Green / Darwin isthmus, with the initial fire support of HMS *Arrow*. We all retired away from Camilla Creek House [the holding position] until start time to make our individual preparations.'

On 28 May, Hughes wrote:

I got the lads up at 01.20 after spending a freezing night ... We brewed up, packed up and moved close into Camilla House, moving off behind Battalion Main Headquarters just after 02.00. Moving with the medical kit divided amongst us, in our bergens ... around the area of Burntside House we came under mortar and artillery fire, quite close, for about ninety minutes ... We were also under fire from a sniper / snipers on the right of the track and at one stage a round whistled inches above my head. It was at this stage that D Company took casualties and we were asked to move forward...

About 11.00 ... we came under heavy bombardment in the gully, with shells whistling not 20ft overhead. The rear slope position saved our bacon ... Shrapnel casualties drifted in, the smoke and cordite streamed through our position doing its damnedest to fog us out at times ... One lad came in almost in tears. He was OK but his mucker, Private 'Chopsey' Gray, was pinned down, dying on the forward slope with his leg blown half off. I knew I had to send a medic forward. It was difficult to ask, I felt almost as if I ought to do it myself, but knew that was out of the question. Bill [Lance Corporal Bentley] accepted the task without qualm. Together with a stretcher party he precariously made his way onto the forward slope to Gray. He completed the partial amputation with his clasp knife and was able to stem the blood loss with a tourniquet. They were then able to bring him into the RAP [regimental aid post]. He had no veins visible anywhere, he had lost so much blood.

Hughes told in his diary how Bentley was in action again with Captain John Greenhalgh: 'At dusk, he [Greenhalgh] had, remarkably, taken his Scout onto the forward slope to drop off Lance Corporal Bentley and to pick up casualties. He had flown, guided by lads on the ground, by a radio version of the "Golden Shot" – "left a bit, right a bit" and "here".'

Bentley filled the helicopter, including his place, with casualties, having to make his way back from the battlefield on foot. He later reported the bravery and flying skills of the pilot, Greenhalgh, for which Greenhalgh was awarded the DFC. Hughes noted how, on 29 May, the Argentine force surrendered its position, adding, 'A television news crew choppered in and tried to film the tragic spectacle of our dead. I sent Bill [Bentley] to see them off.'

Hughes's immensely high opinion of Bentley is revealed in his diary entry for 1 June 1982:

I travelled into Darwin to visit A Company and Lance Corporal Bentley. He is having second thoughts about leaving the Army. It would seem a shame now to lose all the ground we've made in terms of experience – we must consolidate. I must try and keep him. Bill's performance has been nothing short of outstanding. He is both a soldier and a very brave man. From the first time we came under fire he stayed cool and set an example to those around him, including me. He has a calming influence, projected not least by his immense practical sense. If there was nothing else to do whilst we were under shell-fire in the gully, Bill was brewing up! Understandably, just his presence instils confidence in all those around him and the others have come on immeasurably.

Bentley's MM was announced in *The London Gazette* on 8 October 1982, when his citation stated:

Lance Corporal Bentley was a member of the Regimental Aid Post of the Second Battalion The Parachute Regiment throughout the Falkland Islands campaign. During the battle for Port Darwin and Goose Green on 28th/29th May it was of tremendous credit to the Regimental Aid Post that none of the Battalion's thirty-four wounded died. This credit belongs to none more than Lance Corporal Bentley. From the first moment that the Regimental Aid Post came under mortar and artillery fire Lance Corporal Bentley's qualities manifested themselves. His courage and presence of mind in carrying out his job acted as an inspiration, not only to the other medical orderlies, but to all those who came in contact with him. With an immense pack of medical kit on his back Lance Corporal Bentley was to be found wherever the casualties were thickest. Regardless of enemy shell and mortar fire he not only dealt with his casualties in a calm reassuring manner, but boosted their morale with a continuous lighthearted banter.

Typical of his sustained performance during the course of the battle was when a soldier had his lower leg blown off by a mortar bomb. Lance Corporal Bentley, still with heavy pack, ran forward onto a forward slope position and, although under persistent enemy fire, calmly and efficiently carried out the emergency medical treatment that undoubtedly saved the soldier's life.

This incident is just one of many that epitomises the qualities of this brave, resourceful and exceptional man. He acted in, and beyond, the finest traditions of The Parachute Regiment.

After being contacted by me, Bill Bentley generously provided a previously unpublished account that he had written about his experiences at Goose Green. I am reproducing part of his work here, with his permission, because it provides a vivid picture of just how tough the situation was at Goose Green:

Moving along a track towards Goose Green we could hear and even feel the incredible rush of the shells, which were being fired by our ships and artillery, passing overhead in support of our advance. The track was the only practical approach route from our direction. Suddenly we heard what turned out to be horses galloping. Perhaps it was this that also alerted the Argentinians; either way, within seconds, we came under heavy and accurate enemy artillery fire, the shoe was now on the other foot [previously the Argentines had been under fire]. Clearly our approach along the track had been anticipated and a 'defensive fire plan' had obviously been measured up in anticipation of our arrival. We were now in 'the killing zone' and someone had to give the command to spread out. Not an easy decision, as one could just as well assume that the sides of the track had also been mined. After a short wait, I am an impatient beggar, I, as a Lance Corporal, took the initiative over my many superiors and gave the order to spread out. Which was just as well as the track became a death trap just a few seconds later. Whether the sides of the track were mined, we will never know: perhaps the frozen ground had prevented a complete disaster. Soon Dr Hughes took control and we moved forward into dead ground. At least my comrades had started to realise that I was not a bullshitter and I started to quickly gain the respect of the young soldiers and the commanders alike.

Ahead of us on the upward slope, the battle was in full swing and casualties were being brought in to us at the Regimental Aid Post, which was no more than a group of medics and a doctor, all with rucksacks full of medical supplies. One young soldier had been shot in his water bottle, which had exploded, probably breaking his hip. Another [wounded soldier], we could not identify his injury and so I persuaded the PT [Physical Training Corps] Sgt, who was leading a stretcher-bearer team, to shine his torch onto the casualty. The PT Sgt was horrified at the thought of lighting up the darkness while the battle raged just ahead of and above us. Using his own body to screen the light from the direction of the battle, he did as I had requested. We were then able to identify that this young man had also been shot in his webbing, the bullet had ripped through his equipment, travelled along the inside of his belt and had come to rest exactly in his navel. Clearly the lad was shocked and bruised but, as I could find no injury and there were obviously no broken bones, I wanted to send him back to his platoon. After all, they were in the heat of the battle. My boss, Dr Steve Hughes, was more sympathetic and sent the lad back to Ajax Bay for a proper check-up. (This young man rejoined us before the battle for Wireless Ridge where he was then killed.) The battle moved forward ahead of us but we remained in the dead ground where it was much more realistic to treat the casualties than on the battlefield itself.

During quiet moments, we tried to take a nap but the bitter cold made this almost impossible. As dawn broke, we went forward to search for our missing comrades. Along with the Reverend David Cooper, our padre, I carried in our first dead body. The soldier, a friend of mine, had been shot through the head, the bullets had ripped the back of his head off and literally blown his brain out. While carrying his body back into the lines in a poncho, his head kept banging against my knee and giving off a 'hollow echo', a sound that is not easy to forget.

I went out again, this time with Mark James [name changed]. Mark and I decided to split up, the area to cover was considerable and time was critical to the survival of our comrades. I soon became aware of someone sitting or crouching, about a hundred metres ahead of me. Looking for cover I suddenly saw a trench ahead of me and ran to it and jumped in. In the bottom of the trench there was obviously someone hiding under a poncho. Instinctively, I fired a long burst of Sub Machine Gun [SMG], luckily past my own feet into who or whatever was under the poncho. Climbing out, it was as if I was stood on a waterbed with lumps in it. I guess shocked, I sprang back out and moved forward to another trench. Here there was a severely wounded Argentinian soldier who was unconscious [and dying]. Again moving forward, towards the first person that I had seen, I realised that he was also an Argentinian soldier. I moved quickly and cautiously towards him and, as he had made no aggressive gestures, I was also not aggressive. In front of me was a young Argentinian soldier, he had been shot through the leg and was in deep shock. The better side of me, or my training, now took over. The youngster had no weapon at hand and so I hoisted him up over my shoulder, a classical fireman's lift, and carried him into our own lines. Looking back this was quite a risk as he would have been looking down onto my bayonet and it would have been fairly easy for him to have drawn it and stabbed me in the back.

One of the medics indicated to me that another missing friend of mine was 'over there'. I found him alongside another body lying next to his. It was obvious that my friend had been injured first and that the youngster had gone to his aid. The shell dressing and the position of the bodies were unmistakable. They had both obviously taken a prolonged burst of machine-gun fire that had made a real mess. Out of respect for the youngster, I chose to carry him in first. Lying down next to him, I took his arms up over my shoulders and staggered to my feet, as I did this the youngster just rolled to the side and back to the ground. I was still holding one of his arms over my shoulder. Spreading my own poncho out on the ground, I rolled his body onto it and dragged him back towards the rest of the medics. Somebody came out to meet me and helped me drag the body the rest of the way. I desperately needed a rest, we had now been moving in extreme conditions for about fifty hours. I had to ask two other medics to go out and bring in my friend while I had a brew and tried to take a nap.

I was awoken to obvious confusion. Dr Hughes was getting ready to go forward and attend to Lt Col Jones who had been shot. The RSM [Regimental Sergeant Major] would brief us and I should bring up the rest of the medics at the double. The RSM asked us to take forward as much ammunition and weaponry as possible so I stashed my SMG and grabbed a GPMG [general-purpose machine gun] and as much ammo as I could carry. My own load was well in excess of 120lb, my trench-mate Dawson [name changed] was similarly loaded. We two went on ahead of the others. 'Just follow the track' were our only instructions. Upon reaching the crest of the hill, we became aware of a Pucará fighter aircraft bearing down upon us. I immediately opened fire from the hip with the GPMG but got a stoppage [the gun jammed]. Dawson dashed to help me but fell to the ground like a stone. The Pucará flew past us and I moved to help Dawson. Luckily, he had not been wounded but had tripped and was winded by the weight of his load landing on top of him. We looked for the Pucará which was, by now, shooting down one of our helicopters about half a mile away. Immediately upon arrival at A Company's lines we were relieved of our extra weapons and ammunition and so, I for one, now felt naked with only my SMG and at the very next opportunity took an SLR [self-loading rifle] from the dead marine, Cpl Geoff Hunt [name changed]. Several other medics followed suit.

We found Dr Hughes: Colonel Jones was already dead. Others desperately needed our services and, having assisted a couple of casualties, I became aware that one of the young platoon medics, Greg [name changed], with whom I had become very close during the training on the MV *Norland*, needed help. Greg had been shot some hours earlier and had lost a lot of blood and, although he had been patched up by others, he was in danger of also freezing to death when we found him. Dawson ripped open his own shirt and placed an infusion bag against his naked body to try to take off the chill, while I placed the infusion needle into Greg's arm. It was a moment desperately full of emotion that I can only compare with the delivery of my own two daughters into this world. We evacuated Greg on the next available helicopter, regardless of medical priorities. Greg survived as did, luckily, all other casualties who were alive when we reached them. Another young platoon medic, Arthur [name changed], had been shot through the head. A squirt of his brain was visible on the back of his head, like toothpaste that had been squeezed out of a tube. I did not consider that he could survive and told Phil Barnes [name changed] to give him 'a lot of morphine' but Dr Hughes thought that he could 'have a chance' and, with help from Phil and Mark James, he also survived. Thanks to all of them, Arthur Jones is today still a valued friend of ours.

The day passed with moments of intense action and quiet moments. During a heavy barrage, I found myself sharing a shell crater with our padre, what a guy! If anything put me off him it was the extra long spade that he carried, just in case he had to 'dig a quick grave'. He always had a story or a quick joke like 'not being fussy about who I have to bury' and 'I would be proud to do you the favour'! Thanks, Padre.

Steadily the row of our own bodies grew and at some point my good friend Bertie's [name changed] body was brought in. I confess that I broke down and cried. We were not getting any useful medical resupplies: we were all dead tired, hungry, even eating biscuits from the pockets of the dead, friend and foe alike, and the ammunition was running out. Their artillery had us pinpointed, the colonel was dead along with a growing list of officers and men, things were looking pretty desperate.

Fred [name changed], a friend of mine, came staggering down from the crest of the hill towards us, his bayonet still fixed and he told Dr Hughes that yet another platoon medic, Jim Lang [name changed], and another friend, Peter Plant [name changed], were injured on the other side of the hill. Doc [Hughes] looked at me and I heard myself volunteering. Fred led me through our own front line, through a gap in a stone wall, where he suddenly opened fire on two enemy soldiers. I also breached the gap and opened fire. By the time I came up level with Fred, he was thrusting his bayonet into the second soldier, the first was already most definitely dead. We moved on to the forward slope down a small depression to a point where

Fred could point out the casualties to me. It was about 25 metres to them, fully exposed to the enemy down in Goose Green. I told Fred to await the rescue party and then to creep over to us on my signal. I crept over to Jim and Peter. Peter told me to look after Jim who 'is in a bad way'. Jim had gone back to rescue Peter who had been shot through the arm and, in doing so, had himself been hit 'full on' by a mortar bomb which had shattered one leg, broken the other and he was full of fragmentation. I quickly decided it would not be possible to deal with all of this on the spot, and so opted to amputate the shattered leg. By now, somebody had become aware of my presence and bullets were 'pfloping' into the soft ground around us. I placed a tourniquet on Jim's leg and severed the remains of his lower leg with my Swiss Army knife so that I could place a stump bandage. Jim just cringed into the ground, which was already soaked with his own blood. The sweet sickly smell, mixed with the cordite, burnt flesh and fresh earth, is unforgettable. The incoming fire was, by now, increasing and so, turning to help Peter, I gave the signal to Fred to come and get Jim. A young Captain had, however, taken command of the rescue party and he had decided to rush in, grab the wounded and bolt for cover, which is exactly what happened. If a plan works it was the right plan on the day!

When the enemy saw a group of men rushing from cover, all hell broke loose. The ground around us exploded. I remember placing Jim's severed leg on the stretcher then suddenly they were all 10 metres ahead of me. The ground between us erupted, it was alive! I decided to play dead where I was. After what seemed to be an eternity, the rescue party reached safety and the incoming fire faded away. I slowly gathered my equipment together and as many of the 'left behind' weapons from the rescue party as I could carry and, in the now oncoming dusk, made my way back up the hill. I became concerned that I did not know the password to re-enter our lines.

This, however, was not a problem: the lads had seen everything that had happened and welcomed me with open arms. When I asked, 'What is the password?' somebody said, 'Who cares? When we challenge "Who goes there?", if the answer is "*Qua?*" we shoot the bastard!'

I arrived back over the hill in time to see Jim and Peter waiting for a helicopter evacuation. When the helicopter landed, we placed Jim's stretcher in the pod on the outside of the chopper but we could not get the lid to close. Realising that Jim still had his webbing on and the spade that he had been carrying was preventing the pod lid from closing, I sat Jim up to remove his shoulder harness and that's when Jim saw his own leg lying across the end of the stretcher. He stared at me, or rather through me. I gave him a hug, assured him he'd be OK, pressed him back down, closed the pod and waved to the pilot to take off. Enemy artillery had seen the helicopter landing and were again making things most uncomfortable.

In an interview with me, Bentley played down any suggestion that he had been brave during the Falklands War:

People talk about courage, but if you are not afraid you don't need courage. Personally, I was never afraid. Sure, I knew I was taking risks, but they were calculated risks and so I just got on with it. I never did anything that I considered to be foolhardy. I have never felt fear for myself though I have felt it for my family.

Incidentally, the Rev. David Cooper referred to in Bentley's interview is also quite a character. Cooper was in his late thirties by the time the Falklands War broke out, when he was the army chaplain, or padre, to 2 PARA. He was a hugely courageous man and was filmed on 30 May 1982 officiating at the moving field burial service for the eighteen Paras who were killed in the Battle of Goose Green, including Colonel 'H' Jones. During that service, he used the expression 'think on', which became his catchphrase with the media. After the war, he was recommended for the MC, only for it to be downgraded, somewhat controversially, to a Mention in Despatches. Cooper, who was himself a champion shot, also ministered to 2 PARA during its tours to Northern Ireland, when the battalion again suffered heavy losses. After retiring from the army in September 1984, he became Chaplain at Eton College. He is now fully retired and living in Somerset.

Bentley left the army in 1983, and for the next year worked mostly in America for Prince Bandar bin Sultan, the Saudi ambassador to the United States. In 1985, he returned to the UK, where for the next five years he served in the Duke of Lancaster's Own Yeomanry. He finally ended his time in the military in 1990 in the rank of Staff Sergeant, having by then completed three separate stints and accumulated a total of seventeen years' service.

After leaving the army for the final time, he moved to Germany in 1990, marrying for the first time. He has two daughters by his first wife, a German, but the relationship ended in divorce. Bentley later got remarried, again to a German woman. After moving to Germany, Bentley first worked collecting the cash from casinos and then trained as a gas and water fitter. Later, he became a property surveyor and later still an energy consultant. However, Bentley was forced to give up this role in 2011 after many years of ill health, and he lived for the next eight years on a smallholding and off his army pension. However, over the years Bentley became less able to withstand the cold of the northern European winters. So, along with Rahi, in 2019 he moved to the south of Spain. In 2021, fifty-one years after joining the army, Bentley finally received his old-age pension.

THOMAS JAMES CAMP

Service: Army

Final rank: Colonel

FALKLANDS WAR DECORATION / DISTINCTION:

MILITARY MEDAL (MM)

DATE OF BRAVERY: 28 MAY 1982

GAZETTED: 8 OCTOBER 1982

OTHER DECORATIONS / DISTINCTIONS:

MENTIONED IN DESPATCHES (MID)

Tom Camp's army career was remarkable in that he served for more than thirty-one years, during which time he was awarded a gallantry medal as a Corporal, yet later rose to become a full Colonel. His MM was gained during a fierce firefight to recapture Darwin Hill on East Falkland.

Thomas James Camp was born in London on 21 February 1957. His father was a steel erector, and because he worked in the construction business the family travelled the country widely, linked to his work. Camp left school aged sixteen having attended West Bromwich Grammar School in the West Midlands.

Still aged sixteen, he joined the army in September 1973 at the Infantry Junior Leaders Battalion at Oswestry. From 1975 to 1982, he served as a Junior NCO with 2 PARA. During this period, he was deployed to Northern Ireland, the USA and Norway.

Like most servicemen, until 1982 Camp had little knowledge of the Falkland Islands or exactly where they were situated. However, once they were invaded on 2 April and it looked as if war was likely, there was a sense of anticipation from him and his comrades in 2 PARA. He said,

For a time, of course, it looked like there might be a diplomatic settlement. But once it looked as if something was going to happen, everybody in the Battalion was terrified that they weren't going to be involved. This feeling went wider than just the Battalion – everyone was anxious that their unit would somehow be involved.

2 PARA travelled to the Falklands on MV *Norland*, a requisitioned North Sea ferry that was less than ideal as a troop carrier or warship. Camp recalled:

The ship was designed for a two-hour crossing not as somewhere to spend five weeks. Cabins with four-man bunks, two each side, for four paratroopers and lots of kit meant things were pretty tight, space wise. I remember we stored lots of the kit, including our bergens, in the shower room. En route we did lots of weapon training and lots of fitness – as much as you can by running up and down corridors and stairs on a ferry. There was also lots of combat first-aid training relating to drips and essential equipment, plus a lot of kit-checking.

While the *Norland* was sailing to the Falklands via Ascension Island, the war proper started and people began to get killed. Camp, who was married with a baby son, said:

We all realised once the hostilities started that this was serious. With it came a lot of will-writing and signing up for 'PAX' – personal life insurance arranged through the military. A lot of people who had never had the inclination or thought of paying an insurance premium suddenly decided to try to get insured up to the hilt so their wives – their widows – would be looked after financially if they got killed in battle. There was a big effort from the top of the MoD down to make sure people made provisions for their loved ones just in case – though I, in fact, already had insurance. Filling in a life insurance form, however, focused the mind for a few of the lads.

Camp said that he and his men were also fiercely determined not to let themselves down in battle:

> You are dealing with a unit [the Paras] with a tremendous record and therefore you want to live up to the expectations of everyone that is looking at that unit. By that point, in 1982, I had been in the Army for nearly nine years and – apart from Northern Ireland, and we had all done Northern Ireland – this was my first time in action. We knew it was going to be a proper test and everyone was simply looking forward to doing well, to playing their part. We wanted to do the job that we had been trained to do.

After landing at San Carlos Bay on 21 May, 2 PARA went ashore in landing craft. Camp continued:

> We were in the dark and we had no idea what we were going to: it was a pretty unique experience. Landing craft are not really de-signed to be loaded from a ferry so that was an experience in itself. Like most other land-based forces, we just wanted to get ashore where we felt more comfortable. Bobbing around in a little landing craft is not where a Paratrooper wants to be. Then we got wet feet and some people got more than wet feet because there was an 'early beaching' when people got out on something that wasn't the beach – it was a sandbar well off land. So we had to pull off that and go on to what was actually the beach, with some men by then pretty wet and cold.

Camp said that after tabbing to Sussex Mountain, high ground above San Carlos, with heavy ammunition, he and his comrades prepared a defensive position:

> We then spent from the 21st to the 26th on Sussex Mountain, which I can only describe as a bare-arse position: a very boggy, hostile environment. There was a lot of rain and a high water table, so we couldn't really dig in deep because as soon as you dug down a hole it filled with water, so you had to build up turf walls to create protection. We spent five days there, but everyone was champing at the bit to get something done. Then on the 26th, we started advancing southwards.

On the morning of 28 May, the battle for Darwin Hill began. As the Commander of a section of eight men, Camp takes up the story with typical modesty:

> We had spent the night going through our various objectives. At first light, we saw someone moving across in front of us. To start with in the gloom, we thought it was someone walking a dog. We had not expected anyone 'hostile' to be so close to us, but it was in fact an Argentine soldier moving between trenches. Then someone shouted, someone else opened fire and it all started. At that point, we were very close to the enemy – perhaps 50 or 60 metres, almost on top of them. We were in slightly lower ground [to the Argentine force] and in the open, so if I remember rightly, we moved forward and left and tried to get some cover. And then we had to clear some initial trenches to get to what they call 'Gorse Gully'. That gave us some cover from the main position, and there was a succession of attempts to get onto a ridge 20 or 30 metres in front of it to fire down onto the main enemy position. But it became clear very quickly that anyone trying to get onto that ridge was taking

Investigate day: William 'Bill' O'Brien outside Buckingham Palace with his DFM.

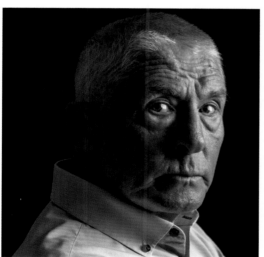

Sid Davidson
Died Falklands 1982

ABOVE LEFT Bill O'Brien DFM, who flew numerous missions in a Gazelle helicopter of 3 Commando Brigade Air Squadron, Royal Marines, lending valuable support to the Paras at Goose Green and Darwin in May 1982: 'I really thrived on the intensity of it … and frankly missed it when I returned to Britain after the war.' Remarkably, he was still flying operationally in Afghanistan in 2009–10, nearly thirty years after the Falklands War.

ABOVE RIGHT Sergeant Sidney 'Sid' Davidson, who served in 'D' Squadron, 22 SAS, at the capture of South Georgia and in a raid mounted on Pebble Island; he helped a wounded colleague in the former action. Described by one comrade as having been 'outstanding from day one, a soldier's soldier', he was among those killed in the Sea King helicopter disaster of 19 May 1982.

The honours and awards of Major Peter Ratcliffe of the SAS, including his DCM on the left. They reflect active service in Dhofar, Northern Ireland, the Falklands War and the First Gulf War, in the last of which he won his DCM. The riband of his South Atlantic Medal bears an oak leaf to denote his Mention in Despatches.

Private Stephen Illingsworth of 2 Para, who displayed supreme courage in the battle for Goose Green and Darwin in May 1982. Having rescued a wounded colleague under 'a hail of enemy fire', he returned to collect the soldier's webbing and much-needed ammunition. As he did so, he was killed. He was originally recommended for a posthumous award of the VC, but in the event he was awarded the DCM.

Peter Ratcliffe, on the right, with HRH the Prince of Wales. On Mount Kent in late May 1982, his four-man SAS team engaged an Argentine patrol and took its surrender. A few days later on another recce, this time at Fox Bay, his team positioned itself right on the edge of the enemy's forward position: 'And the beauty of it was that they had no idea we were there.'

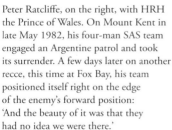

Lance Corporal Gary 'Gaz' Bingley of 2 Para, who was awarded a posthumous MM for his gallantry and sacrifice at the battle for Goose Green and Darwin in May 1982. He was killed storming an Argentine machine-gun post. Major Phil Neame later said, 'It was the sort of immediate get-up-and-go and flair that really got us out of a sticky situation.'

Martin 'Bill' Bentley of 2 Para, who was awarded the MM for his gallantry as a member of the battalion's regimental aid post in the battle for Goose Green and Darwin in May 1982. At the height of the battle he had to remove the shattered remnants of a comrade's leg with his Swiss Army knife.

The honours and awards of Colonel Thomas Camp MM, reflecting active service in Northern Ireland, the Falklands War, the First Gulf War and Kosovo. He was serving as a Corporal in 2 Para at the time of winning his MM on Darwin Hill in May 1982, when he advanced under heavy fire and knocked out an enemy bunker with grenades.

Lance Corporal (later Company Quartermaster Sergeant) Stephen 'Baz' Bardsley of 2 Para, who was awarded the MM for his gallantry in the battle for Goose Green and Darwin in May 1982 when leading his men in a series of close-quarter attacks on enemy positions, in addition to rescuing one of his wounded comrades under heavy fire. One Falklands War comrade described him as a 'legend'.

Lance Corporal 'Les' Standish of 2 Para. He won the MM for a series of ferocious night actions in the battle for Goose Green and Darwin in May 1982, when he cleared the opposition trench by trench in addition to rescuing a wounded comrade under heavy fire. Since then, his courage has not deserted him and he has fought PTSD and other setbacks with equal determination.

Sergeant Ian McKay of 3 Para, who was awarded a posthumous VC for his magnificent courage and sacrifice on Mount Longdon in June 1982.

Investiture day at Buckingham Palace: Ian McKay's widow, Marica, with her son Donald and daughter Melanie: 'I was incredibly proud when he was awarded the VC, but part of me wishes he had hidden behind a rock…'

Marica McKay today, photographed at her Lincolnshire home with her children Donald, fifty-three, and Melanie, forty-three; she is holding a replica VC to recreate the scene outside Buckingham Palace nearly forty years ago.

Ian McKay's funeral at Aldershot Military Cemetery, Hampshire, on 26 November 1982, when he was buried with full military honours. Among the pallbearers were Ian Bailey MM and Desmond Fuller MM.

Corporal (later Captain) Ian Bailey of 3 Para, who won the MM for his gallantry alongside Ian McKay VC on Mount Longdon in June 1982. In the midst of heavy fighting, Bailey received three serious wounds that medics feared would claim his life. However, he eventually made a good recovery and acted as a pallbearer at McKay's funeral.

Sergeant Desmond 'Des' Fuller of 3 Para, who was awarded the MM for his gallantry on Mount Longdon in June 1982. At the height of the battle, on learning of Sergeant Ian McKay's loss, his Commanding Officer told him: 'You're fucking in charge!' He didn't disappoint, rallying and leading his platoon in a series of close-quarter assaults on the enemy.

Peter Marshall, who joined the West Midlands Police on leaving the army. A cook by trade, he was Mentioned in Despatches for his gallantry as a stretcher-bearer in 3 Para on Mount Longdon in June 1982. As one Para put it: 'They say the Toms were good, but the fucking cooks were good as well: those guys were up and down the mountain with the artillery going, still bringing the bodies back and the wounded back.'

British paratroopers carrying out emergency medical treatment on wounded comrades while under fire on Mount Longdon in June 1982.

Sergeant Terence Barrett of 2 Para, far right, who was awarded the MM for his gallant deeds at Goose Green and on Wireless Ridge. At the former battle in May 1982, he 'controlled his fire teams in a masterful way, often exposing himself to machine gun and sniper fire as he personally led forward his fire teams'.

Company Sergeant Major (later Captain) William 'Bill' Nicol and comrades from 2nd Scots Guards. He was awarded the DCM for three separate acts of courage, most notably on Mount Tumbledown on 14 June 1982, when his company came under 'devastating machine gun and sniper fire'. Going forward to tend to a wounded comrade, he was himself wounded in the hand but refused to be evacuated.

Falklands dead arrive home in a freightliner in November 1982.

ABOVE LEFT British diplomat Sir Rex Hunt, Governor of the Falkland Islands at the time of the Argentine invasion, on receiving his knighthood at Buckingham Palace. Having told the senior officers of his defence force that 'it looks like the bastards mean it', he declared a state of emergency in the early morning of 2 April 1982, shortly before the first Argentine commandos set foot on the Falklands.

ABOVE RIGHT The aircraft that helped to win the Falklands War: Margaret Thatcher in the cockpit of a Sea Harrier at the British Aerospace facilities at Kingston upon Thames in December 1982. The aircraft was one of seven under construction to replace those lost in the conflict.

RIGHT Falklands Victory Parade, London, 12 October 1982: thousands of spectators belted out 'Rule Britannia' as the march past of 1,250 military personnel proceeded from Armoury House in Bunhill Fields to the Guildhall. Mrs Thatcher and Admiral of the Fleet Sir Terence Lewin took the salute on the portico of Mansion House, where even the Labour leader Michael Foot was seen to tap his hands in time with the music.

Falklands Victory Parade: General Sir Jeremy Moore KCB OBE MC on the right. He commanded the British Land Forces during the conflict.

HRH the Prince of Wales chats to Welsh Guardsman Simon Weston after presenting him with the South Atlantic Medal at Buckingham Palace on 1 December 1982.

The Union flag flying over the British War Cemetery at San Carlos on 21 February 2012, shortly before the thirtieth anniversary of the Falklands War.

an awful lot of fire. And that was where a lot of our [2 PARA] casualties were taken, along that ridge line. Once we were in this more protected position, we were about 150 to 200 metres from the enemy. I would say the whole action was probably over in two and a half to three hours. I am proud to say all of my men went to the Falklands and all of them came back, which was amazing. I was one of three Corporals in my platoon in 'A' Company, 2 PARA. One was killed, one was seriously injured, but I came back safely.

As previously detailed, during the battle Colonel Herbert 'H' Jones, the CO of 2 PARA, was shot and killed. Camp said, 'It occurred at the culminating point of the whole action. I didn't see him get hit, but I was told very soon afterwards that he had gone down. He was literally 30 to 50 metres to our right.' Of the controversy on whether Colonel 'H' should have been leading his men so close to the front line, Camp said, 'It's a sensitive subject and a lot has been written about it. All I can say is that he was the CO of a Parachute Battalion who was leading from the front.'

Subsequently, on 13 June, the day before the surrender, Camp and his men saw action on Wireless Ridge. 'We were involved in a noisy, night-time attack. It was successful,' said Camp, who is not one to waste words or go into detail about the gruesome scenes that he and others witnessed during their fierce firefights.

After the surrender and once we got into Stanley, we could see it was a mess. There was lots of kit everywhere, thousands of prisoners of war. The whole place was very dirty, pretty abused. The Argentine Army consisted of a lot of eighteen-year-old conscripts who were not very disciplined. It looked as if there had been a party for a thousand teenagers – not a pretty sight. On the outskirts of Stanley, I moved with my section into a schoolmaster's house, which was welcome because the weather was getting worse and worse. I think we spent six or seven days there – the nice bit was we were all allowed to send one short telegram home. Then eventually we were allowed home, sailing back up to Ascension Island and then flying back to Brize [Norton, Oxfordshire].

Before going to the Falklands, Camp had attended a course in Warminster, Wiltshire, to begin being commissioned as an officer.

In September 1982, three months after the war ended, I was in Beaconsfield, Buckinghamshire, at the Army School of Education, doing a pre-Sandhurst course, when I was whistled into the OC's office and told that I had been selected for a decoration. It was nice to be honoured.

His MM was announced on 8 October 1982, when his citation stated:

In the early hours of 28th May, the 2nd Battalion The Parachute Regiment were ordered to attack enemy positions in the area of Port Darwin on the island of East Falkland. The enemy were well entrenched in strength on Darwin Hill and fierce fighting ensued.

Corporal Camp was leading his Section when they came under fire from an enemy bunker: continuing under fire he moved forward and hurled grenades into the bunker. He then manoeuvred his men into positions from where their anti-tank rockets and section machine gun were able to engage and destroy the enemy position. Thereafter, he successfully led his men in further assaults on well defended enemy positions. His courage and leadership in action were outstanding.

It was not until 1983 that Camp was able to go to Buckingham

Palace for his investiture accompanied by his wife, Shelagh, and a close friend. The Queen presented him with his MM, noticing that he was an Officer Cadet – by this point, he was undergoing officer training at the Royal Military Academy, Sandhurst. From 1984 to 1987, by then a Lieutenant, Camp served with 29 Commando Regiment Royal Artillery with deployments to Norway and Denmark. By chance, Plymouth-based 29 Commando Regiment had supported 2 PARA during some of the most intense fighting of the Falklands War. By 1987, Camp was a Captain and was posted to 19 Field Regiment Royal Artillery in Dortmund, West Germany, serving as a forward observation officer, adjutant and Headquarters Battery Commander. Next, he deployed to Northern Ireland and then to the British Army Training Unit Suffield in Alberta, Canada.

After attending the Army Staff College at Camberley, Surrey, he joined Headquarters 1st Armoured Division as it moved to Saudi Arabia as part of the initial deployment for 'Operation Granby' during the First Gulf War. After the liberation of Kuwait, Camp was divisional operations officer at Verden, Germany, from 1991 to 1992. In 1993, he assumed command of 88 (Arracan) Battery of 4 Field Regiment, Royal Artillery in Osnabrück, Germany. And in 1994, he returned with his battery to Northern Ireland, where he was responsible for army support to the Royal Ulster Constabulary (RUC) within the New Lodge area of north Belfast. He was Mentioned in Despatches for his work in New Lodge.

In September 1994, Camp was promoted to Lieutenant Colonel, and he joined the Directing Staff at the Army Staff College, Camberley. He returned to Sandhurst eleven years after being commissioned, a feat of which he is rightly proud. In March 1996, he became the Directing Lieutenant Colonel of 'A' Wing at the Army Junior Division at Camberley, where he was responsible for overseeing the initial staff training of seventy army Captains. Camp commanded the 5th Battalion, Royal Irish Regiment, in Ballykelly, Northern Ireland, from August 1997 to September 1999, where he was responsible for army support to two RUC police divisions. Next, he was posted as a plans officer to NATO's Joint Headquarters Centre in Heidelberg, Germany, as they moved to Kosovo for KFOR 2 (Kosovo Force 2) and where he served in Pristina. On promotion to full Colonel in January 2002, he assumed his final post of Deputy Commander and Chief of Staff, HQ British Forces Gibraltar. Camp retired from the army on 18 April 2005 after thirty-one years and six months of service, during which he had worn a total of six different cap badges.

After leaving the army, Camp concentrated on his hobbies, including motorcycling, cycling and wine-tasting. Along with his wife, in 2005 he moved to a village in south-west France, where he continues to live. The couple have a grown-up son and a grandson. Reflecting on the Falklands War nearly four decades on, he said, 'When I look upon the war, I was fortunate not to get injured and I was very fortunate to be honoured – and I had a good life and a successful career after that. So I consider myself to have been very lucky.'

KEVIN PETER DUNBAR

Service: Army

Final rank: Staff Sergeant

FALKLANDS WAR DECORATION / DISTINCTION:

MENTIONED IN DESPATCHES (MID)

DATES OF BRAVERY: 28–29 MAY 1982

GAZETTED: 8 OCTOBER 1982

OTHER DECORATIONS / DISTINCTIONS:

MILITARY MEDAL (MM)

Kevin Dunbar was Mentioned in Despatches for bravery during the battle for Goose Green. While serving with 2 PARA, he courageously took part in hand-to-hand combat and destroyed an Argentine bunker with an anti-tank rocket. He went on to serve in the SAS, and he was awarded the MM for gallantry behind enemy lines during the First Gulf War in 1991.

Kevin Peter Dunbar, a farmer's son, was born on 29 August 1959 in Shrewsbury, Shropshire, one of fourteen children. He was the ninth-born child, one of seven brothers and seven sisters. However, his father died in 1973, and with his mother struggling to look after such a large family, he went to live with an uncle, who was a brother in the Redemptorist Order. As a youngster, Dunbar attended St Mary's Catholic Primary School in Brewood, Staffordshire, before attending Wolgarston High School in nearby Penkridge.

Dunbar enlisted in the army on 18 November 1976, aged seventeen. After serving in the Junior Parachute Company ('Junior Paras') in Aldershot, Hampshire, he went on to serve in 2 PARA. Between 1977 and 1982, he completed lengthy tours in Germany and Northern Ireland, as well as shorter placements in Denmark and Kenya. During his tour of Northern Ireland, he lost comrades and friends in the Warrenpoint ambush of 27 August 1979. Eighteen soldiers based at the Abercorn Barracks, Ballykinler, were killed and more than twenty injured in the IRA attack in Co. Down, which took place on the same day Lord Mountbatten was murdered when a bomb was planted on his fishing boat in Mullaghmore, Co. Sligo.

When the Falkland Islands were invaded on 2 April 1982, Dunbar, by then aged twenty-two and in the rank of Lance Corporal, was on leave and helping his uncle with farm work. The local police managed to track him down and instructed him that he had to return to his barracks in Aldershot immediately. Days later, 2 PARA was sailing for the Falklands on board MV *Norland*.

Everyone was up for what lay ahead. I was in 'B' Company and luckily we had one of the greatest soldiers who ever lived as our OC – Major [later Colonel] John Crosland. He said it as it was going to be: this was going to be a tough fight and some of us would not be returning. The men really, really respected him – he had just come from Hereford [serving with the SAS]. Everyone knew he was a great soldier and they just did as they were asked. We stayed fit on board and underwent training every day throughout the voyage.

2 PARA arrived in the Falklands at San Carlos Bay on 21 May 1982. In an interview, Dunbar said:

Initially, we got dropped off in quite deep water, whereas we had expected to be taken almost onto a beach. Because we had been up to our chests in water, our uniforms, boots and other clothing got soaking wet – and we got very cold. It meant too that over the next few days quite a few guys got trench foot and were in quite serious pain. We then had quite a long march to get to our first RV point, where we dug in.

Even before the main battle for Goose Green, 2 PARA in general and Dunbar in particular became involved in some dangerous situations, especially as they tried to shoot down enemy planes that were attacking both soldiers on land and British Navy ships off the coast. In his book *2 PARA Falklands: The Battalion at War*, Major General John Frost wrote:

Similar stories [of trying to shoot down enemy planes] were repeated often in the rifle companies. In 'B' Company, for example, Lance Corporal Dunbar and Private Ferguson of 4 Platoon blasted away at a Skyhawk that was following a Mirage. As the aircraft came soaring up the valley towards them, its belly was turned fully exposed to their fire, and soon a smoke trail told of their success. Indeed the Skyhawk had flown so low overhead that they could actually see their tracer hitting the fuselage.

Dunbar confirmed this incident. 'It didn't get light till quite late so I suppose that first attack was about 9.30 in the morning. It was the first time I had fired in anger during the war,' he said.

In his book *Goose Green*, Mark Adkin describes another scene shortly afterwards in which an Argentine pilot was shot down and killed: 'The dead pilot was Sub Lieutenant Miguel who died instantly when his aircraft smashed into the ground among 4 Platoon of B Company near Goose Green. Part of the plane hit Lance Corporal Dunbar, removing two belts of ammunition clean out of his hand.'

Dunbar confirmed this incident too:

Hundreds of us had been shooting from the ground at the enemy plane and it was hit. As the Pucará was coming down, the pilot banked his attack aircraft. It meant that luckily for us it hit the ground in front of us rather than ploughing into us. It must have crashed into the ground about 50 metres from where I was standing and a fragment from the plane, perhaps a bit of the wing, knocked the ammunition belts from my left hand. It was a near miss.

The battle for Goose Green began in earnest on the night of 28 May, and by the next morning Dunbar and his comrades in 'B' Company had been made aware over their radios that Colonel 'H' Jones had been shot and killed. Reflecting on the incident, Dunbar said, 'To be honest, Colonel "H" was a very, very nice chap and a fine soldier. But no Commanding Officer should have been on the front line – his position should have been controlling the battalion from the rear echelons.'

The citation for Dunbar's Mention in Despatches describes his role in the battle:

During the night attack in the battle for Port Darwin and Goose Green on 28/29 May 1982, Lance Corporal Kevin Dunbar showed outstanding leadership skills and courage in the hand-to-hand fighting as the enemy positions were cleared trench by trench. At first light B Company was pinned down by a strong enemy bunker. Lance Corporal Dunbar realising this, and on his own initiative, stood up under enemy fire, and from a range of 150 metres, calmly fired a light anti-tank rocket into the bunker. This action undoubtedly saved the lives of several soldiers and allowed the Company to reorganise in safety and continue to advance. After neutralising the enemy bunker Lance Corporal Dunbar returned to his section and continued to display the same standards of leadership, coolness and courage until the end of the battle.

Recalling the incident, Dunbar told me that he and his comrades from 'B' Company, a force of more than sixty men, had found themselves in a difficult position as they advanced on the night of 28–29 May:

We were basically advancing in line in the dark when we realised there were two enemy positions directly in front of us – both heavy machine-gun positions. I was on the left of the company and Major Crosland stopped the advance because of this threat and told us that we had to try to knock these positions out. It's hard to estimate because it was dark, but I would say one of the positions was going on for 300 metres away. So I fired an anti-tank rocket – a Law 66 – and I hit the enemy bunker smack on. The weapon is usually only good to be fired from no more than 200 metres, but I guess I was lucky and it carried. Some of the other guys attacked the other position and knocked that one out too. After that, it was quite a fluid movement for our advance.

That was the end of the hand-to-hand fighting for Dunbar and his comrades from 'B' Company. After the Argentine surrender, he was involved in rounding up POWs and clearing up ammunition. Dunbar said, 'I lost some good friends in the fighting, including those from "A" Company in which I had originally served.' During their stay in Port Stanley, several men from 'B' Company, including Dunbar, were put up in a bungalow in the town before they sailed for home, feeling proud of what they had achieved. 'On the way back, the 3rd Battalion joined us on the car ferry [MV *Norland*],' Dunbar recalled.

Dunbar's Mention in Despatches was announced in *The London Gazette* on 8 October 1982. He was made aware of it shortly before the public announcement, in a letter from John Nott, the Defence Secretary.

Dunbar told me that even before the Falklands War he had planned to seek selection to the SAS, after some of his friends and comrades from 2 PARA successfully made the switch. He passed selection first time and joined 'A' Squadron in early June 1983 before serving in The Regiment for more than sixteen years and rising to the rank of Staff Sergeant. During his time in the SAS, Dunbar took part in a daring undercover mission in Iraq during the First Gulf War, for which he was decorated with the MM. Dunbar was discharged from the army on 22 December 1999 after more than twenty-three years of army service.

He left with an affectionate testimonial to his professionalism that praised his 'exemplary service' to the army:

During this time he has worked at various employments and roles including active service on sensitive operations abroad. He was Mentioned in Despatches during the Falklands Conflict and in 1991 he was awarded the Military Medal for bravery during the Gulf War.

Staff Sergeant Dunbar MM is a highly motivated man who has a pleasant, friendly manner and disposition. He is very well experienced at managing men and resources which added to his personal skills makes him an excellent team leader. He is a very personable man who can identify with objectives and, with his enthusiastic approach to all tasks, ensures that they are completed to the best of his ability. He mixes easily in professional and social situations.

Staff Sergeant Dunbar's commitment and dedication throughout his service has been outstanding. His inherent qualities of self-discipline, trustworthiness and loyalty will make him an immense asset to any future employer.

After leaving the military aged forty, Dunbar worked in security, including personal protection, from 1999 to 2014. His security work took him to the US, Nigeria, Sudan, the Congo and Liberia. From 2014 to the present day, he has worked in property management. Dunbar, who has three children from his first marriage, lives in south-east England with his second wife. He told me: 'I have loved my career, particularly my time in the army. If I could do it all over again, I would. I wouldn't change anything.'

STEPHEN ALAN BARDSLEY

Service: Army

Final rank: Company Quarter Master Sergeant

FALKLANDS WAR DECORATION / DISTINCTION:

MILITARY MEDAL (MM)

DATE OF BRAVERY: 28 MAY 1982

GAZETTED: 8 OCTOBER 1982

OTHER DECORATIONS / DISTINCTIONS:

BRITISH EMPIRE MEDAL (BEM)

Stephen Bardsley, who was decorated for his actions both in the Falklands War and in the First Gulf War, was at one time the most highly decorated NCO in the British Army. He also had the distinction of serving in the South Atlantic under Colonel 'H' Jones.

Stephen Alan Bardsley, known as 'Baz' to his comrades, was born in Manchester on 31 August 1957. He was the eldest son of Alan and June Bardsley, who had been married two years earlier, and he was educated at Moston Brook High School in Manchester.

After leaving school, Bardsley was determined to join the army. After training and gaining the coveted red beret, he was posted to Northern Ireland with the Parachute Regiment in January 1980, serving at Ballykinler, Co. Down, where six years earlier two British soldiers had been killed and thirty-three others injured in a bomb attack on the Abercorn Barracks. In 1980 too, Bardsley married his childhood sweetheart, Margaret Malthouse, in Manchester.

At the time of the invasion of the Falkland Islands in early April 1982, Bardsley was serving as a Section Commander in 'B' Company. Bardsley embarked for the South Atlantic with the battalion, serving under the command of Major John Crosland, who was awarded the MC during the conflict, and under the overall command of 2 PARA's OC, Colonel 'H' Jones.

Bardsley travelled to the war zone with 2 PARA on MV *Norland*, on which the men spent many hours working on their fitness. None of the young soldiers knew what lay ahead, but they were well-trained, single-minded and 'ready for anything'. They needed to be: the weather when they arrived at the Falklands on 21 May 1982 was challenging, and the terrain on East Falkland was no easier.

It was during the Battle for Goose Green that Bardsley, then a 24-year-old Lance Corporal, displayed such gallantry on the battlefield that he was later awarded the MM. The citation for his decoration takes up the story:

In the early hours of 28 May 1982, 2nd Battalion, The Parachute Regiment launched an attack to take enemy positions in the area of the Darwin and Goose Green settlements on the Island of East Falkland. Lance Corporal Bardsley was a Section Commander during the night advance on Goose Green.

He led his men in a series of close quarter attacks on enemy positions. As dawn came his men were pinned down by enemy fire. Unruffled, he organised an orderly withdrawal. In withdrawing one of his men was wounded; disregarding his own safety, Lance Corporal Bardsley returned to rescue him. Thereafter, he continued to lead his men with distinction in further actions through the day.

Lance Corporal Bardsley showed impressive leadership and courage in action.

His MM was announced on 8 October 1982. In fact, 1982 was a memorable year for Bardsley in many ways as it also saw the birth of his first child: a daughter called Catherine. Two other daughters followed over the next seven years and the Bardsleys were a strong family unit.

Following the Falklands War, Bardsley received promotions, and in the rank of Colour Sergeant in 1990, he was selected for an exchange with the US Army. He was posted to Fort Bragg, attached to the 82nd Airborne Division.

Bardsley was acting as a Platoon Sergeant with the 2/505th Reconnaissance Platoon when orders came through for deployment of the platoon to the Gulf. For his combat operational service in that war, he was awarded the British Empire Medal (BEM) and the US Bronze Star. His BEM was gazetted on 29 June 1991 and stated:

You were posted to the United States Army's 82nd Airborne Division in April 1990. When you were employed as a rifle platoon Sergeant on deployment to the Persian Gulf, you demonstrated your powers of innovation by designing and organising realistic and effective field firing facilities that proved to be critical in achieving required standards of operational readiness in the Battalion. During the operational phase of the fighting it was your display of initiative, the ability to inspire your men and a readiness to share and apply your experience from the Falklands War that contributed so greatly to the success of your unit missions and so, Colour-Sergeant Bardsley, I am commanded by Her Majesty the Queen to present to you the Medal of the Order of the British Empire for meritorious service.

The citation for his US Bronze Star, which was gazetted on 8 June 1993, was given

for exceptionally meritorious achievements in support in actions against a hostile force in the Persian Gulf from 17 January 1991 to 20 March 1991, while assigned to Company C, Second Battalion, 505th Parachute Infantry Regiment, 82nd Airborne Division. As the First Sergeant and Infantry Platoon Sergeant, Colour-Sergeant Bardsley's performance in combat operations was a key factor that enabled the 82nd Airborne Division in conjunction with coalition forces to implement United Nations Security Council resolutions, end Iraqi aggression and free the country of Kuwait. His devotion in duty, aggressiveness and ability to excel while under great pressure contributed significantly to the successful accomplishment of the mission. Colour-Sergeant Bardsley demonstrated the high ideals and professionalism exemplified by the airborne tradition. His outstanding performance in support of the combat mission reflects distinct credit upon himself, the 82nd Airborne Division and the United States Army.

Returning from the Gulf, Bardsley remained with the 82nd until April 1992, when he rejoined the Parachute Regiment and took up the duties of Company Quarter Master Sergeant, Headquarters Company. After further postings, he left the Paras in 2001 after twenty-two years of military service.

Next, Bardsley found another passion: bodybuilding. Along with his younger brother, Mark, he became the co-owner of Powermill Gym in Middleton, north Manchester. The gym soon became *the* bodybuilding centre for the area and produced several leading proponents of the sport, including the brothers who were both competitive bodybuilders.

In 2012, Bardsley sold his medal group at auction for a six-figure sum and used the money to open a new gym aimed at getting youngsters off the streets. Friends said it was typical of the man that he was always trying to help others. He was also humble and rarely talked of his wartime exploits or his many decorations.

Bardsley's life, however, took a turn for the worse when his wife, Margaret, was diagnosed with a brain tumour. She died on 10 December 2013, aged fifty-six, leaving her husband devastated. In fact, he never recovered from her death; they had met each other when they were both ten years old and had been married for thirty-three years.

Bardsley took his own life on 4 June 2014, just over thirty-two years on from the battle at Goose Green which had claimed the lives of fifteen of his fellow paratroopers. He was fifty-seven years old, and the last love letter he received from his late wife was found on his bed. It read: 'I just wanted you to know I love you all the world and more. I can't wait to go away this weekend with you.'

His eldest daughter, Catherine Disbury, a teacher, later told an inquest that it had been a 'terrible blow' for her father when her mother fell seriously ill. He became her full-time carer and he had later told his children that he did not want to be alive and instead wanted to be with his late wife. Bardsley even stopped taking medication for his heart condition in the hope that he would have a fatal heart attack. She told the inquest: 'I was seriously worried about his well-being. It was clear from his behaviour he was not in a good place and was angry.' She added, 'When I was informed that he had taken his own life I was shocked but I was surprised it had taken this long after the death of my mum.'

In a recent blog on a website for Falklands War veterans, Jay Hyrons, a fellow bodybuilder, posted an affectionate tribute to Bardsley which ended with the words:

> It is hard to know the final straw when someone is in that frame of mind to not want to continue with life. Sometimes it is a bit like weight training, that moment when you train to failure and the muscle just cannot go on. Each and every one of us has the potential to get to that point; it's all about the size of the burden and sometimes it is too much to bear. We thank you Baz for your gallant service, rest in eternal peace, you deserve it.

Replying to the online tribute, Vincent Bainbridge, who served with Bardsley in the Falklands, described him as 'a legend'. He suggested his friend had been suffering from PTSD but, like many of his generation, 'just got on with it but suffered in silence, Baz carried a lot of demons like many of us who went to war…'

LESLIE JAMES LEONARD STANDISH
Service: Army
Final Rank: Corporal
FALKANDS WAR DECORATION / DISTINCTION:
MILITARY MEDAL (MM)
DATES OF BRAVERY: 28–29 MAY 1982
GAZETTED: 8 OCTOBER 1982

Les Standish paid a heavy price for his bravery in the Falklands War. His gallantry at Goose Green led to him being awarded the MM, but what he had seen and experienced on the battlefield also resulted in him suffering from severe mental health problems after leaving the army.

Leslie James Leonard Standish was born on 2 April 1961 in Bolton, Greater Manchester. His father, Roy, served in the army, ending up in the rank of Sergeant Major in the 14th/20th King's Hussars. After a nomadic life travelling the world because of his father's job, the family settled in Leigh, Lancashire. He finished the final year of his education in Leigh before leaving school to join the army's Junior Parachute Company on 6 September 1976, aged just fifteen. For the first two years of his service, he was in the Pegasus Gymnastic Display Team. After doing his basic training with the Paras' Recruit Company, he passed out and joined 2 PARA in Ballykinler, Co. Down.

At the time, 2 PARA was a year into its two-year tour of Northern Ireland in the midst of The Troubles. During Standish's time as a Private based at Forkhill in South Armagh, in August 1980 Sergeant Brian Brown, one of Standish's comrades and a father of three, was blown up and killed by an improvised explosive device placed near an army post.

For the next two years, Standish was based at Aldershot, Hampshire, doing various training exercises. In the spring of 1982 he got married, and he and his new wife, Trudi, were on honeymoon in Spain when the Falklands crisis began to unfold. In an interview from his home in Bolton, Standish said, 'We were the standby battalion [for any emergency]. While on honeymoon, I received the code word – Bruneval – which meant I had to return to camp straight away. I was a week into our fortnight's honeymoon when I headed back to Aldershot.'

Standish and his comrades from 2 PARA travelled to the Falklands on board MV *Norland*:

> When we first heard we were off to the Falklands we didn't know where it was. If I am being honest, the majority of us thought it was somewhere in Scotland. Even when we knew where it was and we were going down there, we thought it would all be sorted out politically. We didn't expect that we were going to war.

However, things changed dramatically on 25 May 1982, when SS *Atlantic Conveyor* was hit by two air-launched Exocet missiles. The container ship, owned by Cunard, had been requisitioned for the war but had no 'active' nor 'passive' defence system. When she was hit twice on her port quarter side, twelve men were killed, including the ship's master, Captain Ian North, who was awarded a posthumous DSC. 'It was only when we got the news that the *Atlantic Conveyor* had been sunk that we realised it was all going to kick off. I thought, "This is it,"' Standish said.

> We did all the weapons training and everything on board the ship to prepare for the landing. We landed in San Carlos Water, East Falkland – codename Blue Beach 2. Our landing craft stopped short of the shore, the front went down and the pilot of the landing craft shouted, 'Out troops, out troops.' We didn't move to start with because that was Royal Marines terminology. It was only when our Sergeant Major shouted, 'Go!' – our PARA terminology – that we all ran out of the front of the landing craft and into the sea. At that point, we didn't know whether it was an opposed landing or an unopposed landing. In the event, it was an unopposed landing.
>
> From there we got ourselves together and reorganised. Then we tabbed up to the top of Sussex Mountain on the west side of East

Falkland. It was the hardest thing I have ever done in my life without a doubt. We were each carrying between 140 and 180lb of kit because each man had two mortar bombs. My section was the SF [sustained firing] section so we had a machine gun and a tripod, and it was really hard-going because the terrain was really tough as well.

At one point on the first day – and also on other days later that week – the Argentine Air Force attacked our ships in San Carlos Water. We were firing our small-arms rifles into the valley to try to hit the enemy planes. After we had been on the island about a week, our Section Commander got trench foot and was taken off the mountain to go to the hospital in Bluff Cove. So that meant I was the acting Section Commander – in charge of eight men.

We spent every morning doing clearance patrols. One morning, while we were patrolling on foot, we came across an enemy patrol in a Land Rover and with another soldier on a motorbike. We weren't expecting them, and they weren't expecting us. As soon as we saw them, we pointed our weapons at them. That was my first contact, though in fact there was no firefight. The soldiers came out of the Land Rover and put their hands in the air. They basically froze and came out of their vehicle straight away. We took four prisoners – the one on the motorbike and three in the Land Rover.

Our next contact was Goose Green itself after we had been on top of the mountain for just short of two weeks. We had slept each night in a hole in the ground in a trench. We had some dry, windy days to dry out our kit but mostly it was freezing cold and wet. But we got into a good routine and we were well-trained so it was OK.

As for Goose Green itself, we all got our briefing. Then we did a night march to the start line. We got to a place called Boca House, but then the BBC World Service broadcast that an attack on Goose

Green was imminent so we had to lie up in a field for a day because the radio announcement delayed the attack as it had warned the enemy. The army Commanders were furious with the BBC.

This meant we had eaten all our rations, so in fact we attacked Goose Green [in the early hours of 28 May] on an empty stomach. Colonel 'H' was our CO and he was very popular and well-respected. On the day of the battle, we got to the start line. I was in 5 Platoon, the rear section; 4 and 6 Platoons were the two point [attacking] sections. We advanced the contact during the night.

As soon as the contact started at about 2 a.m. or 3 a.m., all the Shamoolies went up. That's a big flare that comes down on a small parachute in order to light up an area of about 1 square km so we could see what we were attacking. At that point, the shit hit the fan and all the fighting started. It was organised chaos – very lively. Early in the battle it came over on the radio, 'Sunray is down.' Sunray was the codename for our CO: Colonel 'H'. I thought, 'Fucking hell.' Then 'The White Shark' took over – that was our nickname for Major Chris Keeble because of his shock of blond hair.

I was responsible for eight other guys in the section and for myself too. We fought side by side – we really were brothers in arms. We had to perform for ourselves and for one another. We were one group going forward together ... We got through quite a lot of trenches under a heavy fire. We would throw in grenades, jump in the trench and kill the enemy. In the trench, it was him or me. Then we moved on to the next one: the adrenaline takes over. During the fighting that day, I killed three of the enemy for definite – I was up close and saw the fear in their faces and the whites of their eyes. It was kill or be killed – I didn't have time to stop and think. I shot them with my rifle. It was what I was trained to do – I was doing my job.

But nothing can prepare you for what actually happened. Now, I see the fear in the Argentine faces that I killed. They were trying to kill us, but we were elite forces in a battle with conscripts aged eighteen or nineteen. They did not have a cat in hell's chance. 'Bang, bang,' and away you go.

There was a young boy who knew he was going to die when I shot him. He was not pointing his weapon, but he had it in his hand and potentially he could have shot me. When you get into contact with someone you can see their face just go white, their eyes wide open, and he just knew he was going to die. At the time, I had no time to reflect on what I had done.

At one point, the rest of the platoon had retreated back over a hill. But at first light we got caught on a forward slope. We had sniper fire coming down on us and we couldn't move at all. Every time we moved the rounds came in about a foot away, hitting the ground where we were standing.

I had a choice as the Section Commander to either go forward down the slope and into a dip and separate ourselves from the rest of the platoon or to go back up the mountain to rejoin the rest of the platoon. By this point, we were about 100 yards from the rest of our men. In the end, I decided to move back and the rest of the platoon gave us covering fire as we moved in twos back up. Most of my section got back into dead ground. But one of my lads, Private Jim Street, got shot in the leg by the incoming rifle and machine-gun fire from about 500 to 1,000 yards.

I was nearly up to the top, the dead ground, when I realised that he had been shot. He was screaming. So me and another one of my Privates, Andy Brooke, we both went down the slope with rounds coming in all the time close to us. We basically got hold of Jim and dragged him up the hill still constantly under fire. How we did not get hit I do not know to this day. Then there was a bit of a respite before we advanced again because the Argentinians had pulled back to the settlement. We then advanced trench by trench. They put up a light defence, and we had to be careful because there were civilians in the church house so we couldn't retaliate too heavily.

Eventually, when we were outside Goose Green, [Major] Chris Keeble gave the Argentinians the chance to surrender – but they didn't initially. Then two Harrier jets flew across Goose Green and dropped some cluster bombs and 'The White Shark' told the Argentinians [senior officers], 'Look, if you don't surrender, the planes will be back and you will be responsible for a lot of deaths, including civilian deaths.' The enemy surrendered soon afterwards.

When I asked Standish about the controversy of Colonel 'H' – whether he had been foolhardy and asked his men to do too much – he replied:

You can't criticise if you weren't there. He made a decision in a split second in the middle of a battle. There is no such thing as being 'too brave'. You do what you have to do for the people you are fighting next to. If anyone else had been where 'H' Jones was, would they have done exactly the same? Of course they would. He wanted his battalion to be successful in the battle – and it cost him his life. Because he got killed, the rest of the war was fought for Colonel 'H'.

The most traumatic event Standish witnessed actually took place shortly after the Argentinian surrender at Goose Green. Once again, he takes up the story:

When they surrendered, the Argentine prisoners got put in the sheep pens in the middle of the settlement. They had booby-trapped their own field guns. My job was to take an Argentine soldier and make the guns safe, so that we could use them if the need arose. When the Argentine went to make the guns safe, the incendiary device blew up and in doing so blew the flesh and muscles off his legs, from the waist down. His bones were intact, his feet were still there. But you can imagine that from his waist up he was fine, from his waist down he was just bones. Because it was an incendiary, all his veins had fused so he was not bleeding. He was just kicking his bones up and down. The flesh from his legs went all over me and another Argentine prisoner nearby. We had both been standing about 10 or 15ft apart from each other when the explosion happened. He was there with all this gunk of human flesh and muscle all over him, and I was there with all this stuff over me, and we had this Argentine soldier kicking his legs and asking for his mother. So we picked him up and took him to our aid post.

I will never forget it. It was a big wooden table, because that is all we had, and all you could hear were his bones, his legs, banging on the table, tapping on the wood as he shouted for his mother. We tried to get a line in him to give him fluids. We couldn't find his veins because they had retracted. So we had to get our Medical Officer, Steven Hughes, to cut his wrists – it is called a 'cut down' – and we got a line in his wrist and pumped a load of fluid into him. And I will never forget it… Tap. Tap. Tap. Tap. Tap. You could hear his legs banging on the table like that, crying for his mum, his bones exposed. There was not much flesh on them at all. You can imagine a skeleton, skeleton legs and from the waist up a normal body. And we just watched him die on the table. We just couldn't do anything.

In fact, Standish also got injured shortly after the battle, but not seriously.

There was a stack of Argentinian bombs at Goose Green. We

looked at them to see if they were booby-trapped or wired up. But one of the bombs in the stack rolled off and landed on my right foot, breaking my big toe. So that was basically the end of my war. I ended up taking the prisoners [Argentine POWs from Goose Green] on the *Norland* to Montevideo. We searched them as they came aboard, then fed them and looked after them until we reached Montevideo. Then we sailed on to Ascension Island and got a VC10 flight to RAF Brize Norton.

Standish's MM was officially announced in *The London Gazette* on 8 October, when his citation stated:

In the dark early hours of 28 May 1982, the 2nd Battalion, The Parachute Regiment launched an attack to take enemy positions in the area of the Darwin and Goose Green settlements on the Island of East Falkland. Lance Corporal Standish was a Section Commander.

During the advance on Goose Green he led his section in a series of ferocious night actions. The enemy had to be cleared trench by trench. Shortly after dawn, enemy fire caught his men in the open; he calmly withdrew them to dead ground. In withdrawing a private soldier was wounded. Disregarding his own safety, Lance Corporal Standish returned through enemy fire to drag him to safety.

Throughout the battle Lance Corporal Standish commanded his section with the utmost distinction and courage.

On the day of the announcement of his MM, he received a telegram from the Prince of Wales, the Colonel-in-Chief of the Parachute Regiment, which read: 'On receiving the news of your award I send you my warmest congratulations. I have the greatest possible admiration for the gallantry you displayed and for the way in which you maintained the very highest traditions of the Regiment.'

Standish was surprised, even shocked, when he learnt of his decoration:

It never crossed my mind that I would receive a decoration for what I had done ... To be honest, I didn't really know what the MM was until I read the history of the medal.

When I was told, I rang up my dad and said, 'Dad, I have won the Military Medal.' And he replied, 'Son, you don't *win* the Military Medal, you get *awarded* it.' He had served in the army so he knew the terminology. It was when my citation came through that I felt really proud and thought, 'I am the member of a very small club.' I felt proud and honoured – I was only twenty-one.

My only bone of contention is that Private Andy Brooke and I did exactly the same thing. Yet, Andy Brooke got a Mention in Despatches and I received the Military Medal. So why didn't he get the MM as well? Apparently it was because I was twenty-one years old and the Section Commander and it was also everything I did prior to the action. So I just had to accept it at the end of the day.

I received my decoration at an investiture hosted by the Queen at Buckingham Palace. I went with my wife, my dad Roy, my mum Maureen and my brother Peter. The thing I remember most about meeting the Queen was her handshake: for such a small, petite lady, she had a really strong handshake. She gripped me like a bloke would do and it took me back a bit.

For the first six months after we came back, I couldn't put my hand in my pocket for anything. It was the same for everyone. We'd done a good job out there and we became national heroes. We were proud soldiers. We were very young and were proud of what we did.

I stayed in the army for four more years after the Falklands War and left in 1986 in the rank of full Corporal. I had to decide whether to stay in the army and make a career of it or leave and make a career in 'Civvy Street'. By then I had done two tours of Northern Ireland, the Falklands War and trips to Belize, the Oman and Kenya. I thought I had done enough.

In 1987, Standish joined the prison service as a physical education instructor.

I was a prison officer during the Strangeways riot [which started on 1 April 1990 and lasted for twenty-five days, during which an inmate and a prison officer died]. I was more scared in the riots than I had been during the war. They were throwing scaffolding poles at us, and it was such close contact. Unlike being in the army, I wasn't sure that I could trust the man [fellow prison guard] next to me. In the army you always knew the guy next to you had your back, but in the prison service you were not sure. Army and civilian people are a totally different breed. It was all quite hairy and that's when things started to go haywire in my brain. I had flashbacks to some of the things that happened during the Falklands War and seeing the people that I had killed.

After the Strangeways riots, I started drinking heavily – I guess it was the usual sort of spiral downhill. My marriage broke up in about 1992 and by that point we had two children – a boy and girl. I ended up homeless: I felt alone and had no help from anyone. I was suffering from PTSD and I mixed with the wrong crowd in Bolton. I made bad decisions that I wouldn't have made if I was in a stable position.

Around this point, Standish, using his connections in the Bolton underworld, joined an illegal circuit of bare-knuckle fighters who travel around Britain being paid to fight and sometimes wagering money on themselves against their opponents. For eighteen months, he fought in warehouses, empty factories and barns, where up to 200 bloodthirsty gamblers would turn up at the fights. Standish says he fought nineteen times, won seventeen, drew one and got badly hammered in one other. The fights were vicious affairs: the last man standing was the winner.

'When I was still working as a prison officer, I got arrested. I used to collect money for a drug dealer. I wasn't involved in drugs other than collecting the money. But I got caught and I was sentenced to three years in prison for conspiracy to supply cannabis,' he said.

Initially, while awaiting trial, Standish was kept in solitary confinement for his own safety, because he had been a prison officer and might have faced great hostility from prisoners. This left him, after three months, planning to commit suicide in his cell; he was, by his own admission, at 'rock bottom'. Fortunately, however, he came into contact with Dr Dafydd Jones, who ran a clinic for ex-servicemen called Ty Gwyn in Llandudno, north Wales. Standish says that this was a turning point, and he credits Dr Jones with saving his life.

Standish was allowed by the Home Office to serve his prison sentence at Denbigh Hospital in north Wales, where Jones was the consultant psychiatrist. Standish was then taken as a day patient to Ty Gwyn, where he underwent prolonged treatment. Part of his counselling involved him writing down his dreams. 'I get little white flashes that simulate bullets coming through my head and then I am back in the war and I remember everything, and I just relive it over and over again,' he said.

My time at Ty Gwyn helped me hugely. I was under a psychiatrist, and I had to relive everything I had been through – the Falklands,

Strangeways and other things. I was taught to box everything up and lock it away – then I was in control over when I open the box and bring it out, then put it back in the box again.

When I came out of prison in 1996, I found there were a lot of people in the same position as I was, and I started working with some of them through Colonel Simon Brewis, who had been in charge of the South Atlantic Medal Association. We worked together to find other soldiers with PTSD and then made sure that they received the same treatment that I had. That was all voluntary work – not paid work.

In 2002, Standish met a soldier who he had fought against in May 1982:

This Argentinian soldier came onto our Parachute Regiment website asking to contact anyone who had fought at Goose Green. He got a bit of abuse from some of the lads – unnecessarily, I thought. I just replied to him and said I was a Section Commander at the battle. In fact, I later found out I was in the right-hand attacking section and he was in the left-hand trench defending Goose Green. So at some point we would have been shooting at each other. We exchanged emails, then I did some charity events to raise money for him to come over to England. His name is Alejandro Videla, and he was a Corporal in the 12th Infantry Regiment in 1982. He came to Bolton and he stayed at a hotel in the town. I liked him and there were no hard feelings about the war – we were both just doing our jobs. It was therapeutic to meet him and we are still in touch by email even now, almost another twenty years on. I hope to go and see him in Argentina one day.

In February 2002, Standish got married again. However, he was still suffering from PTSD, so that marriage also failed and the couple divorced eight years later. For a time, he was homeless and living in a van, but he got a flat with help from the charity Soldiers Off The Street. After his divorce, he travelled around the world, and today he lives with his current partner, Julie, in Bolton and is enjoying his retirement.

CHAPTER 7

THE BATTLE FOR THE MOUNTAINS, PART 1: PORT HARRIET AND MOUNT LONGDON

3 Commando Brigade had, from the moment it arrived in the South Atlantic, planned a short, sharp campaign aimed at winning the war within weeks, not months. The operational problems of fighting a war 8,000 miles from home, plus the worsening winter weather, were key factors in plotting a rapid campaign. There was also a fear that, although British public opinion was generally behind the war, there might not be the stomach for a prolonged conflict once the body bags started arriving home and the funeral numbers mounted. So, political and diplomatic pressures also encouraged the planning for a decisive assault.

It soon became apparent that there would be what has been called 'The Battle for the Mountains'. Mount Kent on East Falkland was soon in British hands because the enemy, perhaps foolishly, chose not to defend it. This prevented the Argentine forces from using the vantage point to attack British ships. However, if the British were to advance on Port Stanley, they needed to break through a defensive line of mountains and hills including Mount Harriet, Mount Longdon, Two Sisters, Mount Tumbledown and Sapper Hill.

The lesson the British military Commanders had learnt from Goose Green, the first major land battle of the war, was that the enemy were adept at doggedly defending prepared positions. This meant the British could expect fierce opposition from the Argentine troops if they

attacked the mountains and hills that protected Port Stanley. The tar-
gets of Mount Harriet, Mount Longdon, Two Sisters, Mount Tumble-
down and Sapper Hill were all defended by minefields and significant
firepower, including heavy machine guns.

The fiercest fighting in the Battle for the Mountains took place
during the Battle of Mount Longdon, but in the build-up to that sus-
tained firefight there were many incidents of bravery. Once again, this
is not the book for a detailed account of the Battle of Mount Longdon
because other military historians have already completed that task. The
battle was fought over 11–12 June between 3 PARA, led by Lieutenant
Colonel (later Lieutenant General Sir) Hew Pike, and elements of the
Argentine 7th Infantry Regiment reinforced by Special Forces snipers.
The imposing Mount Longdon loomed like a fortress between 3 PARA
and the western end of Port Stanley. To the south lay a vast minefield,
to the east lay Wireless Ridge and in between lay the enemy, who were
well dug in and up for a fight. The battle raged for twelve hours as the
enemy put up fierce resistance. The fighting was costly to both sides:
3 PARA lost twenty-three men, including two soldiers attached from
other regiments, and forty-seven others were wounded. Two of the
3 PARA dead – Privates Ian Scrivens and Jason Burt – were only sev-
enteen years old, while Private Neil Grose was killed on his eighteenth
birthday. The enemy casualties were higher – thirty-one killed and
more than 100 wounded. 3 PARA also took at least thirty-nine POWs.

Some of the fighting was brutal, especially as most of the troops on
both sides were seeing combat for the first time. One young Argentine
conscript later described being at the receiving end of an intense bom-
bardment at the height of the battle. He said, 'The rocking was tremen-
dous; it was like an earthquake, as if everything was going to fall apart.
I thought my eardrums were going to burst. We'd been told that, in the
case of a bombardment, we had to open our mouths wide and try to
scream because otherwise we ran the risk of going deaf. It was our first
bombardment and we all tried to do what we'd been taught in a split

second. Some shouted because we'd been taught to; others screamed from fear. I suddenly had terrible earache; it was as if liquid was pouring out of my ears; I felt my face but there seemed nothing there.'

During the battle – much of it fought in driving rain, strong winds and heavy mist – many members of 3 PARA displayed outstanding bravery in the mixture of ranged combat and hand-to-hand fighting. The courage of 3 PARA was typified by the selfless actions of Sergeant Ian McKay, who sacrificed his own life to help his comrades. For his valour, McKay was awarded a posthumous VC – one of only two given for the entire war. I purchased the McKay medal group privately in 1989, and I feel privileged to be the custodian of this brave soldier's gallantry and service medals. His family have indicated that they are equally delighted that the medal group is on public display at the Imperial War Museum.

Other decorations for courage displayed at the Battle of Mount Longdon included one DSO to Lieutenant Colonel Hew Pike, two MCs, two DCMs, three MMs and numerous Mentions in Despatches.

Success at the Battle of Mount Longdon and at other encounters in the Battle for the Mountains meant the British Forces could advance towards Port Stanley. The victory that the British military Commanders had been seeking for the past month suddenly looked a reality, but with the momentum behind the British Forces, could they bring off a swift and decisive end to the war?

IAN JOHN McKAY

Service: Army

Final rank: Sergeant

FALKLANDS WAR DECORATION / DISTINCTION:

VICTORIA CROSS (VC)

DATE OF BRAVERY: 12 JUNE 1982

GAZETTED: 8 OCTOBER 1982

Ian McKay was awarded 'the last VC of the twentieth century' for an act of outstanding bravery more than 8,000 miles from his Yorkshire roots. His gallantry award was announced in *The London Gazette* on the same day as Colonel Herbert 'H' Jones's VC, but McKay's decoration appeared after the senior officer's because of his lower rank. These were the only two VCs to be awarded as a result of the Falklands War.

Ian John McKay was born in Wortley, near Sheffield, on 7 May 1953. He was the son of Kenneth McKay, a foreman in a Sheffield steelworks, and his wife Freda (née Hargreaves). Young Ian was educated at Roughwood Primary School in Rotherham, Yorkshire, and Rotherham Grammar School. He left school with six O-levels, and despite being a talented footballer, he turned down the chance to join Doncaster Rovers. As teenagers, McKay and his friends played war games with rules such as, they could not shoot each other if there was a tree or a bush in the line of fire to protect them. McKay's father was keen for him to pursue a career as a physical education teacher, but the young man was having none of it.

Instead, McKay was determined to pursue a career in the army, and he joined up on 3 August 1970, less than three months after his seventeenth birthday. While still only seventeen and having passed out into the Parachute Regiment, he made his first tour of Northern Ireland at the height of The Troubles. His family was concerned for his safety, especially after three Scottish soldiers were murdered by the IRA within a week of his arrival. McKay was on duty with his company from the 1st Battalion, the Parachute Regiment (1 PARA) on 30 January 1972, when thirteen civilians were killed and more than fifteen injured in the Bogside, Co. Derry, at what became known as 'Bloody Sunday'. At the subsequent public inquiry into the shooting, McKay gave evidence under oath but anonymously for his own safety as 'Soldier T'. Later, he served as a weapons training instructor at Aldershot, Hampshire. On 4 December 1976, McKay married Marica Vickers, who was six years his senior and already had a son, Donald, from her first marriage. The couple, who met while McKay was serving in Germany and his bride-to-be was married to another soldier, later went on to have a daughter, Melanie, whom Ian adored. He also took his duties as a stepfather very seriously.

In 1981, McKay was promoted to acting Sergeant, a rank that was confirmed the next year. He was hugely admired by both his subordinates and his superiors. Lieutenant Colonel (later Major General Sir) Hew Pike, who got to know McKay well during this time, said of him:

> His manner was outgoing, self-confident and extremely enthusiastic yet he was also clearly a thinker, a man with ideas, who was always looking for a better, more professional way of tackling a problem … As a leader, he was strong but compassionate – a man greatly respected and trusted by his soldiers, because of his obvious professional competence, his infectious confidence and his utter sincerity.

On 9 April 1982, McKay embarked for the Falklands as a Sergeant with 4 Platoon, 'B' Company, 3 PARA. His leave, and his time with his family, had been cut short by the events 8,000 miles away in the South Atlantic. After playing football, he had received a call to say he needed to return to barracks. 'He came in and went out,' Marica McKay later recalled. 'I put his dinner in a Tupperware container and he went straight away. He just said, "I've got to go." I never saw him again.'

On the way to the Falklands, on board SS *Canberra*, an ocean liner part of the P&O Cruise fleet, McKay wrote a postcard to his parents and brothers, joking that if he'd had to pay for his cabin it would have cost £5,000 for a ninety-day cruise. He also told a friend: 'I've no intention of taking any risks and getting killed. If I do … then it will be to protect my men, to save lives.' The voyage to the Falklands was not wasted time, however; McKay used it for up to three fitness sessions per day and extensive training for him and his men. Along with his comrades from 3 PARA, he landed at Port San Carlos on the western coast of East Falkland on the night of 21 May. Soon, they had to 'dig in', knowing that if they remained visible, they would be easy targets for the Argentine Air Force. For several days, there was no chance of attacking the enemy as they were waiting for reinforcements to arrive.

After exhausting marches on the nights of 27–28 May and 28–29 May, during which they covered 40 miles in total, the Paras arrived at Mount Estancia, East Falkland. Each man had carried loads of up to 120lb during the marches, and the total area covered on foot since landing amounted to more than 50 miles. By this point on 29 May, and after their gruelling tab, the Paras were ready for the final push on Port Stanley. At this point, McKay and his men became aware of the death of Colonel 'H' Jones and fourteen others from 2 PARA during the hard-won victories at Darwin and Goose Green. They also knew that many other Paras had been wounded, but it was time to press on.

On 2 June, some members of 3 PARA had gone on a 'probing patrol' on Mount Longdon while McKay's patrol had moved forward to Murrell Bridge. However, here they had come across well-placed Argentine mortar fire and were forced to pull back and once again dig in. Over the next week, more patrols put out feelers, and on 6 and 7 June there were modest firefights but no full-scale battles.

McKay even found time on 8 June to write a letter to his parents and two brothers, in which he said:

I have never known a more bleak, windswept and wet place in my life. We spend our life with wet feet trying to dry out and keep warm. The wind blows constantly but it is cooling rather than drying. You cannot walk fifty paces anywhere, even on the mountainsides, without walking into a bog. To be quite honest once we have given them a hammering and put them back in their place the Argentines can have the place. It really is fit for nothing. I thought the Brecon Beacons was bad but this takes the biscuit.

It would be his last letter home and it was signed, 'All my love to you all, Ian.'

Meanwhile, the tactics to end the enemy's occupation of the Falklands were being worked out, and Mount Longdon was seen as the key point of the Argentine defences. The final push began on 11 June. By dawn the men were preparing themselves for the impending battle, and McKay was, in the words of one comrade and friend, ready to 'look after the lads almost like a mother hen'. He had twenty-eight men in his platoon, including himself, and he had a strong feeling that he might not survive the battle. Company Sergeant Major John Weeks said later:

> I remember Ian coming up to me this side of the Murrell – just before we crossed the river, before the battle for Mount Longdon and again, it's always stuck in my mind. He said, 'Remember what I told you? I am not going to come back from this.' This was maybe an hour before we crossed the river and got into our formations for the battle. And sure enough he did not come back.

The long citation for McKay's posthumous VC takes up the story of a single episode in the long, fraught and confused battle:

> During the night of 11th/12th June 1982, 3rd Battalion The Parachute Regiment mounted a silent night attack on an enemy

battalion position on Mount Longdon, an important objective in the battle for Port Stanley in the Falkland Islands. Sergeant McKay was platoon sergeant of 4 Platoon, B Company, which, after the initial objective had been secured, was ordered to clear the Northern side of the long East / West ridge feature, held by the enemy in depth, with strong, mutually-supporting positions.

By now the enemy were fully alert, and resisting fiercely. As 4 Platoon's advance continued it came under increasingly heavy fire from a number of well-sited enemy machine gun positions on the ridge, and received casualties. Realising that no further advance was possible the Platoon Commander ordered the Platoon to move from its exposed position to seek shelter among the rocks of the ridge itself. Here it met up with part of 5 Platoon.

The enemy fire was still both heavy and accurate, and the position of the Platoons was becoming increasingly hazardous. Taking Sergeant McKay, a Corporal and a few others, and covered by supporting machine gun fire, the Platoon Commander moved forward to reconnoitre the enemy positions but was hit by a bullet in the leg, and command devolved upon Sergeant McKay.

It was clear that instant action was needed if the advance was not to falter and increasing casualties to ensue. Sergeant McKay decided to convert this reconnaissance into an attack in order to eliminate the enemy positions. He was in no doubt of the strength and deployment of the enemy as he undertook this attack. He issued orders, and taking three men with him, broke cover and charged the enemy position.

The assault was met by a hail of fire. The Corporal was seriously wounded, a Private killed and another wounded. Despite these losses Sergeant McKay, with complete disregard for his own safety, continued to charge the enemy position alone. On reaching it he despatched the enemy with grenades, thereby relieving the position of beleagured [sic] 4 and 5 Platoons, who were now able to redeploy with relative safety. Sergeant McKay, however, was killed at the moment of victory, his body falling on the bunker.

Without doubt Sergeant McKay's action retrieved a most dangerous situation and was instrumental in ensuring the success of the attack. His was a coolly calculated act, the dangers of which must have been too apparent to him beforehand. Undeterred he performed with outstanding selflessness, perseverance and courage. With a complete disregard for his own safety, he displayed courage and leadership of the highest order, and was an inspiration to all those around him.

McKay, who died aged twenty-nine, had displayed astonishing courage in the heat of battle. It was entirely appropriate for him to be awarded Britain and the Commonwealth's most prestigious gallantry award for bravery in the presence of the enemy.

Corporal (later Captain) Ian Bailey, whose own story is told in this book, said of McKay's final moments: 'The last time I saw Ian McKay alive, he was still moving on my right. I was hit, went down, tried to get up and never saw him again. There was firing going on, two explosions then it stopped and then there was nothing. Ian died in the trench.' It is understood that as he lay dead or dying in the trench, McKay was hit by at least three bullets. He had sacrificed his life in order to save the lives of his friends and comrades.

McKay's daughter, Melanie, was just four years old. At the time his VC was announced, McKay's distraught widow said that she feared his decoration and his bravery 'would all be forgotten in twenty years' time'. Fortunately, she was wrong, and nearly forty years on his VC and his gallantry are very much still remembered.

McKay's mother, Freda, had been told the news of his death on the phone and reacted by screaming the word 'No' four times. His father, Ken, later said of the award: 'I'm the proudest man in the world – but I would rather have Ian alive.' They were heartfelt sentiments echoed privately by the remainder of McKay's family.

Among the many tributes and letters of condolence to McKay's family was one to his parents from Lieutenant Colonel Hew Pike, who had known the young Sergeant for many years. In his letter dated 10 October, the senior officer wrote:

Dear Mr and Mrs McKay,

We are so proud and delighted about the news of Ian's Victoria Cross, albeit so terribly sorry that his magnificent achievement cost him his life. We all mourn his loss deeply, and shall continue to do so, for he was a wonderful man.

But you must feel justly proud that your son has achieved a unique recognition for his bravery and leadership. He is the first Victoria Cross ever to be awarded to a member of 3 PARA, including all our actions of World War Two. That perhaps is indication enough of his supreme self-sacrifice.

We all rejoice with you, and salute him. It was particularly touching that you should have said … that the award is the battalion's as well as Ian's. I know Ian himself would have thought this, and every soldier in the battalion feels inspired and a better man for Ian's example – we all do.

I was privileged to know your son well – he was a corporal in 'A' Company when I was the OC. He was an outstanding instructor, and obviously an up-and-coming NCO in every way – intelligent, energetic, firm and determined. He was, as you know, a talented sportsman – I myself used to play quite a lot of squash and tennis with him and often enjoyed watching him play football. Above all, perhaps, he was a person whom it was always a pleasure to have about – bright, cheerful, enthusiastic, outgoing, interesting, and utterly dedicated to his profession. Even I, not even related, feel a dreadful sense of loss – miss him terribly and I feel the whole Regiment does. Such a loss cannot be replaced and the loss cannot be compensated...

It only remains to say again, how immensely proud we all are. Every soldier in the army salutes Ian's memory – indeed, I believe the whole nation does so. As for all of us in 3 PARA we feel a special sense of pride and of sadness. I shall never forget him, nor I think will any of us.

On 9 November 1982, in an investiture at Buckingham Palace, the Queen presented McKay's posthumous VC to his widow at a ceremony that was also attended by his daughter and stepson. Melanie, by then aged five, was photographed wearing her father's decoration pinned to her black velvet dress.

Over the decades, McKay's widow has given very few interviews to the media. However, after learning of her husband's posthumous VC late in October 1982, she gave a newspaper interview in which she spoke of her love for her late husband and his affection for their daughter:

We met and we knew. Simple as that. We were married for six wonderful years. Melanie was his joy. You'd have thought he was the first man to have a daughter. He wasn't the sort to mind being seen pushing a pram either. We could talk about anything. We were the sort of people who went out to dinner and never noticed anyone else in the restaurant.

I used to miss him most late at night and in the early mornings. Now I'm beginning to realise that I've also lost my greatest friend.

McKay's body was eventually recovered and brought back to England for burial. He was buried along with fifteen comrades from the battle in a funeral with full military honours at the Aldershot Military Barracks in Hampshire on 26 November 1982. The last two men to see him alive were among the pallbearers: they were Corporal Ian Bailey, who was shot and badly wounded just minutes before McKay was killed, and Colour Sergeant Brian Faulkner, who said of his friend: 'Mac was the bravest of the brave.'

On 19 July 1983, a Commonwealth War Graves Commission headstone was erected at Aldershot Military Cemetery, Hampshire. The words chosen by McKay's widow for his epitaph were:

> TO THE WORLD A SOLDIER
>
> TO US THE WORLD
>
> TILL WE MEET AGAIN

Since McKay's death, there have been several monuments and memorials in his honour, including the McKay Memorial Cottages in Barnsley, Yorkshire; the Ian McKay VC barrack block at the Army Foundation College, Harrogate, Yorkshire; the McKay conference room at Permanent Joint Headquarters in Northwood, Middlesex; a Territorial Army centre at Rotherham called the McKay VC Barracks; and an NCO accommodation block named McKay House at the Defence Academy, Shrivenham, Berkshire. There is also a portrait of McKay at the 3 PARA Sergeants' mess and a painting of his VC action at the 3 PARA Officers' mess.

Freda McKay also gave few interviews about her son's death over the decades. However, she did open her heart to a journalist, Elizabeth Grice of the *Daily Telegraph*, in June 2007, to mark the twenty-fifth anniversary of her son being killed in battle.

There are so many stages of grief. You blame yourself, you blame them for dying, you blame the politicians. But I never blamed those who killed Ian. The Argentinian soldiers were doing the same as he was doing – and most of the time none of them knew what the hell they were doing.

She admitted that she was bitter for a long time and that she blamed Margaret Thatcher for warmongering. In her interview, Ian's mother also disclosed that her marriage had broken down as she and her husband faced grief in such different ways: her wanting to talk about Ian's death and him not wishing to do so.

Freda McKay revealed that over the space of just sixteen years, she had lost the five men in her life, starting with Ian's death in 1982. Ian had two younger brothers, Graham and Neal, who both had cystic fibrosis and were not expected to survive childhood. As adults, they underwent heart and lung transplants, but Neal died in 1989 aged thirty-two, and Graham in 1995 aged thirty-nine. After her marriage failed, Freda met a new partner, Jeff Agar, at a dancing club. However, Jeff died of cancer in 1994, a month after being taken ill on holiday in Spain. In 1998, just as relations between Freda and Ken were improving, he died suddenly of a heart attack – on Armistice Day as he prepared to attend a Remembrance Day parade.

In 2012, to mark the thirtieth anniversary of the Falklands War, Jon Cooksey published his well-researched biography, *Falklands Hero Ian McKay: The Last VC of the 20th Century*. Military historian Andrew Roberts wrote the Foreword to Cooksey's book and said:

> The word 'hero' is used all too easily and often nowadays, even to describe sportsmen and entertainers. This fine book is about a genuine hero, someone who at the age of twenty-nine quite deliberately sacrificed his own life in battle so that others – his comrades in the 3rd Battalion, the Parachute Regiment – might live.

On 23 March 2015, a further memorial to McKay was unveiled on the Falkland Islands by three veterans from 3 PARA. The inscription on the memorial ended with the words: 'Greater love hath no man than this, that a man lay down his life for his friends.'

In an interview at her home near Lincoln, Marica McKay recalled her late husband with affection and pride. She told me: 'Ian was a real gentleman. He was a family-orientated man with a good sense of humour. He was straightforward and quite private – there were lots of things in his past career that he never discussed with me and that I only learnt about after his death.'

Mrs McKay recalled that she was at her army home in Aldershot when she learnt her husband had been killed in battle but that, like him, she'd had a strong feeling he would not return from the Falklands.

> I had said to someone I was working with at the hospital, 'Ian is not coming back.' I just knew that things would change after the British sank the *Belgrano*.
>
> I heard the news of his death on a Monday. A friend had just rung me to say her kettle had broken and could I get her a new one. Then the doorbell rang, and it was Colonel Simon Brewis and Sue Patton, the wife of another senior officer. I knew then, as soon as I came down the stairs, that Ian had been killed. Sue came in with a bottle of brandy and I said, 'I don't drink brandy.' News of his death was not a surprise because I had been expecting it.

Mrs McKay revealed that she knew little about her husband's incredible bravery until four months after his death when his prestigious decoration was announced:

> I was incredibly proud when he was awarded the VC but a part of me just wishes he had hidden behind a rock. It was a bitter-sweet award. Ian had no fear and his thoughts would have been to protect

his men. If Ian was alive today, he would say his VC was not just for him, it was for all his comrades.

She said that her late husband and his only child, Melanie, had a close relationship.

> When he was away she could be a little madam, but as soon as he walked back through the door, she was fine. He missed out on so much by not seeing her grow up, become a teacher and have a son [Harry, aged seven]. To become a grandfather would have made Ian's day.

Mrs McKay said that she never saw Melanie cry over her father's death and that her daughter was reluctant to talk about him for many years. Melanie did not attend Ian's funeral because she was so young, but she did later visit his grave and, pointing to the ground, said, 'My daddy's in there.'

Mrs McKay also talked about going to the investiture at Buckingham Palace with her two children and her husband's parents:

> I bought Melanie a beautiful new dress for the day, but she wouldn't wear it. She insisted on wearing a black velvet dress. She kept practising her curtsey beforehand, but when she was introduced to the Queen she didn't do it! The Queen told me: 'Your husband was a very brave man.' In the weeks afterwards, I found it harder and harder to cope without Ian.

A few years after her husband's death, Mrs McKay said that while at home she was 'visited' by an image of her husband, who was ironing one of his shirts. He told her: 'I wouldn't have changed anything.'

Mrs McKay, who is now seventy-three, went on to have another child, a son called Simon, in another relationship, but she never remarried after Ian's death. Nearly forty years on, she said:

> I still think of Ian a great deal – I suppose he was the love of my life even though we were only together for quite a short time. I am delighted that his VC is in the Lord Ashcroft Gallery at the Imperial War Museum because it will mean he will never be forgotten and his bravery might inspire other people too.

IAN PHILIP BAILEY
Service: Army
Final rank: Captain
FALKLANDS WAR DECORATION / DISTINCTION:
MILITARY MEDAL (MM)
DATES OF BRAVERY: 11–12 JUNE 1982
GAZETTED: 8 OCTOBER 1982

Ian Bailey was a 22-year-old Corporal when he charged close by Sergeant Ian McKay on Mount Longdon at the height of the battle to regain the Falkland Islands. Neither man would emerge from the battle unscathed or undecorated. Bailey, who received horrific injuries that left him close to death, eventually made a good recovery and was awarded the MM. He served for a further twenty years in the Parachute Regiment, and it was only some time after he left the army in 2009 that he became aware of still having an Argentine bullet and shrapnel in his body, as a result of his wartime wounds from nearly thirty years earlier.

Born in Silverdale, Staffordshire, on 3 April 1960, the eldest of four children, Ian Philip Bailey came from a family with strong military roots. His grandfather, Wallace Bailey, had fought in both world wars, being awarded the MM in the First World War, while his father, Roy, served with the 16th/5th Lancers as a tank driver and wireless operator. His family moved to Wales when Bailey was a young boy, and after attending Abergele High School in north Wales, he enlisted on 10 January 1977, aged sixteen, as a boy soldier in the Infantry Junior Leaders Battalion. After a year, he graduated as a boy Regimental Sergeant Major. He then went to Depot PARA in January 1978, passing out in April the same year. He was posted to 3 PARA, based in Germany, the following month, beginning his career as a Private.

In April 1982, Bailey was serving as a Corporal with 3 PARA when he and his comrades were transported to the Falkland Islands on board SS *Canberra* as part of the Task Force. At the time of the Argentine invasion, *Canberra* had been cruising in the Mediterranean, while Bailey was staying at the home of his fiancée, Tracy, in Winchester, Hampshire. Soon he was bound for the Falklands, where he took part in the action at Mount Longdon which claimed more lives than any other battle during the Falklands War.

The mountain was some 5 miles to the west of the capital, Port Stanley, on the island of East Falkland. A vivid description of the battle appears in Martin Middlebrook's book *The Falklands War* (now published by Pen and Sword Books but previously known by the title *Operation Corporate: The Story of the Falklands War, 1982*), in which Bailey and others were interviewed about their wartime experiences.

As part of the advance on Port Stanley, 3 PARA was given the objective of reclaiming Mount Longdon, which lay within a large government-owned property leased to a local sheep farmer. Of the units involved in the three-pronged assault, 3 PARA's began first, with Lieutenant Colonel Hew Pike concluding that the best way of attack was frontally at its west end. The plan was that 'A' Company on the left would try to seize a feature that was codenamed 'wing forward'. It was intended that this would in turn act as a fire-support base for another attack by 'B' Company on the main Longdon mountain, on which two parts were codenamed 'fly half' and 'full back'. Finally, it was intended that 'C' Company would move up if, as was hoped, there was a collapse by Longdon's Argentine defenders, who were part of the conscripted and overburdened 7th Regiment.

On 11 June 1982, when the British artillery was facing no more than the normal evening harassment, the Paras moved off after dusk for the approach march to the start line. Bailey was given a role as a Section Commander in 'B' Company, which along with 'A' Company reached the start line some fifteen minutes later. In an interview with Martin Middlebrook, Bailey said:

We were only on the start line a few minutes. I went round the lads and checked everybody and had a joke with my mates. The lads were quiet, each man whispering to their own very good friends, having a last drag. It was a time for being with your own mates. They knew some of them were going to get killed. For some reason, most of them fixed bayonets; I put mine on and looked round to find all the others were putting theirs on too.

We stepped over the stream and set off. It was a very clear night, cool, but it didn't feel cold; there was too much adrenalin flowing. We knew we had got a punch-up on our hands. It was uphill, a fairly steep gradient, lots of rocks, tufts of grass, holes where you could break your ankle easily – just like a good training area. You could see 200 or 300 metres ahead of you. As we went up, we were funnelled together into a space between the main Mount Longdon and a large separate rock. At one time, we were shoulder to shoulder, so we tried to spread out, some men waiting while others moved on faster. That was only about 20ft from their main position but that first position turned out to be empty.

At this point, everyone was trying to be as quiet as possible as they approached well-constructed and heavily manned defences, but this ploy was ruined when a Corporal who was a Section Commander in 'B' Company's left forward platoon stepped on a mine, severely injuring his leg. The explosion, coupled with his agonised screams, informed the Argentines that the battle they had been anticipating was about to begin. 'B' Company came under fire before it reached the main enemy positions, and the Paras found themselves forced into a vulnerable series of steep and narrow rock channels. From their vantage points further up the mountains, the Argentines could fire their weapons and toss grenades. Furthermore, it was not possible to bring the British artillery close enough to engage the enemy.

Once again Bailey takes up the story:

Then we got the first grenades; they were just bouncing down the side of the rock face. We thought they were rocks falling, until the first one exploded. One bloke caught some shrapnel in the backside. He was the first one in the section to get injured, not badly but enough to put him out of the fighting. The small-arms fire followed soon after. People were getting down into cover again then. Because we had got funnelled, we weren't really working by sections now; the nearest Private soldier to you just stuck with you. Corporal McLaughlin, the other leading section commander, was ahead of me now. He and his men were getting the small-arms fire. It was keeping his group pinned down but no one was being hit in either of our sections. There was a lot of fire on the right, where 6 Platoon was going up but it was quiet on the left where 4 Platoon was coming up after hitting the minefield.

My men started firing their '66s' [handheld 66mm anti-tank rockets]. Whoever was in the best position to spot targets fired; the others passed spare rockets to them. It was a very good bunker weapon; there wasn't going to be a lot left of you if your bunker or sangar [a small, raised, protected structure for observation or used as a firing point] was hit by one of those. We could see their positions by now, up above us, possibly 30ft or so away, we could even see them moving, dark shapes. Their fire was sparse to start with but then it intensified. Some of them were very disciplined, firing, moving back into cover, then coming out again and firing again or throwing grenades.

The next cover to get forward to was in some rocks with one of their positions in the middle of it. Corporal McLaughlin's GPMG [general-purpose machine gun] gave us cover and we put about four grenades and an '84' round into the position, which was a trench with a stone wall around it and a tent, which was blown over. We went round and on, myself and whichever 'toms' [Privates in the Parachute Regiment] were available, and the two men with the '84' launcher. It was all over very quickly. We ran across, firing at the same time. Just as we went round the corner, we found one Argentinian just a few feet away. Private Meredith and I both fired with our rifles and killed him. The rest of the post – two men – were already dead, killed by the grenades or the '84' shrapnel. We put more rounds into them, to make sure they were dead and weren't going anywhere; that was normal practice.

Elsewhere on the mountain, men from 'B' Company were having a tougher time of it. Lieutenant Bickerdike's 4 Platoon had become pinned down by one of the heavy machine guns and was largely out of contact with the Company Commander. However, three men from 5 Platoon put the enemy machine gun out of action, thereby freeing up 4 Platoon to rejoin the fray. With the advance route on the left under formidable fire, Bickerdike eased 4 Platoon to the right, and two of his sections became intermingled with

5 Platoon. However, their progress became blocked by a second heavy machine gun, and this in turn caused some casualties. Bickerdike himself was thrown backwards after being hit in the thigh.

The next phase of the action was led by Sergeant McKay with some of his men from 4 Platoon and with Corporal Bailey's section from 5 Platoon. Once again, Bailey describes the thick of the action:

> Ian and I had a talk and decided the aim was to get across to the next cover, which was 30 to 35 metres away. There were some Argentinian positions there but we didn't know the exact location. He shouted out to the other Corporals to give covering fire, three machine guns altogether, then we – Sergeant McKay, myself and three Private soldiers to the left of us – set off. As we were moving across the open ground, two of the Privates were killed by rifle or machine-gun fire almost at once; the other Private got across and into cover. We grenaded the first position and went past it without stopping, just firing into it, and that's when I got shot from one of the other positions which was about 10ft away. I think it was a rifle. I got hit in the hip and went down. Sergeant McKay was still going on to the next position but there was no one else with him. The last I saw of him, he was just going on, running towards the remaining positions in that group. I was lying on my back and I listened to men calling to each other. They were trying to find out what was happening but, when they called out to Sergeant McKay, there was no reply. I got shot again soon after that, by bullets in the neck and hand.

Bailey was eventually stretchered down the mountain and given first aid for separate injuries to his neck, hip and hand. After being treated at the company and regimental aid posts, he was deemed unlikely to survive his injuries. However, he was later transported by Wessex helicopter to the hospital ship SS *Uganda*, where he underwent seven operations. Later, when back in the UK, he was treated at an RAF hospital in Wroughton, Wiltshire. His unit, 'B' Company, had suffered heavy casualties in the battle to recapture the Falklands: twenty-three dead and more than forty injured.

Bailey was discharged from hospital in September 1982 and resumed his military career. His MM was announced on 8 October, when his short citation read:

> In the early hours of 12th June 1982, the 3rd Battalion The Parachute Regiment assaulted enemy positions on Mount Longdon, 8km to the West of Port Stanley on the Island of East Falkland. Corporal Bailey's Section were tasked to aid a Platoon pinned down by heavy automatic fire.
>
> Under covering fire, together with Sergeant McKay, he attacked the enemy's position with grenades. Whilst closing on the enemy, Corporal Bailey was wounded. His brave actions helped to destroy the enemy and relieve the pressure on the Platoon that was pinned down.

On the same day that the MM was announced, the Prince of Wales sent Bailey a telegram that read: 'On receiving the news of your award I send you my warmest congratulations. I have the greatest possible admiration for the gallantry you displayed and for the way in which you maintained the very highest traditions of the Regiment. Charles.'

The posthumous award of McKay's VC was announced in *The London Gazette* on the same day as Bailey's MM. Bailey had known McKay prior to the battle in which the Sergeant died, although Bailey was in 5 Platoon while McKay served with 4 Platoon. 'I knew Ian to be a good footballer and always smart. We would pass the time of day, but we did not know each other well,' he said.

Bailey had not realised that McKay had been killed on Mount Longdon until he was returning home on the hospital ship.

However, McKay's body was later exhumed from the Falkland Islands and brought back to England, where it was re-interred with full military honours at Aldershot Military Cemetery, Hampshire. Bailey, though still recovering from his wounds, was one of the pallbearers. He also took part in the London Victory Parade on 12 October 1982, when 300,000 people lined the 1-mile route to pay their respects to those servicemen who had taken part in the war.

Bailey received his gallantry medal from the Queen at an investiture at Buckingham Palace in January 1983, which was also attended by his parents. Furthermore, when he was shot, his dog-tag identification discs had been lost on Mount Longdon. Yet in 1983, as the Royal Engineers cleared the battlefield, they found the bloodied tags and they were returned to Bailey.

In an interview at his home near Aldershot, Bailey told me how he made an emotional return to Mount Longdon as part of an army exercise in 1998:

> I walked the route that we had taken sixteen years earlier. It enabled me to look at it from every angle and to see if we had done anything wrong. But, with all the information we had at the time, there was no way we could have launched the attack any better.

During a distinguished army career, Bailey was involved in training programmes for the Royal Marines, the Royal Irish Home Service and the Parachute Regiment. In 2000, he received a commission as a Captain, but he resigned it three years later and retired from the army due to the injury to his neck and the possible fusion of his spine. By then, Bailey had served for nearly twenty-seven years, including completing tours in Northern Ireland and Kosovo.

Shortly after leaving the army in 2003, he began to have problems with the bullet wound to his hip opening up, and after seeing a medical consultant he was amazed to learn that he still had the head of an Argentine bullet, as well as numerous smaller fragments of shrapnel, lodged inside him. In June 2009, the wound required an operation to remove the metal debris, and in order to undergo the surgery Bailey had to resign from his senior job within the security industry in Nigeria. During the operation, the bullet and forty-two tiny pieces of shrapnel were all removed.

Bailey said:

> On leaving the army in 2003, I started to have problems with discharge from my hip injury ... Over the next six years the discharge became more frequent and the pain more intense, culminating when I went into hospital to have [the shrapnel] removed. This took some three hours on the operating table and some five days in hospital. They found many bits of shrapnel, including the head of the bullet. These offending items had been in my body since June 1982 and no one had bothered to mention it!
>
> My injuries remain a bone of contention between the army and me: I was shot three times serving my country and left with long-term problems, yet I only receive a small military pension.

Since leaving the army, he has worked in the security industry, spending time in Iraq, Nigeria, Afghanistan, Libya and London. However, this career was ended in the summer of 2014 by a heart ailment. Over the past seven years, Bailey has done a number of jobs, including teaching fly fishing. For two and a half years, until October 2020, he worked for the National Rifle Association as a safety and ammunitions supervisor.

Today, Bailey remains married to Tracy, who was his fiancée at the time of the Falklands War. The couple married in Winchester on 7 May 1983 and have a grown-up son and daughter and one grandson.

Like many veterans, Bailey is alarmed at how many men who served in the Falklands have suffered from mental health problems over the past four decades, including there being a large number of suicides. He said:

> The Falklands War was a bit more down and dirty than more recent conflicts. I think as a result of this a lot of people have suffered from a few different issues. When I listen to some of the eulogies to former comrades who have died, I can't believe I am hearing about the same people that I served with in the military. The war has had a negative impact on a large number of people.

I am particularly delighted to have Bailey's medal group in my collection of decorations, for earlier, in 1989, I had purchased the VC medal group of Ian McKay. It means the gallantry medals of these two courageous men can, appropriately, lie side by side, just as the two men fought shoulder to shoulder nearly forty years ago.

DESMOND PAUL FULLER
Service: Army
Final rank: Sergeant
FALKLANDS WAR DECORATION / DISTINCTION:
MILITARY MEDAL (MM)
DATES OF BRAVERY: 11–12 JUNE 1982
GAZETTED: 8 OCTOBER 1982

Desmond Fuller showed outstanding courage under the most trying of circumstances during the battle for Mount Longdon. He took command of a 3 PARA platoon after Sergeant Ian McKay was killed in battle. Fuller rose to the challenge in spades and was later decorated with the MM for his actions in leading his men during one of the fiercest battles in the war.

Fuller, who was always known as 'Des', was born in Norwich, Norfolk, on 8 October 1950. His father, John, was a Sergeant in the Royal Signals; as a result the family travelled widely and Fuller, the second of four sons, was educated at several different schools. He enlisted into the army on 28 April 1966, aged fifteen, and served in 4 Platoon, 'B' Company, 3 PARA all around the world, including tours to Malta, Cyprus, Ghana, Italy, France, Germany and Northern Ireland. A typical all-action PARA, he completed a 'HALO' (high altitude low opening) free-fall parachuting course, a mountaineering course, a weapons course and was a signals cadre and twice passed out as a ski instructor.

In the aftermath of the invasion of the Falklands, 3 PARA was based at its barracks in Tidworth, Wiltshire. On the day after the invasion, Fuller, who at this time was a Platoon Sergeant with the Junior Parachute Company in Aldershot, and others were making preparations in the Depot Sergeants' mess for the Easter Ball. In an interview with Christian Jennings and Adrian Weale for their book *Green-Eyed Boys: 3 PARA and the Battle for Mount Longdon*, Fuller said:

> We all had to turn up about 10 o'clock Saturday morning [3 April] – all the NCOs on the Entertainments Committee – to put up the decorations, hang the 'chutes and tart the place up a bit. We were all there whingeing and talking about it, and the RSM [Regimental Sergeant Major] there was Ron Lewis, and we were all going up to the RSM and saying, 'How are we going to get there?' and he was just telling us all to 'Piss off, you're here and this is where you are staying.'

How wrong he was: Fuller and his comrades were later told to be outside their CO's office on Sunday morning. There were about a dozen instructors from 2 and 3 PARA present, and the CO said that the battalions wanted the men back but only on a voluntary basis. Those who wanted to volunteer were asked to take a step forward – and everyone took a step forward. On Monday morning, Fuller was on his way to Tidworth to rejoin his battalion.

Soon, Lieutenant Colonel Hew Pike was briefing his men in person:

Gents, just to let you know the full implications and developments. We will be going to Southampton on Wednesday or Thursday to embark on a ship yet to be named. We will then sail south. There will be a lot of running about between now and then, so please be patient. You will have tomorrow off and by then, Monday the fifth, you will have a better idea of the coming events. Good day.

Fuller and his comrades were all up for whatever lay ahead. By 9 April, wives and girlfriends were gathered at Southampton dock to wave off their husbands and boyfriends for their 8,000-mile journey south on board SS *Canberra*. The band of the Parachute Regiment played the 'Ride of the Valkyries' on the quayside. Fuller and other NCOs were allocated the first-class cabins, and P&O waiters served them five-course breakfasts every morning. However, everyone was apprehensive too: would the enemy surrender before a shot was fired or would there be battles that would cost men from both sides their lives?

Just before arriving at Ascension Island on 20 April, 3 PARA heard the welcome news that 2 PARA, commanded by Colonel Herbert 'H' Jones, would be joining them in the South Atlantic. Arriving at Ascension, 3 PARA cross-decked to HMS *Fearless*, the assault craft. While moored off Ascension for the next two weeks, members of 3 PARA went ashore for various live-fire drills and other training exercises. As 3 PARA prepared for what lay ahead, South Georgia was reclaimed by the British on 25 April. And five days later the Argentine cruiser *General Belgrano* was found by the submarine HMS *Conqueror* and the enemy ship was sunk on 2 May.

On 14 May, back on the *Canberra* and three days from the Falklands, 3 PARA was told that they would go ashore when they arrived at their destination, where there were already 11,000 enemy troops. The strength of 3 PARA was 671 men, including forty men from 9 (Parachute) Squadron, Royal Engineers. By 20 May, 3 PARA was preparing to cross-deck to HMS *Intrepid* for the landing at San Carlos. The next day they did just that before boarding landing craft for the final leg of their journey through San Carlos Bay and on to Sandy Bay.

On 27 May, as 3 PARA tabbed towards Teal Inlet, about halfway to Port Stanley, 2 PARA prepared to begin their famous assault on Darwin and Goose Green. Fuller later told Jennings and Weale:

> We looked at the map: sixty miles. No big deal over a few days, but being on the top of the mountains it was rather firmer, and once you got down there every other step was a pothole or a peat bog. God, it was horrendous! The worst thing was that the first night, the bloody OC's signaller went and twisted his stuffin' ankle; course [Major Mike] Argue knew I was an ex-signaller and I ended up with the radio. I was really chuffed!

3 PARA arrived at Teal Inlet on the night of 28–29 May to discover the Argentine patrols had gone, though there was soon a small contact with the enemy. After twenty-four hours at Teal Inlet, 3 PARA continued their march, this time in bitterly cold conditions on to Estancia House, which consisted of a house, a barn and some outbuildings on the outskirts of Port Salvador inlet. Fuller

admitted that at times he was so cold he wanted to shed tears: 'We sat there, we put a poncho round us and just huddled shivering, and I was so pleased to get the order to move [from Teal Inlet],' he said. By the time the battalion regrouped at Estancia House, their objective had been decided: Mount Longdon. In early June, there were several reconnaissance patrols on the mountain. By 9 June, as the attack plans were being formulated, 3 PARA was told it must take Mount Longdon and if possible move on to Wireless Ridge. Although the target was only 782ft high, it presented a massive challenge – an east–west orientated ridge about 1,200 metres long and some 200 metres wide.

As the battle progressed on 11–12 June, 4 Platoon found themselves in a deadline situation. In an interview with Jennings and Weale, Fuller takes up the story:

The word came over that [Lieutenant Andy] Bickerdike was down, that 'Sunray 21' was down and that 'Sunray Minor' – Ian McKay – 'had gone off and was missing'. And that's when Mike Argue told me to go … words to the effect that I should meet up with Ian and discuss who was the senior and who would be the platoon commander and who would be the platoon sergeant. This was as I walked past, and I didn't want to get into an argument or anything like that, but I would have been quite happy for Ian to take over … he was the platoon sergeant, so it would have been the logical thing for him to take over and me to take over as platoon sergeant. But as I walked past John [Weeks], he just very bluntly said, 'Des, you're fucking in charge.' That was it…

So there I was, wandering up and down the mountain, looking for them … the only one I knew there was [Corporal] 'Ned' Kelly so I started shouting for Ned and listening for voices. I was a bit worried about making too much noise and giving the enemy my position, but eventually I got to the end of 4 Platoon and Ned came and met me. He briefed me very quickly that Bickerdike was down and Ian McKay had gone and I said, 'Well, let's go and speak to Bickerdike and see what he can tell me.' He was just laying there in a lot of pain, shot through the thigh and couldn't tell me too much, and there was a Tom [soldier] with him, and I just said to the Tom, 'Stay with him,' and got Ned and said, 'Fill me in more,' and he told me that Ian McKay had gone off on a recce, or whatever with 'Beetle' Bailey's section and two of the guys who were actually stop-gap guys, mess stewards or something. But apparently he was now between the enemy and us and he'd been shouting to the guys, and we were trying to find out where the enemy were 'cause there was no movement, they were not shooting at us at that time, apart from the sniper who was some distance away … and I just asked Ned to go and get all the section commanders together. Des Landers was the only one there, but he said, '"Scouse" McLaughlin's up on the high ground just on the right side of us.' He was with his section, he'd kept his section totally together. I didn't know where [Sergeant] John Ross was, I didn't know where [Lieutenant Mark] Cox was, and so I called Scouse down; he didn't know either. So I made a plan to carry on going forward, it was as simple as that really. We actually couldn't see where the enemy were, the guys were saying: 'They're out in front, they're over there, they're there,' but it was pitch black. So I told Scouse to go back and give us covering fire; I told him what I wanted him to do; that we would continue to go forward until such time as we came upon them or they opened up on us; and Scouse was to give us covering fire all the way through.

From the time we started moving, he started firing into the likely positions – that was the idea – and it was coming over our heads. Of course, as soon as we actually broke out into the open, then they started firing at us, and the only thing to do now, now that we were actually in the open, was to push on forward.

I'm not sure quite how far we'd gone when Ned went down but I saw him hit – Ned was just in front – and I sort of ran past him and patted him on the leg and said – it was a stupid thing to say – 'Stay there Ned, I'll come back for you.' He wasn't going anywhere.

Basically, once Ned had gone, I'd lost all my experienced guys, my section commanders, so I was running up left and right, pushing the guys into the sangars. The guys were top, excellent, superb. They had a job to do: they knew what they had to do; they'd been trained to be able to operate on their own, not necessarily with a guy screaming and shouting at them. Mine was just encouragement, I wasn't telling guys, 'Take those two out!' 'cause I couldn't see what they were doing, or where they were. It was just, 'Keep going forward! Keep going forward!'

As the fighting continued, Fuller and his men 'hit a really bad path' under fire from the enemy. He continued:

They must have stayed low, hoping we'd go away, and didn't want to give their position away, but again, another huge barrage of fire came down … I actually didn't see any of my Toms go down but then I went further and one of the section gunners – GMPG guy – he'd actually been shot in the finger, he'd been shot in the trigger guard or the pistol grip of his gimpy. One of the guys there was trying to give him morphine, and what he'd done was, as opposed to pushing the needle in and breaking the seal, he's managed to pull the bloody thing out: fuck knows why. I spent five or six seconds in the pitch black trying to find this bloody hole to put this pin back in so this poor bugger could have his morphine.

Then I went forward again and that's when we came up to the sangar with about three or four of our Toms there and one said, 'This is Ian McKay,' and I'd assumed we'd taken the position, there was no more firing and we started shouting, 'All clear, all clear.' I told the guys to get in and go firm.

Fuller was at the forward edge of 'B' Company's assault and was deciding what to do next:

I was laying there and I'd called for Scouse McLaughlin to come down to me, 'cause we were firm and I wanted to do another 'step' forward, and I wanted Scouse to go ahead of us. There was a little ridge ahead of us and Scouse had seen people scurrying about, or his section had seen them running and he was still firing at them [the enemy]. That's why it took a bit of shouting to get Scouse down.

Later in the battle, and having taken casualties, 'B' Company's progress stalled. Fuller again takes up the story as they planned an evacuation of the wounded:

So I went off with [Lance Corporal] Phillips to go and find these guys. I don't know how far we'd gone but we had two grenades thrown at us ... one went off, I don't know, 2 or 3 metres away – it appeared to be that close – but it had no effect on us at all. I didn't feel any shrapnel or any blast or whatever ... but eventually I bumped into [Company Sergeant Major] John [Weeks] with the remainder of his guys and we actually came down and we started to extract the wounded, with the wounded out of the way, we could carry on. Although we were slightly depleted, we had Scouse's section to bolster us.

We had some of the guys down there and we were organising getting the wounded out. Ned [wounded soldier] wouldn't be carried out, he walked out, but every time someone got up, the sniper was there, zapping off from a great distance. I went to pick Andy

Bickerdike [wounded Lieutenant] up and carry him out and managed to get him on my shoulder and take about two paces and all he did was scream in my ear. So I put him down, saying, 'This guy's going to have a stretcher,' and John just pushed past, grabbed him, threw him on his shoulder and let him scream.

By dawn the next morning the battle was virtually over – and won. Fuller and others had the grim task of collecting their dead. However, Fuller could not face the prospect of finding McKay's dead body. He later recalled:

After first light, John and the guys were going to go down to the actual battle area and go and gather our dead and wounded and all that sort of stuff. And I said, 'John, I'm fucking not going down there today. I don't want to go and see Ian,' so he said, 'All right. I'll go down there. You do round here.'

Sadly, Corporal Stewart 'Scouse' McLaughlin was among those who had been killed by a mortar attack.

The recommendation for Fuller's MM gives more detail to the story:

During the attack by 3rd Battalion, The Parachute Regiment on the 11–12 June it was reported that the Platoon Commander [Lieutenant Bickerdike] of 4 Platoon had been wounded and that the Platoon Sergeant [Ian McKay] was missing, believed dead. Sergeant Fuller was a supernumerary Senior Non-Commissioned Officer grouped with Company Headquarters. He at once volunteered to go forward and take command of 4 Platoon.

On arrival forward, he joined OC 4 Platoon where he had fallen wounded but was able to get enough information from him to assess his tactical task. Sporadic enemy fire was being directed from positions east along the ridge and also from the base of the slope, where he was told were some enemy sangars. He understood that this was the position recently attacked by the Platoon Sergeant and some members of 5 Platoon. Sergeant Fuller could not locate OC 5 Platoon.

Gathering 4 Platoon and the left section of 5 Platoon Sergeant Fuller organised a further assault on the enemy sangars. He positioned a gun team on the right and skirmished the assault group forward. They were soon again under effective fire, which caused a number of casualties in quick succession. Nevertheless, under his leadership, the group cleared the nearest sangars of enemy, some being seen to flee to the east...

Sergeant Fuller's action in taking command of a platoon under fire and in contact with the enemy, and subsequently leading them through a successful assault, was an example of the highest standards of leadership and courage.

In the aftermath of the battle, there was confusion and almost tragedy in the shape of two friendly-fire, or 'blue on blue', incidents. Once again, Fuller described to authors Jennings and Weale the events as he was escorting a party of enemy POWs down from Mount Longdon:

I was told to take all the prisoners down to find Lawrie Ashbridge [sic], the RSM [Regimental Sergeant Major] ... I came over this crest and looked down, and I went to ground straight away and told all these other guys to get down as well because 70, 80 metres away ... there were these seven or eight guys and they were all in green so they were Argentine – we'd been told to keep our helmets on and were in cammo [camouflage] so that we could distinguish ourselves – and I shouted to them: 'Argentinos, do you surrender? Argentinos, do you surrender?' ... I actually stood up and shouted at them, and there was this big rock or boulder and I was edging round that and they just took a bomb-burst [military slang for running off in all directions] and I let go with half a magazine into the general area, and fortunately I never hit anyone 'cause it was a fucking PARA burial party, with the padre, Tom Smith the cameraman and some other guys.

However, in the fog of war, the situation then escalated, as Fuller detailed:

At that stage I saw, on the right-hand side, all these fucking heads pop up from this rock feature, and all hell let loose ... and [Private] Southall and I were under this bloody boulder and all the Argies were just laid out in the open. Not one got hit, they must have been firing at us for ten minutes ...This was 9 Squadron engineers, battalion headquarters, the RAP [regimental aid post] firing at us, thinking we were Argies... and young Southall and I were in there, and we were screaming: 'We're 3 PARA! We're 3 PARA!' 'cause I could hear English-speaking voices: I actually heard [Colour Sergeant] Brian Faulkner giving fire-control orders! In the end it was the old fucking beret out ... and throw the beret over the rock, and then we started hearing, 'Cease fire! Cease fire! Stop firing, they're ours.' But it still took me two or three minutes before I dared put my fucking head out.

It was only when he rested at the RAP that Fuller began to take in the number of casualties that 3 PARA had taken during the battle:

I really felt it then because I could see... I think there were four or five body bags laid out, and the helicopters were coming in, taking away the wounded ... and you started hearing now, who's there, you know, from 6 Platoon... 'A' Company... Support Company... very, very good friends ... Nobody had seen Scouse McLaughlin at the time. So I sat there, had a cup of tea and chatted to Brian [Faulkner]. But I actually had to leave because I could feel the tears welling up in my eyes because every minute, or two or three minutes, when I looked over there was another body bag. You know, they say the Toms were bloody good, but the fucking cooks were good as well: those guys were up and down the mountain with the artillery going, still bringing the bodies back and the wounded back.

On the morning of 14 June, 3 PARA was again preparing for battle, with 'C' Company poised to attack a position known as Moody Brook before trying to retake Port Stanley. However, there was no need for further fighting because the Argentines surrendered. Fuller said:

We were told they'd fucking surrendered, so helmets off, berets on, and we were taking off like jackrabbits down the mountain just to beat the Marines in – which we did! Although in the papers they were putting the Union Jack up, having taken it down from when 2 PARA put it up the first time. Going into Stanley, it was something out of a bloody movie; there was bodies laid on the floor, there was Argie wounded just lying there, there were weapons laid all over the place, there were broken-down trucks. It actually looked like something that you'd see in a war movie.

3 PARA later helped supervise the clear-up around Port Stanley, and their last duty was the provision of escorts for the mass of Argentine POWs that were returned home on the *Canberra*. The battalion finally left the Falklands on 25 June 1982. Of the 671 men who had left Tidworth just over two months earlier, twenty-three were dead and nearly fifty were wounded. They were joined by

their comrades from 2 PARA on MV *Norland* for their journey to Ascension Island, from where they flew back to Britain.

Fuller's MM was announced in *The London Gazette* on 8 October 1982, and it came as a shock. Fuller told me:

> I was in Aldershot at the time and OC, 'B' Company Major Mike Argue called me into his office and told me I had been awarded the MM – something which was a total surprise. I was also very proud, and that night I called my dad to tell him. He was extremely proud of me too as he had kept a whole scrapbook on my military career.

Fuller's joy at his own decoration was tempered by his anger that his friend and comrade Corporal Stewart 'Scouse' McLaughlin was not also awarded a posthumous decoration:

> He and his section were incredibly brave to hold a position to enable the wounded to be evacuated and Scouse also led a charge towards Argentine machine-gunners. I was disgusted that his courage was never recognised. In fact, it was recognised by all who served with him. But for a lost piece of paper he gets nothing.

The 'lost piece of paper' is a reference to an apparent recommendation for his friend's posthumous gallantry medal being misplaced. Some comrades referred to McLaughlin putting in a 'man of the match' performance during the battle, yet no gallantry award was ever forthcoming.

News of Fuller's own decoration led to several senior officers writing letters of congratulation to the young sergeant. Major Argue, who was decorated with the MC for his own bravery, said in a hand-written letter:

There is no doubt in my mind that it was a fitting tribute to your sheer guts and determination throughout the events on Longdon and you can be quite sure that it was well and truly earned. Needless to say 'B' Coy [Company] has much to be proud of and I think those of us who have been honoured, more perhaps than others, will never forget the bravery and sacrifice over the battle for Stanley and what it cost us in friends and comrades.

Fuller was one of the pallbearers at the funeral of Sergeant Ian McKay VC after his body was repatriated to the UK and was buried, as previously mentioned, along with fifteen comrades from 2 and 3 PARA with full military honours at Aldershot Military Cemetery. 'In all, I was tasked with organising three funerals [for fallen comrades] and attending several others,' he said.

Fuller was discharged from the army after eighteen years of service on 1 March 1984, when his military conduct was described as 'exemplary'. His testimonial from his Commanding Officer read:

Sgt Fuller has made an excellent contribution to the Army. He is enthusiastic, determined and fit, and at his best in a leadership situation under pressure. He is very reliable and loyal and easily commands respect. He is intelligent and articulate with a good down to earth common sense approach. He displays initiative and works very hard without supervision. He will be successful in civilian life.

Shortly after leaving the army, Fuller moved to Zimbabwe. After a brief period with the British Military Advisory and Training Team, he began working in the transport industry. He then had a farm in Zimbabwe for twelve years, but it was seized from him in 2001 under President Robert Mugabe's rule. After that sorry episode, which cost him his life savings, Fuller returned to work in the transport industry.

Fuller has been married twice; he has three children by his first marriage and two stepchildren from his second. Today, he lives on a golf estate in Zimbabwe, which accounts for his sixteen handicap in the sport. Looking back on his part in a war from nearly forty years ago, Fuller said:

I am extremely proud of the role I played and also the role of the soldiers who served with me, especially the youngsters. A lot of those guys were ex-Junior Paras, just seventeen and eighteen years old, who were in my Platoon as juniors two years before. Not once did they falter [in battle] and it was an honour and a privilege to serve with them. I still think a lot about those young men who didn't make it back, and it still hurts me to think of them getting killed. I sometimes think to myself, 'Did I do the right thing? Should I have done something differently?' But I come back to the same conclusion that I did what I was told to do and that was it.

PETER JAMES MARSHALL

Service: Army

Final rank: Warrant Officer Class 1

FALKLANDS WAR DECORATION / DISTINCTION:

MENTIONED IN DESPATCHES (MID)

DATES OF BRAVERY: 11–12 JUNE 1982

GAZETTED: 8 OCTOBER 1982

Peter Marshall showed incredible courage while leading a team of stretcher-bearers in support of the soldiers from 3 PARA during the battle for Mount Longdon. He and his men repeatedly risked their lives, often under heavy fire, in order to ensure that the wounded from the battle received medical treatment as quickly as possible. On two occasions he was knocked off his feet by the blasts from shells that had landed close to him, but in both incidents he escaped injury. Marshall's bravery was recognised with the award of a Mention in Despatches for his gallantry on 11 and 12 June 1982.

Peter James Marshall was born in Hammersmith, west London, on 20 July 1951. His father was an accountant, his mother a nurse, and he was the joint eldest of six children (including a twin brother). As a young boy, he lived in west London and later in nearby Wimbledon before moving to Kent in 1962, aged eleven. There, he was educated at Hayes School, near Bromley. Marshall enlisted into the army at Blackheath, south-east London, as a boy soldier aged just fifteen, on 1 September 1966. He had wanted to join the Parachute Regiment but was advised to join a Corps and learn a trade, so he joined the Army Catering Corps, embarking on a three-year apprenticeship. He ended his apprenticeship as a junior Regimental Sergeant Major and took the passing-out parade in 1969. Later that year, in August 1969, he joined the 7th Parachute Regiment (Royal Horse Artillery), better known as simply 7 PARA (RHA). He completed parachute training in December 1969 and was awarded his wings and red beret. Marshall then went on to serve with 16 PARA Brigade until 1973, completing three tours of Northern Ireland and undergoing jungle warfare training in Malaya, as well as completing parachute jumps in the UK, Denmark, Cyprus and Northern Ireland. In 1973, he was posted to the British Forces Germany, representing his unit in many sports, including athletics and cross-country. Further senior postings followed until he joined 3 PARA in 1981. The following year, aged thirty-one and in the rank of Sergeant, he was deployed to the Falkland Islands with 3 PARA as part of 'Operation Corporate'.

Marshall wrote later about his feelings at being deployed:

3 PARA were the spearhead battalion and we were 'stood to' and prepared to be deployed. At that time most of us had to be told

where the Falklands were and we expected to be recalled before getting there. [The] battalion moved to Southampton where we boarded the *Canberra*, a passenger liner requisitioned to transport the battalion southbound to the Falklands. Once on board and sailing through the Bay of Biscay it started to sink in that we were going to get involved.

Due to my previous experience as a military skills trainer, I was tasked with training the Headquarters staff and updating their military skills: this included cooks, REME [Royal Electrical and Mechanical Engineers], mechanics, medics and members of The Parachute Regiment and other attached arms. We all kept fit by running around the deck, push-ups, sit-ups. When we got to Ascension Island we had the opportunity to fire our weapons on the ranges there, practise our skills and swim in the Atlantic. We also had to cross-deck a large amount of equipment and ammunition as much of it had been loaded on the wrong ships. Very difficult moving large crates containing Milan missiles along narrow corridors and up and down stairways designed for the movement of passengers. The civilian staff on board *Canberra* were great: they welcomed us on board and throughout the journey south did as much as they could to make us comfortable on board. As we got closer to the Falklands, news was relayed to us about what was happening in the Falklands, including the attacks on British ships and personnel. We were now all looking to what lay ahead and the part we would play.

At 5.20 a.m. on 21 May, *Canberra* weighed anchor and entered San Carlos Water to disembark her troops in the knowledge that an air attack was likely at any moment. Once again, Marshall takes up the story with his written notes:

Landed at Port San Carlos after having to cross-deck into a landing craft from a passenger ship, something I would not like to repeat as we had to wait for the swell to bring the landing craft high enough for us to jump across from the side entrance of the ship. Once we landed we began to get ourselves sorted out and dig in, digging in defences and bringing in all the stores from the landing area. This was exhausting, hard work as everything had to be manhandled from the shoreline up to the shearing sheds. Whilst digging a large hole to store jerry cans full of fuel, we came under attack from Argentinian aircraft who flew in so low that we could see the pilot quite clearly. Without thinking, most of us took shelter behind the stack of fuel containers. Whilst at Port San Carlos, we were under regular attacks from the air.

We moved out from Port San Carlos and as the battalion began to move across the island [East Falkland] we were tasked with moving as much of the equipment up to support them, much of this was done at night. We were assisted by the Falkland Islanders with their 4x4 vehicles, which were overloaded. I have never spent so much time digging out vehicles from mud and water to keep them moving. Eventually, we set up at Estancia House where the battalion prepared. As this was going on, we were tasked with providing listening posts between our lines and the Argentinian lines. The padre came around and talked to as many of us as he could for a chat, many of us talking to him about our families.

As the British forces started to gain the upper hand, the Battle of Mount Longdon took place on 11 and 12 June, but even in the run-up to the main fighting Marshall and his men came under fire. He continues the story:

One night whilst dug in under a rocky outcrop with a young lad called Tommy Onions, a creeping barrage advanced on our position. At this point, Tommy whispered to me: 'Fucking hell, I am shit scared.' I replied, 'That makes two of us.' We were both relieved when the barrage stopped about 200 metres from our position.

When the battalion moved forward for the attack on Mount Longdon, we moved up in support carrying large amounts of ammunition, our own kit and extra medical supplies. As we moved forward the battalion began to draw enemy fire from the positions high above us, much from well-placed snipers. As the battle continued and the battalion took casualties, we took on our roles as stretcher-bearers and we went up as far forward as possible to treat and bring back the injured to the RAP.

It soon became obvious that, once we crossed an invisible line on the ground, we were coming under fire, and we had to move forward to help the wounded. Once this line was crossed, we continued on with the task in hand. It seemed to go on for ever with us going back and forth up the hill to treat and collect the wounded. I was very proud of the young lads who were with me as not once did they question me as I told them that we had to go back up again. Many times we all came close to being killed as comrades next to us were hit with either shell fire or small-arms fire. The following day we had the task of going out and recovering the dead bodies of our comrades. This we did whilst continually being harassed with artillery fire. I can remember RSM [Regimental Sergeant Major] Laurie Ashbridge coming over to us with a cup of tea, which was the best ever.

On 14 June, the enemy surrendered, and Marshall and many others travelled back to Ascension Island on MV *Norland*. Marshall recalled: 'Then we flew home to be welcomed by HRH Prince Charles at Brize Norton. The local butcher sold out of fillet steak that night as we all celebrated being back home and remembered our fallen comrades.'

Marshall's Mention in Despatches (MID) was announced in *The London Gazette* of 8 October 1982, along with many other of the Falklands War honours. The unpublished recommendation for his award, from Lieutenant Colonel Hew Pike, the CO of 3 PARA, read:

> During the night of the 3 PARA attack on Mount Longdon and subsequent clearance operations throughout 12 and 13 June, the stretcher bearers of the battalion earned the undying respect of their comrades as they continuously risked their lives in an unselfish manner in order to retrieve the wounded under extremely hazardous conditions. Sgt Marshall was leading a team of stretcher bearers and his example was outstanding throughout this period. Always heading and encouraging the stretcher bearers, particularly when they were exhausted, his men performed great feats under his direction. The stretcher bearers had, as an initial step to the attack, carried large amounts of ammunition over difficult terrain and many were exceptionally tired before the attack began.
>
> Throughout the daylight of the 12 June the battalion came under repeated attacks of accurate artillery fire and casualties were incurred. Sergeant Marshall, without any concern for his own personal safety, continuously encouraged his bearers to work under these conditions. Twice he himself was knocked off his feet by the force of nearby shells – but miraculously remained uninjured.
>
> He is an outstanding credit to the Corps, and has earned the greatest respect from his comrades in The Parachute Regiment. His courageous and humane service deserves full recognition.

After the MID was announced, Pike wrote a warmly worded letter of congratulations to Marshall in which he said, 'I was delighted and proud to hear of your well deserved Mention in Despatches – well done indeed. It represents the great dedication and gallantry you displayed as a stretcher bearer, and a number of soldiers have good cause to be grateful to you. Many congratulations!'

The other well-wishers included the Prince of Wales, who sent Marshall a telegram that read: 'Having heard of your Mention in Despatches I wanted to send you my warmest congratulations. I have immense admiration for the way in which you carried out your duty in such conditions and upheld the gallant traditions of the regiment. Charles.'

Furthermore, Marshall featured in a painting called 'Lull in the Battle', painted by artist Terence Cuneo. He is portrayed on the outskirts of Port San Carlos standing in the middle of a small group of soldiers from the Army Catering Corps, sipping a mug of tea. Cuneo, who was the official artist for the Queen's Coronation in 1953, loved painting military scenes.

The month before his award was announced, Marshall had been promoted to Staff Sergeant and posted to 59 Commando, Royal Engineers, for a six-month tour of Canada. Further promotions followed – to WO Class 2 in 1983 and WO Class 1 in 1987. He retired from the army on 19 July 1991, the day before his fortieth birthday, having completed just under twenty-five years' service.

In 1991, he joined West Midlands Police, where he received a commendation for bravery in 1992 after tackling a man armed with a hammer. This incident resulted in him being attacked and injured. Later, Marshall worked for Warwickshire Police, retiring from the force on 31 July 2017.

The previous year, Marshall had taken time to write up a short account of his life and career, signing and dating it 12 July 2016. The final sentence of this write-up read: 'Still married (forty-four years) to Patricia who has supported me throughout and who without I may not have coped with what I saw and experienced on Mount Longdon. Plus we have two grown-up children and five grandchildren who give me great joy every day.' Now married for forty-nine years, the couple also have one great-grandchild, called Jaxon, and live near Coventry. Reflecting on the events of 1982, Marshall told me:

> After forty years I still feel pride in what we did to recover the Falkland Islands – for the people who live there and for Britain. This is tinged with the sadness for the friends and comrades who died and the ones whose lives were changed by the conflict – injuries and mental welfare.

CHAPTER 8

THE BATTLE FOR THE MOUNTAINS, PART 2: TWO SISTERS, TUMBLEDOWN AND WIRELESS RIDGE

The Battle for Mount Longdon was undoubtedly a vital victory for the British forces, but in the second week of June there were other key positions that needed to be gained before the final push on Port Stanley could begin.

On the night of 11–12 June, the British fought three battles as part of a brigade-size operation. Other than the Battle of Mount Longdon, the other two were the Battle of Mount Harriet and the Battle of Two Sisters. Two Sisters was a mountain with two peaks which, because of its location and height, provided the Argentines with a useful vantage point from which to prevent the British advance towards Port Stanley. It was situated some 2 miles south-west of Mount Longdon.

In late May and early June, there had been some heavy exchanges between the British and Argentine forces in and around Two Sisters. For example, on 6 June, a patrol from 45 Commando was lying up when a party of twenty enemy troops came across their position. A fierce firefight ensued in which the British killed twelve Argentines and wounded three.

However, it was 11–12 June that saw the heaviest fighting for Two Sisters in an all-night battle. 45 Commando was ordered to seize the mountain and, if time allowed, proceed onto Tumbledown Mountain too. The heavy resistance from the enemy meant that the second phase had to be abandoned in the short term.

45 Commando was supported by the 8th Battery, 29 Commando, Royal Artillery, while HMS Glamorgan was offshore to give more fire support with her 4.5in. gun. 45 Commando was commanded by Lieutenant Colonel Andrew Whitehead and his force of some 600 Royal Marines was opposed by an Argentine company, some 350 strong, drawn from the 4th Infantry Regiment. The enemy, of course, had the major advantage of being dug in on the advantageous higher ground. A major artillery attack was followed by heavy fighting between the two sides. In total, the enemy killed some seventeen British troops, while another four died as a result of friendly fire. More than forty others were injured. The Argentine casualties were similar in number: twenty killed and fifty wounded, with a further fifty-four men taken as POWs.

HMS Glamorgan stayed in position longer than intended to offer support to the troops on the ground, and on 12 June she was hit by an Exocet missile fired from the land, killing fourteen of her crew (thirteen immediately and one from his injures several days later) and causing massive damage to the ship.

By the evening of 13 June, after a highly successful forty hours on the battlefield, the British forces were preparing to resume their assault on the enemy, this time with another three key targets. The 2nd Battalion, Scots Guards, with support from the Welsh Guards, were tasked with assaulting Tumbledown Mountain; the 7th Gurkhas were ordered to take the adjacent Mount William, and further north 2 PARA had been transferred back to 3 Commando Brigade and were instructed to attack Wireless Ridge. The support for these assaults was provided by five batteries of artillery, four warships and eight tanks.

The attack on Tumbledown started first with a smaller diversionary advance to the south, then the main assault from the west. Lieutenant

Colonel Mike Scott, commanding the Scots Guards, was aware of the difficult terrain: a sheer drop to the north, while on the gentler drop to the south there was open ground that was well-defended. Tumbledown itself has a long, narrow, rocky ridge.

The fighting lasted for some twelve hours, and the Argentines defended their position fiercely knowing that if they lost Tumbledown, Port Stanley was there for the taking and then the war would be lost. However, the British, with a force of nearly 650 men, won the day with nine killed and more than thirty wounded. The larger enemy force was defeated with thirty men killed and forty-five wounded. Thirty others were taken as POWs.

Tumbledown, *a television drama, was screened in 1988, starring Colin Firth as Lieutenant Robert Lawrence MC, who, aged twenty-one, was shot in the head by an enemy sniper. It was controversial because, apart from depicting the brutality of war, it highlighted the alleged indifference shown by government and the public to the returning wounded from the Falklands War. The drama was based on Lawrence's book, co-written with his father, John:* When the Fighting Is Over: A Personal Story of the Battle for Tumbledown Mountain and Its Aftermath.

Fresh from its hard-fought victory at Goose Green, 2 PARA marched around the back of Mount Longdon to take up their positions for the assault on Wireless Ridge. Wireless Ridge was one of seven strategic hills within 5 miles of Stanley that had to be taken in order for the island's capital to be approached. The Argentine 7th Infantry Regiment was in opposition, but by 4.30 a.m. on 14 June, following an assault that had started late the previous day, the Argentines were defeated. A British force of some 600 men saw only three killed and eleven wounded. The enemy force, believed to be some 500 strong, suffered much heavier losses: twenty-five killed, 125 wounded and thirty-seven taken prisoner.

With Two Sisters, Tumbledown and Wireless Ridge all in enemy hands after less than twenty-four hours of fighting, the situation for the Argentines was hopeless, and it looked only a matter of time before Port Stanley would be captured. The war to regain the Falkland Islands was all but won.

TERENCE IRVING BARRETT

Service: Army

Final rank: Sergeant

FALKLANDS WAR DECORATION / DISTINCTION:

MILITARY MEDAL (MM)

DATES OF BRAVERY: 28–29 MAY 1982 AND 13–14 JUNE 1982

GAZETTED: 8 OCTOBER 1982

Terence 'Ted' Barrett was decorated for two prolonged periods of bravery at crucial moments during the Falklands War after circumstances had conspired, unexpectedly, to put him in charge of his platoon. Initially, prior to the battle for Darwin and Goose Green he displayed great courage during heavy fighting, and he again showed outstanding gallantry in the attack on Wireless Ridge just over a fortnight later.

Terence Irving Barrett was born in Chelmsford, Essex, in 1950. He was the eldest of seven children and his parents were strict but loving. Stressing the importance of family values, they wanted their children to be upstanding members of society. From an early age, Barrett was known to most friends as 'Ted'.

Barrett left school at fifteen and initially intended to go straight into the army. It appears that the inspiration for his choice of career was a family friend, Sid Day, who had served with Airborne Forces as a glider pilot at the Battle of Arnhem in September 1944. However, his parents opposed the proposal and made him spend another year in education, attending a local college. At the end of his college year, he was still determined to join the army, and as his seventeenth birthday approached he set off to join the Parachute Regiment with three friends.

Barrett was accepted into the Parachute Regiment, where he was to remain for seventeen years, largely serving in 2 PARA under the command of Colonel Herbert 'H' Jones. During the earlier years of Barrett's army career, he served in both Northern Ireland and Belize.

As the Falklands War loomed in the spring of 1982, he was serving as Platoon Sergeant of 1 Platoon, 'A' Company. By this point, he was an experienced and highly professional soldier. He was tall, fit, lithe, energetic, had a dry sense of humour and sported a thick moustache.

A week after 2 PARA landed on East Falkland, Barrett found himself temporarily in command of 1 Platoon, as 2 PARA was committed to recapture Darwin and Goose Green. After a brief skirmish during the hours of darkness on 28 May, 'A' and 'B' Companies went to ground. Dawn the next day revealed entrenched enemy positions with no cover in the barren countryside. On the Left Flank of the advance, 'A' Company fought a sustained action to capture Darwin Hill after five hours of fighting. During this fraught time, Barrett's leadership was outstanding. Grouping machine-gun teams together, he harassed the enemy's furthest trenches, playing a key role in their eventual surrender. Thriving on the challenge and always in the thick of the action, he encouraged his men to victory.

The citation for his MM, published on 8 October 1982, told how Barrett had been at the centre of the fighting in both late May and mid-June:

Sergeant Barrett was a Platoon Sergeant in A Company 2nd

Battalion The Parachute Regiment during the Falkland Islands campaign. On the final approach march prior to the battle for Port Darwin and Goose Green on 28th/29th May 1982 Sergeant Barrett's Platoon Commander was injured and he took command of the Platoon. Throughout the five hours battle for Port Darwin in which A Company destroyed twenty-two enemy bunkers, Sergeant Barrett's Platoon was given the task of providing covering fire. Sergeant Barrett organised and controlled his fire teams in a masterful way, often exposing himself to machine gun and sniper fire as he personally led forward his fire teams. His outstanding leadership and personal bravery coupled with his cool appreciation of what was needed proved a fine example to his Platoon and was a significant factor in his Company's ultimate success. Again on the night of 13–14 June 1982 in the attack on Wireless Ridge A Company came under artillery fire during the final assault. Sergeant Barrett's example and leadership were a significant factor in maintaining the momentum of the attack. Throughout the campaign Sergeant Barrett has shown outstanding conduct, professionalism and coolness under fire that have been an inspiration to his Platoon and a steadying influence on the younger soldiers.

Furthermore, he had narrowly escaped serious injury or even death during the battle for Darwin and Goose Green: at one point, a tracer round had embedded itself and burnt out in his radio battery. After returning from the Falklands, however, Barrett struggled to fall back into the routine of army life, and in 1983 he left 2 PARA, aged thirty-three.

His main work after leaving the Armed Forces was in the haulage business. Living with his wife Carol in Hull, Yorkshire, his final job was as a driver for Riby & Son. Sometimes his wife accompanied him on his long drives across Europe. His employer,

Mr Riby, described him as 'an impeccable driver, a lovely man, for whom no job was too much to ask'.

However, his work for the firm was to be cut short by the onset of cancer. With typical determination, Barrett told his boss: 'Don't give my cab away, I am coming back!' However, he died in December 2000, aged fifty, leaving a widow and two sons, Jamie and Danny. A large number of family and friends filled the Catholic church in the centre of Hull for a moving service on 2 January 2001, at which they said farewell to a soldier who had courageously served his country in its hour of need.

In March 2001, Dave Connolly, who had served with Barrett in the Falklands, penned a moving obituary to his former colleague on the 'Airborne Assault: ParaData' website. Headlined 'Ted Barrett MM: A Soldier's Soldier', his tribute ended with the words: 'His story, though not unique by any means in the history of the Parachute Regiment, is still testament to the quality, leadership, ability and bravery that is displayed by individuals from this regiment when facing an enemy of this country in a life or death struggle.'

WILLIAM McINTOSH NICOL

Service: Army

Final rank: Captain

FALKLANDS WAR DECORATION / DISTINCTION:

DISTINGUISHED CONDUCT MEDAL (DCM)

DATES OF BRAVERY: 6–14 JUNE 1982

GAZETTED: 8 OCTOBER 1982

Bill Nicol received one of just eight DCMs awarded for the Falklands War as part of a distinguished career with the military spanning almost forty years. His decoration was the result of his bravery during the Battle of Tumbledown Mountain in the final stages of the conflict in June 1982. Nicol was shot and injured while rescuing a mortally wounded comrade, showing great composure under heavy fire and then refusing to be evacuated until all other casualties had been removed, despite his injuries.

William McIntosh Nicol was born on 16 December 1950 in Falkirk, a town in the Central Lowlands of Scotland. The youngest of three children, he was made a ward of court aged just five and was brought up in children's homes. Having seen potential in the young boy, the local town council sent him to Elmfield Rudolf Steiner School in Stourbridge, West Midlands, where he boarded from the age of eleven to fifteen. After leaving school in 1961, he joined the army as a boy soldier, but he was earmarked for likely promotion and was sent to the Infantry Junior Leaders Battalion at Oswestry, where future NCOs were trained.

Nicol next joined the Scots Guards and served with the unit in Malaysia and Borneo during the 'confrontation' with Indonesia from 1963 to 1966. Having earned a reputation as a fine, practical soldier, he was selected to become an instructor at the British Army Jungle Warfare Training School in Johor Bahru from 1968 to 1970. During this time, Nicol and his fellow instructors were training Americans, Australians and New Zealanders who were about to fight in Vietnam. To this day, he considers jungle warfare to be his forte.

Next, Nicol served in Belize and Northern Ireland; from 1977 to 1980 he was posted to Dungannon, Co. Tyrone, part of the infamous 'murder triangle'. His job was to train the local Ulster Defence Regiment – an initial two-year posting that was extended by a further year. After completing this role, he served in Ballymurphy, a staunchly nationalist area of Belfast, with his own unit.

By then married with a young son, Nicol sailed for the South Atlantic on 12 May 1982 after completing two weeks of unit training in Sennybridge, South Wales. He was on board the *QE2* as part of the 5th Infantry Brigade and 'Operation Corporate'.

The official Ministry of Defence account of the war noted:

After landing at San Carlos on 2 June, the 2nd Battalion Scots Guards was taken in HMS *Intrepid*, three days later, to Bluff Cove, a settlement not 25km from [Port] Stanley. There the Battalion dug in, in appalling weather and awaited the expected order to move forward to Stanley. In the week the Battalion was there, good intelligence was received from the recce platoon in a covert patrol base well forward in Port Harriet House. This intelligence subsequently had a profound effect on the Brigade plan for the advance on Stanley. During this week the disastrous Skyhawk raid occurred against the *Sir Galahad* and *Sir Tristram*, dealing a sad blow to the Welsh Guards [who took heavy casualties]. If there was any consolation in this attack, the Battalion accounted for certainly two, if not three, enemy planes with small arms fire.

During the night 11–12 June, 3 Commando Brigade took Mount Longdon, Two Sisters and Mount Harriet. The 5 Infantry Brigade plan then was for the Battalion to take Mount Tumbledown from the west and, when firm, to provide fire support for 1/7 Gurkhas to assault Mount William. The Welsh Guards were subsequently to be prepared to take Sapper Hill. The Battalion plan was for a silent night attack in three phases. The fire plan was to include fighter ground attack, five batteries of 105mm Light Guns and Naval Gun fire from HMS *Active* and *Yarmouth*. The mortars of 42 Commando and 1/7 Gurkhas were also available. Each phase was to involve a Company attack on a different part of the objective. Phase 1 was for G Company to take the first part of Tumbledown. Thirty minutes before G Company crossed the start line, there was to be a diversionary attack from the obvious southerly approach. Phase II involved Left Flank moving through and assaulting the main part of the mountain, and in Phase III Right Flank would secure the final part.

Nicol was one of the first on the scene when the Left Flank's No. 13 Platoon ran into serious opposition during the assault on Mount Tumbledown on 13 June. He later described his experiences in Martin Middlebrook's book *The Falklands War*:

When we came under fire, everyone went to ground and was returning fire. There was a staggering amount of noise. I had gone off 'floating' around the left leading the platoon, doing what I saw as a company sergeant-major's job, giving the boys encouragement – not that they needed it. They shouted for me and I went across to [Guardsman] Tanbini and tried to pull him back into cover; if I had tried to lift him, we would have both been exposed and hit. I suggested that he tried to push back with his feet, while I pulled him, but he said, 'Sir, I've been shot' – typical Guardsman, the way he addressed me as 'Sir' – and then he died.

Someone else was screaming for me then. It was the platoon sergeant [John Simeon], he had been badly shot in the thigh. I jumped up and ran across to him and, as I got to him, I was hit. I was just about to kneel down beside him when the bullet hit the centre of my rifle which was across the front of the centre of my stomach in the approved manner, ready for action. If I hadn't been holding that rifle in the manner in which I had been teaching people for years, I would be dead by now. The bullet ricocheted off the barrel and went through my right hand. Tanbini, John Simeon and I had all been shot in one line by the same sniper, I think. I had just received a letter from my wife to say she was pregnant and this went through my mind. I thought I was going to be next. There was nothing I could do about it. That sniper was good; I would like to have met him.

In short, even though Nicol had almost been shot dead by the enemy sniper, he could not, as a professional soldier, hide his admiration for the man's shooting skills.

The official Ministry of Defence account of the incident continued the story:

> At approximately 0230 hrs, artillery rounds landed accurately in front of the right forward platoon and the platoon commander, together with the company commander and company headquarters, led an attack on the forward enemy positions. This assault was successful and the momentum of the attack was maintained. About eight enemy were killed with grenades, rifles and bayonets. The company commander himself killed two and bayoneted a third. Although one section commander, L/Sgt C. Mitchell, was killed, the assault continued up the hill, with sangars and bunkers being taken at the point of the bayonet. The demands of clearing these positions and guarding prisoners resulted in only seven men of Left Flank reaching the top of the mountain and the end of their objective. Below them were the lights of [Port] Stanley and enemy running away. Of these seven, three including Lt Mitchell were immediately cut down by machine gun fire from Right Flank's objective.

By about 8.15 a.m., Tumbledown was in the hands of the 2nd Battalion, Scots Guards, although eight men had been killed and forty-three wounded.

At the time, Nicol also spoke about his admiration for (then) Major John Kiszely, the Company Commander of Left Flank and the man who recommended him for his DCM. At the point when

Nicol was injured, Kiszely was away from his unit, having required treatment for his own wound.

Nicol said, 'The citation came as a total surprise. As far as I was concerned, I was just doing my job.' Nicol returned from the Falklands on 10 August 1982 and his twin daughters were born shortly afterwards. His DCM was announced less than two months later – on 8 October 1982 – and singled out three separate acts of bravery spanning nine days:

WO2 Nicol was the CSM [Company Sergeant Major] of Left Flank, 2nd Battalion Scots Guards throughout the campaign in the Falkland Islands. During this time he maintained exemplary standards of personal courage and leadership which inspired similar standards in all members of his company. Three particular occasions stand out: on 6th June, after a six-hour sea voyage at night in open boats in which most men were completely soaked, the Battalion was ordered to occupy defensive positions on high ground in freezing rain and sleet. Due to CSM Nicol's efforts, although a number of exposure casualties were taken in other companies, none occurred in Left Flank.

On 8th June some twelve enemy aircraft involved in an attack on shipping at Fitzroy flew in three sorties at low level over the company's positions at Bluff Cove. No warning of the enemy aircraft was received but despite this CSM Nicol so rapidly and skilfully organised and controlled his company in firing rifles and machine guns, moving from sangar to sangar with no thought for his own safety, that two or three enemy aircraft were brought down by the Battalion.

On 13 June at Tumbledown Mountain, his company were ordered to take a strong enemy position as part of a Battalion night attack.

After the initial assault, the company came under constant and

devastating machine gun and sniper fire. One of the platoon sergeants was wounded, and CSM Nicol went forward under accurate
sniper fire to rescue him. Wounded in the hand while doing so, he
continued to tend the dying sergeant.

He remained cool and calm under heavy fire encouraging and
exhorting his men and, at the same time, advising one of the young
platoon commanders how to defeat a seemingly impregnable enemy
position.

He remained unperturbed by the weight of enemy small arms,
artillery and mortar fire thus instilling great confidence in men
who might well have been frightened. He refused to be evacuated
himself, until all the other casualties in the company (twenty-six in
all) had been evacuated. CSM Nicol's distinguished conduct and
conspicuous personal bravery throughout the campaign and in particular on the three occasions described proved an inspiration and
example to all ranks and have made an outstanding contribution to
his company's exceptional achievements.

In the spring of 1984, Nicol was with the Scots Guards in Cyprus
before once again being posted to Northern Ireland, this time
serving with the Northern Ireland Training and Advisory Team in
Co. Down.

Nicol left the army in 1986 in the rank of Captain after twenty-
five years' service and went to live and work in Northern Ireland.
He continues to be feted for his bravery in the Falklands. In June
2012, in an interview with his local paper to mark the thirtieth
anniversary of the war, he described the scene where he was
involved in the action that led to him being awarded the DCM.
'The place was just a blaze of tracer. I've never seen anything like
that in my life. Never seen it in a war movie. It was unbelievable,'
he recalled.

Nicol, who has three children and three grandchildren, retired in late 2014, after his sixty-fourth birthday, from his final job working in court-room security. Speaking at his home in Northern Ireland, where he still lives with his wife, he said, 'I have been very fortunate. I have had a marvellous life.'

JULIAN BURDETT
Service: Royal Marines
Final rank: Corporal
FALKLANDS WAR DECORATION / DISTINCTION:
DISTINGUISHED CONDUCT MEDAL (DCM)
DATES OF BRAVERY: 11–12 JUNE 1982
GAZETTED: 8 OCTOBER 1982

Julian Burdett was awarded the DCM for outstanding bravery during a daring assault on an enemy-held mountain-top position. As an experienced climber, he served in the Royal Marines as part of 3 Commando Brigade at the time of a major offensive against Argentine Forces. However, as he scaled the craggy ridge of Two Sisters Mountain in the dead of night he was wounded so badly by mortar fire that it looked as though his left leg would have to be amputated above the knee.

Julian Burdett was born in Somerleyton, Suffolk, on 19 October 1952. The son of a costing clerk, he was the youngest of three brothers. Educated at several local schools, Burdett left Denes High School in Lowestoft aged eighteen to work as a farm hand, and over the next seven years he worked in agriculture, ending up as a dairy herdsman. During this time, he was a keen rock climber and skier, and he saw a career in the military as enabling him to turn his pastimes into his job. So he applied for a role in the Royal Marines, being accepted in October 1977, close to his twenty-fifth birthday. After passing out as a Marine, he successfully applied to join 45 Commando in Scotland, it being a mountain and Arctic warfare unit. After three years, he passed his junior command course, and after being promoted to Corporal he went on to become a Mountain Leader, passing out as top Mountain Leader II on the course and top student in the Military Parachute Course at Brize Norton.

Burdett was driving from Wales, where he had been climbing, back to Scotland when he learnt, on 2 April 1982, that the Falkland Islands had been invaded. He remembers the moment clearly because he was stopped for speeding on the motorway that afternoon. When the police officer saw he was a Royal Marine, he told him about the invasion and that 45 Commando were being recalled to Arbroath. Three days later, Burdett was heading towards the Falklands on RFA *Resource*, a weapons and ammunitions store ship. From Ascension Island, he and his comrades went on to the Falklands on RFA *Sir Tristram*, SS *Canberra* and finally, just the day before the landing, HMS *Fearless*.

After a short stay at Ajax Bay, East Falkland, overlooking 'Bomb Alley', Burdett and his fellow Marines undertook a near 60-mile, three-day yomp, or battle march, from Port San Carlos to Mount Kent via Douglas Settlement and Teal Inlet in readiness for an attack. By the time they arrived at the bottom of the Two Sisters ridge they were facing a daunting task – weather conditions were appalling and the enemy was well dug in on high ground. The Argentine troops, including some Special Forces units, were protected by well-concealed machine guns and minefields, and the steep incline gave an impregnable feel to their position.

3 Commando Brigade set about gaining intelligence on precise enemy positions with a view to mounting a night-time attack. The information was gathered by reconnaissance patrols of Marines,

Paras and SAS soldiers, and armed with this new intelligence they decided to launch a combined attack on the night of 11–12 June. The main attack, intended to be silent up the north slope, was delayed for two hours as 'X' Company approached up 'Long Toenail' carrying heavy Milan launchers that would provide fire support once two other companies made contact with the enemy.

In an interview, Burdett takes up the story of the events of 11–12 June:

> I was in one of two fighting companies which attacked from the north slope with X Company advancing up from the west on the spine of a long ridge. We had the usual formation, two Troops up, one back, and I was in the rear 9 Troop. The road across the Murrell Bridge was parallel to our start line and, after lying up for two hours, we advanced in the darkness and the cold for about a kilometre undetected. The ground was very difficult being covered with 'rock runs' [areas of loose flat boulders lying on top of each other]. We must have taken about two hours to get into position on the lower slopes with the forward Troops getting within 50 metres of the enemy positions. We were a bit further back, perhaps 200 metres away.
>
> I had an IWS [individual weapons sight, for thermal imaging] with me. As I was scanning the area, I picked out a large boulder in front of us and I could see someone standing on it. It was an Argentinian, perhaps a sentry. For some reason, he threw a flare but it silhouetted him up against the mountainside. For the forward two Troops, that was the start of the engagement. He came under fire straight away. By now it was well after midnight.
>
> We had a clear view of the ridgeline and most of the fire was coming down on our position at the rear. 9 Troop was just showered with tracer rounds. You could have just reached up and plucked

them out of the darkness. We could pick out their positions quite easily from where we were but we didn't fire because our two Troops were so well advanced and we feared a 'blue on blue'. We were exposed by this point and had gone to ground, sheltering behind rocks from machine gun and automatic rifle fire. At about 2 a.m., we were subjected to mortar fire and one of the rounds landed in the middle of my Section just beside me. There was a big blast and I was thrown in the air and landed on my back. Initially, I didn't feel any pain because I was in shock. Then I realised I had been hit. It was near freezing but I felt this warm sensation in my back and my shoulders. I was lying on the slope with my head downhill and all the blood from the wound on my leg was collecting at my back. In fact, my left leg had almost been severed below the knee and I had lost a couple of toes. My right knee was also injured and I had been hit in the backside. The same round hit Marine Gordon MacPherson, who was in my Section, and he later died of his wounds.

At that time, we couldn't get anyone [the wounded] off the battlefield. The helicopters couldn't fly in because of the enemy artillery fire – it was too dangerous. My wounds were being treated by my Section. We all had first-aid training and each company had a Naval medic too. I was conscious: I had one dose of morphine and, when that didn't work, they gave me a second dose. As I lay there, I could hear the battle raging, particularly the artillery fire with many rounds, thankfully, not exploding and being sucked into the peat. As it started to snow, myself and another wounded [man] were covered up under waterproof sheets for several hours – until a Scout helicopter flew in at about 9 a.m. I wasn't in much pain as the cold prolonged the effect of the morphine.

Eventually, the battle eased and the helicopters could come in. I was lifted up and pushed onto a Scout. We flew to the regimental aid post around from Mount Kent. I was leaning against the [helicopter] door because when the medics opened it, I fell out, into their arms. The doctor and the medics looked me over with a torch – as it was still dark at that time in the morning – and they said, 'There's nothing we can do for you.' We took off again and contoured down to Teal Inlet where we had one of our two field hospitals. I went in, was placed on the table and the next thing I knew was waking up on the hospital ship, *Uganda*, at ten to four in the afternoon. It was surreal because I was surrounded by nice clean sheets and pillows.

Initially, during the daytime, *Uganda* was out in the open sea, in the 'Red Cross Box', and at night-time we sailed into San Carlos Water for shelter. The ship stayed illuminated because it was a Red Cross ship but then they realised the enemy were using it as a guide point to fly in and attack other targets – so after that we stayed out at sea all the time. We remained there after the surrender because they had to clear [Port] Stanley Harbour of mines before it was safe for us to enter. I stayed on *Uganda* for quite some time: eventually, there were just four of us left, all pretty badly injured with one in intensive care. At one point after one of my operations, someone asked me to sign off having my left leg amputated. I said, 'Well, I'd rather not sign it yet – get me back to the UK first.' I didn't want to lose my leg that quickly and they didn't remove it because I wouldn't sign the form. On 14 July, the four of us were helicoptered to the runway at Stanley and flown in a Hercules, over 3,000km, to Ascension Island – a flight which included air-to-air re-fuelling a couple of times. After a night at the cottage hospital, we were stretchered onto a VC-10 and we were flown on to Brize Norton via Dakar [Senegal] for re-fuelling. On reaching Brize, the Scots Guards, who accompanied us from Ascension, were piped off the plane to a victors' welcome from families. When the celebrations finished, a blacked-out bus reversed up to the plane and we were secreted off: the orders were that no wounded should be seen by the public – a bad image for the politicians. We were taken away to be reunited with our families at RAF Wroughton hospital in Wiltshire.

Burdett was soon moved to Haslar Royal Navy Hospital in Gosport, Hampshire, where he remained for another three months. Altogether, he underwent eleven operations on his left leg, which was held together with an external fixation. He also had several skin grafts.

Burdett had become engaged on New Year's Day 1982, and he had always been due to get married in Glasgow, his bride Lorraine's home city, on 9 October. On his wedding day, when he was still in plaster and on crutches, Burdett was informed that he had been awarded the DCM. 'A newspaper reporter came up to me on the steps of the church and told me. My wife wasn't too pleased: she later said I had stolen the limelight on her wedding day.' In fact, the announcement of Burdett's and other war decorations had been the previous day and the Royal Marines had sent a congratulatory telegram to where they believed Burdett was still in hospital in Gosport. He had left to prepare for his wedding before the telegram arrived, which explains why news of his decoration came as a surprise to him on their big day.

The ferocity of the battle and of Burdett's own courage are apparent from the citation published in *The London Gazette* on 8 October 1982:

On the night of 11/12 June 1982, on the Island of East Falkland, 45 Commando Royal Marines launched a silent night attack against strongly held enemy positions on the craggy hill feature of Two Sisters, 10km to the west of Port Stanley. As Section Commander, Corporal Burdett was leading his Section when they came under heavy fire from enemy mortars. Two of his men were killed instantly and he himself severely wounded. Despite these setbacks, he continued to encourage and steady his Section as they moved forward.

Ignoring his wounds, Corporal Burdett also continued to pass further important reports of enemy positions. Simultaneously, he organised the evacuation of his wounded colleagues until he himself was carried from the scene of fighting. Despite serious losses, Corporal Burdett's selfless and distinguished leadership inspired his men to continue their advance.

In January 1983, while still in plaster, Burdett had a fall and broke his left femur, resulting in another two-month hospital stay. However, he remained in the Royal Marines and rejoined his unit, initially on light duties. He attended his investiture at Buckingham Palace with his wife and mother in July 1983, when he received his decoration from the Queen on the same day that Sir Rex Hunt, Governor of the Falkland Islands, received his knighthood.

Burdett left the Marines in 1986 after nine years' service, leaving in the rank of Corporal. After running his own business refurbishing kitchens for eight years, he returned to his first love – farming – looking after dairy herds in Angus and Aberdeenshire. He retired on his sixty-fifth birthday and now lives with his wife in Fife. The couple have three grown-up children.

Nearly forty years on, Burdett reflected on how the war took its toll on those who fought, in both the short and long term. He told me:

I was looking recently at a photograph of us, the troop, taken on HMS *Fearless* the day before we landed on the Falklands and then another of the troop in Stanley after the fighting had finished [Burdett is not in the second photograph because by then he had been wounded]. In the second picture, it was the look on their faces, what I would call 'combat stare'. They were just looking through the camera and beyond. The experience had left its mark and, as with many other combatants, it would haunt them for the rest of their lives.

CHAPTER 9

SURRENDER AND AFTERMATH

By the morning of Monday 14 June 1982, the Argentine position was desperate; they were surrounded on all sides by advancing British forces. With Port Stanley set to fall, Major General Mario Menéndez indicated that he was willing to talk. Later that afternoon, Colonel Michael Rose, Captain Rod Bell (a Royal Marines officer who spoke fluent Spanish) and a signaller with a satellite link to London flew into Port Stanley in a Gazelle helicopter that had a white parachute trailing beneath it. As the negotiations began in Government House, Menéndez, who had spoken with General Galtieri earlier that day to explain the hopelessness of his position, indicated to Rose that he had no intention of fighting on.

Once the terms of the capitulation were agreed, Menéndez shed some tears before shaking hands with Rose and Bell. Poor weather then delayed the arrival of Major General Jeremy Moore, whose presence was required to sign the surrender. At 9 p.m., the two rival Commanders put their signatures to the document that ended the war with the submission of all the enemy forces on the island. The surrender was in fact contrary to the Argentine Army code, which stated there would be no capitulation unless more than 50 per cent of the men were casualties and 75 per cent of the ammunition was spent.

That evening, Mrs Thatcher informed the House of Commons: 'They [the Argentines] are reported to be flying white flags over

Port Stanley.' Hearty congratulations, including from the Labour leader Michael Foot, soon followed: the so-called Iron Lady was understandably triumphant.

Some 8,000 miles away there were jubilant scenes in and around Port Stanley, with soldiers and islanders alike stunned by the swiftness of the surrender and the huge supplies of unused enemy weaponry they found. In the days after the Argentine capitulation, 11,313 enemy prisoners were repatriated, while the British also began the task of restoring water and power to Port Stanley, cleaning up and assessing the vast minefields laid by the invaders.

On 20 June, the British retook the South Sandwich Islands and declared hostilities to be over after removing the enemy's garrison. The war had lasted seventy-four days, with 255 British and 649 Argentine servicemen killed, along with three civilian Falkland Islanders. By the end of June, most of the servicemen who had won the war were on their way home, many to a heroes' welcome when they eventually arrived back at British ports, notably Southampton, Portsmouth and Plymouth.

A service of thanksgiving for Britain's victory in the Falklands was held on 26 July at St Paul's Cathedral. Those who attended included senior members of the royal family, the Prime Minister and many leaders from the victorious Armed Forces. Less than three months later, on 12 October 1982 – Columbus Day – a victory parade was staged. The Prime Minister talked of a 'Falklands spirit' that had resulted from a job well done. For the Falkland Islanders life would never be the same, but a British force tasked with protecting them had replaced an Argentine force tasked with supressing them. 14 June has been a public holiday in the Falkland Islands since 1984, officially called 'Liberation Day'.

For many British servicemen too, life would never be the same. On top of the 255 men killed, 775 were wounded, some of them maimed for life. Many others would suffer from mental illness, including PTSD. In some cases the PTSD was apparent very quickly; in others it did not surface for many years, even decades.

The British losses included seven ships sunk and ten others badly damaged. Two Sea Harriers and three Harrier GR3 aircraft were shot down by ground fire, and four Sea Harriers were lost in accidents. Twenty-four helicopters were also lost. However, far more enemy aircraft were brought down, and as Max Hastings and Simon Jenkins concluded in their book *The Battle for the Falklands*, 'Rear Admiral Woodward did all that could be achieved with the force at his command.'

The bravery displayed by the British Armed Forces in the most brutal of conditions was nothing short of incredible. Around 30,000 South Atlantic Medals were eventually awarded – this was a campaign medal given to British military personnel and civilians who served during the war and to members of the media who travelled to the South Atlantic to report on it.

More importantly perhaps in terms of this book, in October 1982 many of the servicemen who had displayed outstanding valour during the Falklands War were decorated, on top of the June awards that had been announced for gallantry in defending South Georgia. A *Supplement to The London Gazette* was published detailing the full honours list, all approved by the Queen, which began with the two posthumous VCs awarded to the Parachute Regiment's Lieutenant Colonel Herbert 'H' Jones and Sergeant Ian McKay. Both men had showed inspirational leadership and astonishing valour in the heat of battle. (See the Appendix to this book for more details on the Falklands War honours list.)

Ahead of the creation of the VC in early 1856, Queen Victoria had been advised to inscribe the new medal 'For the Brave'. Apparently advised by Prince Albert, she wisely decided against this in case there was an implication that non-recipients of the decoration were *not* brave. The Queen much preferred the suggestion that all her soldiers and sailors were courageous, so instead the inscription on the VC read, and still reads, 'For Valour'.

Similarly, I believe that all the servicemen and women who sailed or flew to the South Atlantic in the spring of 1982 were brave – they did not know what sort of enemy they would face and there was no guarantee that they would make the return journey – many, of course, did not. So, those individuals who were decorated as a result of their gallantry should, in my view, be looked upon very much as 'the bravest of the brave'.

Back in 1982, Marica McKay, the widow of Sergeant Ian McKay VC, said that she feared his decoration and his bravery 'would all be forgotten in twenty years' time'. I suspect other widows and relatives had similar thoughts about their loved ones who were killed or wounded. However, I am pleased to say that has not happened, and it must not be allowed to happen. *Falklands War Heroes* is my humble contribution to making sure that the courage of all those who risked, and in some cases gave, their lives in the South Atlantic in 1982 is *never* forgotten.

FALKLANDS WAR 1982: TIMELINE

2 April: Argentina invades the Falkland Islands. Within five hours of the first troops being dropped by helicopter, they control the islands.

3 April: The UN Security Council demands the immediate withdrawal of Argentine forces.

5 April: Lord Carrington, the British Foreign Secretary, resigns his Cabinet position and the first ships in the Task Force set sail for the South Atlantic 8,000 miles away.

19 April: Argentina rejects the peace proposals put forward by Alexander Haig, the US Secretary of State.

25 April: South Georgia is retaken by British forces and Mrs Thatcher tells the nation to 'rejoice' at the news.

1 May: A Vulcan bomber is launched on Stanley airfield and four Argentine aircraft are shot down.

2 May: The Argentine cruiser *General Belgrano* is torpedoed and sinks with the loss of some 323 sailors.

4 May: The British destroyer HMS *Sheffield* is hit and sinks with the loss of twenty lives.

14–15 May: The SAS launches a surprise attack on enemy-held Pebble Island, an outpost which could give early warning of the arrival of the British fleet.

20 May: UN peace talks fail thereby ending hopes of a diplomatic solution to the crisis.

21 May: Some 3,000 British troops land at San Carlos Bay on East Falkland but in a day of heavy fighting HMS *Ardent*, HMS *Antrim* and HMS *Argonaut* are all bombed with heavy losses of life.

23 May: The British frigate HMS *Antelope* is hit and later sinks.

25 May: The British destroyer HMS *Coventry* is bombed with the loss of twenty lives and the container ship *Atlantic Conveyor* is hit with the loss of twelve crew.

28–29 May: British forces win the battles for Darwin and Goose Green but Colonel Herbert 'H' Jones is among those killed in the heavy fighting.

8 June: British troops are ferried from San Carlos Water to Bluff Cove and Fitzroy but both RFA *Sir Galahad* and RFA *Sir Tristram* are bombed with the loss of more than fifty men.

11–12 June: Mount Longdon, Two Sisters and Mount Harriet are taken by the British but during a naval bombardment of Port Stanley three islanders are killed.

12 June: The British destroyer HMS *Glamorgan* is hit by a shore-launched Exocet killing thirteen men (a fourteenth died later on).

13–14 June: The final Argentine positions of Mount William, Wireless Ridge and Mount Tumbledown are taken.

14 June: British forces march into Stanley almost unopposed. The Argentine forces lay down their arms and surrender. The ceasefire is announced at 3.30 p.m. local time.

20 June: British forces declare an end to the hostilities and the TEZ is replaced by a smaller Falklands Protection Zone.

11 July: SS *Canberra*, the ocean liner requisitioned as a troopship, arrives back in Southampton to a rapturous welcome.

BIBLIOGRAPHY

Adkin, Mark, *Goose Green: A Battle Is Fought to Be Won* (Barnsley: Leo Cooper, 1992)

Arthur, Max, *Above All, Courage: Personal Stories from the Falklands War* (London: Cassell Military Paperbacks, 1985)

Ashcroft, Michael, *Heroes of the Skies* (London: Headline Publishing Group, 2012)

— —, *Special Forces Heroes* (London: Headline Review, 2008)

— —, *Special Ops Heroes* (London: Headline Publishing Group, 2014)

Barker, Nick, *Beyond Endurance: An Epic of Whitehall and the South Atlantic Conflict* (Barnsley: Pen & Sword Books, 1997)

Barnes, William, *Ultimate Acceptance: The Last Patrol* (Isle of Wight: Sandhills Management Consultancy, 2012)

de la Billière, General Sir Peter, *Looking for Trouble: SAS to Gulf Command – The Autobiography* (London: HarperCollins, 1994)

Bilton, Michael, and Kosminsky, Peter, *Speaking Out: Untold Stories from the Falklands War* (London: André Deutsch, 1989)

Burden, Rodney, Draper, Michael, Rough, Douglas, Smith, Colin, and Wilton, David, *Falklands: The Air War* (London: Arms and Armour Press, 1986)

Cooksey, Jon, *Falklands Hero Ian McKay: The Last VC of the 20th Century* (Barnsley: Pen & Sword Military, 2012)

Delves, Lieutenant General Sir Cedric, *Across an Angry Sea: The SAS in the Falklands War* (London: Hurst & Company, 2018)

Ethell, Jeffrey, and Price, Alfred, *Air War South Atlantic* (London: Sidgwick & Jackson, 1983)

Falconer, Duncan, *First in Action: A Dramatic Personal Account of Life in the SBS* (London: Little, Brown, 1998)

Frost, Major General John, *2 PARA Falklands: The Battalion at War* (London: Buchan & Enright, 1983)

Hart Dyke, David, *Four Weeks in May: A Captain's Story of War at Sea* (London: Atlantic Books, 2007)

Hastings, Max, and Jenkins, Simon, *The Battle for the Falklands* (London: Michael Joseph, 1993)

Jennings, Christian, and Weale, Adrian, *Green-Eyed Boys: 3 PARA and the Battle for Mount Longdon* (London: HarperCollins, 1996)

McCallion, Harry, *Killing Zone: A Life in the Paras, the Recces, the SAS and the RUC* (London: Bloomsbury, 1995)

McManners, Hugh, *Forgotten Voices of the Falklands: The Real Story of the Falklands War* (London: Ebury Press, 2007)

— —, *Falklands Commando: A Soldier's Eye View of the Land War* (London: William Kimber & Co, 1984)

— —, *The Scars of War* (London: HarperCollins, 1994)

Middlebrook, Martin, *The Falklands War* (Barnsley: Pen & Sword, 2012)

Naya, Michael, *War Medic Hero: A Portrait of Sergeant Pierre Naya* (Cirencester: Mereo Books, 2014)

Prebble, Stuart, *Secrets of the Conqueror: The Untold Story of Britain's Most Famous Submarine* (London: Faber & Faber, 2012)

Ramsey, Gordon (ed.), *The Falklands War Then and Now* (Old Harlow: Battle of Britain International, 2009)

Ratcliffe, Peter, *Eye of the Storm: 25 Years in Action with the SAS* (London: Michael O'Mara Books, 2000)

Richardson, Matthew, *Deeds of Heroes: The Story of the Distinguished Conduct Medal 1854–1993* (Barnsley: Pen & Sword, 2012)

Rossiter, Mike, *Sink the Belgrano: The Dramatic Hunt for the Argentine Warship* (London: Bantam Press, 2007)

Southby-Tailyour, Ewen, *Exocet Falklands: The Untold Story of Special Forces Operations* (Barnsley: Pen & Sword, 2014)

The *Sunday Times* Insight Team, *The Falklands War: The Full Story* (London: Sphere Books, 1982)

Thompson, Julian, *3 Commando Brigade in the Falklands: No Picnic* (Barnsley: Pen & Sword, 2008)

Underwood, Geoffrey, *Our Falklands War: The Men of the Task Force Tell Their Story* (Liskeard: Maritime Books, 1982)

Ward, Commander 'Sharkey', *Sea Harrier over the Falklands* (Barnsley: Leo Cooper, 1992)

Way, Peter (ed.), *The Falklands War: The Day by Day Record from Invasion to Victory* (London: Marshall Cavendish, 1983)

Woodward, Admiral Sandy, *One Hundred Days: The Memoirs of the Falklands Battle Group Commander* (London: HarperCollins, 1992)

Websites used for research purposes include:
www.airspacemag.com
www.bbc.co.uk
www.express.co.uk
www.independent.co.uk
www.iwm.org.uk
www.mirror.co.uk
www.paradata.org.uk
www.standard.co.uk
www.telegraph.co.uk
www.theguardian.com
www.thehistorypress.co.uk
www.thesun.co.uk
www.thetimes.co.uk
www.wikipedia.org

APPENDIX: A SUMMARY OF THE DECORATIONS AND DISTINCTIONS AWARDED FOR THE WAR IN THE SOUTH ATLANTIC

SOUTH GEORGIA

The following gallantry awards for South Georgia were announced in *The London Gazette* on 3 June 1982:

Royal Navy
Distinguished Service Order (DSO): 2
Distinguished Service Cross (DSC): 1

Royal Marines
Distinguished Service Cross (DSC): 1
Distinguished Service Medal (DSM): 1

In addition, six members of the Royal Navy were Mentioned in Despatches and two members of the Royal Marines were likewise honoured, these last two distinctions being announced in *The London Gazette* on 8 October 1982. Two other Marines were awarded the Commander-in-Chief's Commendation.

THE FALKLANDS

The following gallantry awards for the Falklands were announced in *The London Gazette* on 8 October 1982:

Royal Navy
Distinguished Service Order (DSO): 11
Distinguished Service Cross (DSC): 21
Air Force Cross (AFC): 2
Distinguished Service Medal (DSM): 8
George Medal (GM): 1
Queen's Gallantry Medal (QGM): 4

Royal Marines
Distinguished Service Order (DSO): 2
Distinguished Service Cross (DSC): 1
Military Cross (MC): 5
Distinguished Flying Cross (DFC): 2
Distinguished Conduct Medal (DCM): 1
Distinguished Service Medal (DSM): 3
Military Medal (MM): 10
Distinguished Flying Medal (DFM): 1
Queen's Gallantry Medal (QGM): 1

Royal Fleet Auxiliary
Distinguished Service Order (DSO): 2
Distinguished Service Cross (DSC): 3
George Medal (GM): 2
Queen's Gallantry Medal (QGM): 2

Merchant Navy
Distinguished Service Cross (DSC): 1
Queen's Gallantry Medal (QGM): 1

Army

Victoria Cross (VC): 2

Distinguished Service Order (DSO): 4

Distinguished Service Cross (DSC): 1

Military Cross (MC): 11

Distinguished Flying Cross (DFC): 2

Distinguished Conduct Medal (DCM): 7

Conspicuous Gallantry Medal (CGM): 1

Military Medal (MM): 24

Royal Air Force

Distinguished Service Cross (DSC): 1

Distinguished Flying Cross (DFC): 5

Air Force Cross (AFC): 4

Queen's Gallantry Medal (QGM): 2

NOTES

In addition, multiple appointments to the Order of the Bath and the Order of the British Empire and awards of the British Empire Medal (BEM) were announced on the same occasion.

Many other members of the armed services were Mentioned in Despatches and some members of the Royal Air Force received the Queen's Commendation for Brave Conduct or Valuable Services in the Air; such distinctions sometimes stemmed from an original recommendation for a gallantry medal.

Further awards were announced at later dates, but the recommendations often reflected services in the Falklands *and* subsequent events. A case in point would be awards of the BEM.

As is made clear by some of the individual stories related in *Falklands War Heroes*, not a few of these awards and 'mentions' were won for gallant actions under fire.

PICTURE CREDITS

CREDITS TO PLATE SECTION 1

p. 1: top © Anthony Devlin / AFP via Getty Images; middle © PA Images / Alamy Stock Photo; bottom supplied by Keith Mills

p. 2: top © Lord Ashcroft; middle © Lord Ashcroft; bottom left © Rafael Wollmann / Gamma-Rapho via Getty Images; bottom right supplied by Dix Noonan Webb

p. 3: top © PA Photos / TopFoto; middle left © Lord Ashcroft; middle right © Lord Ashcroft; bottom © David Bagnall / Alamy Stock Photo

p. 4: top © PA Images / Alamy Stock Photo; bottom left © Lord Ashcroft; bottom right © Monty Fresco / ANL / Shutterstock

p. 5: top left © Lord Ashcroft; top right © Lord Ashcroft; bottom © Lord Ashcroft

p. 6: top © Martin Cleaver / PA Images / Alamy Stock Photo; bottom left © Lord Ashcroft; bottom right © Lord Ashcroft

p. 7: top © Lord Ashcroft; bottom left © Lord Ashcroft; bottom right © Lord Ashcroft

p. 8: top © Jim Hutchison / ANL / Shutterstock; bottom left © Lord Ashcroft; bottom right © Lord Ashcroft

CREDITS TO PLATE SECTION 2

p. 1: top © Lord Ashcroft; bottom left © Lord Ashcroft; bottom right © R. Thomasson

p. 2: top © Lord Ashcroft; middle left © Lord Ashcroft; middle right © Lord Ashcroft; bottom supplied by Spink

p. 3: top © SSPL / Getty Images; middle © Lord Ashcroft; bottom © Cavendish Press

p. 4: top left © Lord Ashcroft; top right © Pictorial Press Ltd / Alamy Stock Photo; bottom right © Lord Ashcroft

p. 5: top © PA Images / Alamy Stock Photo; bottom left © Lord Ashcroft; bottom middle © Lord Ashcroft; bottom right © Lord Ashcroft

p. 6: top © PA Photos / TopFoto; middle © Lord Ashcroft; bottom © Lord Ashcroft

p. 7: top © Roger Bamber / TopFoto; middle left © Fox Photos / Hulton Archive / Getty Images; middle right © Neville Marriner / *Daily Mail* / Shutterstock; bottom © SSPL / Getty Images

p. 8: top © Neville Marriner / ANL / Shutterstock; middle © Popperfoto via Getty Images / Getty Images; bottom © Peter Hazell / Getty Images

INDEX